The American Presidency

CORE DOCUMENTS

The American Presidency

~ CORE DOCUMENTS ~

Selected and Introduced by

Jeremy D. Bailey

ASHBROOK PRESS

Excerpts from pp. 254–6, 266–71 [1140 words] of Frost/Nixon: Behind the Scenes of
the Nixon Interviews by Sir David Frost with Bob Zelnick. Copyright © 2007 by David
Paradine Televesion Inc. Reprinted by permission of HarperCollins Publishers.

Library of Congress Cataloging-in-Publication Data
The American Presidency; Selected and Introduced by Jeremy D. Bailey
      p.   cm.
Includes Index
1.   United States—Politics and government.
ISBN 978-1-878802-44-6 (pbk.)

Cover images, above the title, left to right:
Alexander Hamilton, a painting by John Trumbull (1746–1843) photographed
    between 1900 and 1912 by Detroit Publishing Company. Library of
    Congress Prints and Photographs Division, LC-DIG-det-4a26168.
Woodrow Wilson, photo by Harris and Ewing between 1900 and 1920,
    Detroit Publishing Company Photograph Collection, Library of
    Congress Prints and Photographs Division, LC-DIG-det-4a26353.
Justice George Sutherland, photographed between 1905 and 1945 by Harris
    and Ewing, Detroit Publishing Company Photograph Collection, Library
    of Congress Prints and Photographs Division, LC-DIG-hec-20296.
Robert H. Jackson, ca. 1945, photo by Harris and Ewing. Library of
    Congress Prints and Photographs Division, LC-USZ62-38828.
Senator George McGovern, photographed by Warren K. Leffler, Library of
    Congress Prints and Photographs Division, LC-DIG-ppmsca-19602.

Cover image, below the title:
*Gutzon Borglum's model of Mt. Rushmore memorial—Washington,
    Jefferson, Roosevelt & Lincoln*, c. 1936. Library of Congress Prints
    and Photographs Division, LC-USZ62-105079.

Interior design/composition: Brad Walrod/Kenoza Type, Inc.

Ashbrook Center at Ashland University
401 College Avenue
Ashland, Ohio 44805
www.ashbrook.org

Contents

General Editor's Introduction

This collection of documents on the presidency continues the Ashbrook Center's extended series of document collections covering major periods, themes, and institutions in American history and government. The volume begins with Alexander Hamilton's commentary on those sections of the Constitution related to the executive branch; it ends with President Barack Obama's address to the nation defending his interpretation of executive authority under the Constitution to use force against the Syrian regime. It covers not only the role of the executive branch in our constitutional order, but also the specific questions of presidential selection, term limits, and impeachment. Its documents also explore the president's responsibility to oversee the executive branch (including the removal power, the power to remove executive branch officials from office) and his authority as commander in chief and in regards to foreign policy. This collection and its companion volumes—*Congress, The Separation of Powers, The Judicial Branch, Federalism,* and *Political Parties*—will comprise a detailed account of America's major political ideas and institutions. The document volume series will also include a collection of the most important Supreme Court decisions, as well as two volumes on the First Amendment. One will cover religious freedom and the other the freedoms of speech and assembly.

When the series of Ashbrook document collections is complete, it will be comprehensive, as well as authoritative, because it will present America's story in the words of those who wrote it—America's presidents, labor leaders, farmers, philosophers, industrialists, politicians, workers, explorers, religious leaders, judges, soldiers; its slaveholders and abolitionists; its expansionists and isolationists; its reformers and stand-patters; its strict and broad constructionists; its hard-eyed realists and visionary utopians—all united in their commitment to equality and liberty, yet all also divided often by their different understandings of these most fundamental American ideas. The documents are about all this—the still unfinished American experiment with self-government.

As this volume does, each of the volumes in the series will contain key documents on its period, theme, or institution, selected by an expert and reviewed by an editorial board. Each volume will have an introduction highlighting key documents and themes. In an appendix to each volume, there will also be a thematic table of contents, showing the connections between various documents. Another appendix will provide study questions for each document, as well questions that refer to other documents in the collection, tying them together as the thematic table of contents does. Each document will be checked against an authoritative original source and have an introduction outlining its significance. Notes to each document will identify people, events, movements, or ideas that may be unfamiliar to non-specialist readers and will improve understanding of the document's historical context.

To promote readability, we have in most instances modernized spelling and in some instances punctuation. Occasionally, we have inserted italicized text, enclosed in brackets, to bridge gaps in syntax occurring due to apparent errors or illegibility in the source documents. With regard to capitalization, however, we have allowed usage to stand where it is internally consistent, even when varying from today's usage, since authors writing about the proper assignment of powers to the three branches of our federal government may signal their understanding of the authority belonging to each through capitalization.

In sum, our intent is that the documents and their supporting material provide reliable and unique access to the richness of the American story.

Jeremy D. Bailey, Professor of Politics, University of Houston, selected the documents and wrote the introductions, notes, and study questions. It was copyedited by Ellen Tucker. Ali Brosky and David Tucker provided editorial support. Brad Walrod magically transformed the words into an actual book through his artful typesetting and pre-press support. This publication was made possible through the support of a grant by the John Templeton Foundation. The opinions expressed in this publication are those of the editors and do not necessarily reflect the views of the John Templeton Foundation.

Sarah A. Morgan Smith, Fellow

Introduction

Woodrow Wilson was probably right when he said that it is easier to speak of presidents than it is of the presidency.[1] Because the presidency is held by only one person at a time, and because there have been only forty-five men who have held the office, the study of the presidency invites biography as its most obvious mode of analysis. This approach undeniably has some benefits for the student who wishes to know how a leader's character, education, and experience affects the decisions he makes. In this sense, the study of the presidency offers the study of statesmanship by offering case studies in decision-making.

This volume, however, is aimed at a different approach, as it aspires to study the presidency above and beyond the men who have been president. More precisely, this volume treats the presidency as an ongoing series of questions, questions about the president's duty to defend the Constitution and execute the laws while at the same time leading and representing a changing constitutional democracy. Thus this volume treats the presidency as a dialogue among those who have made it. These persons include presidents, but they also include members of Congress and justices on the Supreme Court, as well as the intellectuals whose writings have shaped important changes to the office.

The volume adopts this approach because the presidency today continues to challenge analysis just as it continues to rise above biography as the best means of analysis. Does the president have the power to reclassify the immigration status of millions of persons? Can the president fire an independent counsel? What does it mean to say the president can decide whether there will be war or not? These questions are ripped from the headlines, but the headlines could be from this decade or any of several others.

This uncertainty over the length and breadth of the president's power comes not only because the Constitution does not and cannot settle every political controversy, but also because the Constitution begins its own presentation of the presidency with a kind of puzzle. Article Two states, "The executive power shall be vested in a President of the United States of

---

[1] Woodrow Wilson, *Constitutional Government in the United States* (New York: Columbia University Press, 1908), 54.

America." This presumes that there is a power or a set of powers that can be identified as executive even before there is a constitution. That means that either by nature or by custom, the executive power exists and can be identified. This is further suggested by the fact that Article One gives Congress only the legislative powers "herein granted," that is, those specifically listed in the Constitution, presumably in Article One, Section 8. The problem, however, is that Article Two also goes on to list the powers given to the president in Section Two, leading many commentators to argue that Article Two should be read in the same way as Article One. Others argue that the Constitution intended the difference between Articles One and Two, and that this difference suggests that the president has *all* the executive power, while Congress only has those legislative powers herein granted.

This puzzle is only partially the result of the language of the text, because there is a deeper problem in designing the presidency. The job of the president, as the executive, is to execute the laws. This is the first principle of separation of powers: he who makes laws cannot execute them. In the context of England, separation of powers was first and foremost a check on kingly power. In the context of the United States of the 1780's, however, separation of powers was accepted as an article of faith, but it was employed to be a check on legislative power. So the Framers of the Constitution made special effort not only to have a separate executive, but also an *independent* executive, that is, a president with his own electoral constituency and source of authority. But even with this innovation there remained an underlying feature of monarchical discretion. The person who executes the laws will also be the one to determine whether and when to execute the laws. Even if this does not mean the president has the power to make new law, it does reveal that the president as executive is not necessarily simply the enforcement arm of Congress. Rather, as Madison explains in *Federalist* No. 51, each department is given a "will of its own." With its own will, and with the unusual wording of the Vesting Clause at the beginning of Article Two, the presidency is an institution that forces serious reflection on what it means to live under the rule of law.

Each of the selections in this volume can be grouped with others and is meant to start a conversation about the presidency. Does the Constitution give the war power to the president or to Congress? Who elects presidents and whom do presidents represent? Can the president remove any executive branch official for any reason, or can Congress create offices that exist beyond the supervisory role of the Chief Executive? Does the Constitution give the president the power to break the law? These questions are enduring not only because we disagree about their answers but also because we disagree about *how* we should answer them, or rather about *who* should answer. This volume, then, is first and foremost an invitation to teachers and students to join the dialogue suggested by the documents. Rather than offering a series of precedents or important historical events, the documents offer opportunities for close study and will reward the instructor who can find the time for extended discussion.

It is important to note that my claim that these questions are enduring has some bearing on an important part of teaching the presidency. I have in mind the modern presidency. Several selections in this volume will invite students to reflect upon the emergence and importance of a modern presidency, but others will invite students to ask whether a deeper continuity is the more important story when it comes to the development of the presidency. That is, teachers and students should not take the modern presidency thesis for granted. Like other textbook accounts of the presidency, it has to be assessed in light of the evidence.

In closing, I am grateful to Allison Brosky, who transcribed these documents. Two anonymous readers for the press helped me decide which texts were important and pointed me to several that I had not considered. Sarah Morgan Smith and David Tucker were generous and clear in their editorial guidance. Finally, I want to thank the professors who taught me the presidency, including Michael Nelson at Rhodes College, Sid Milkis at Brandeis University, and Marc Landy and Bob Scigliano at Boston College. Thanks to these men, I have been thinking about these documents since 1992, and I hope it gives them some pleasure to see my own attempt to pull them into a single volume.

Jeremy Bailey
University of Houston

The American Presidency

CORE DOCUMENTS

The Federalist

Alexander Hamilton, writing as Publius

1788

*I*n late October 1787, three supporters of the newly drafted Constitution—*Alexander Hamilton, James Madison, and John Jay—began authoring a series of essays under the pen name Publius. Written for the New York newspapers, the essays countered attacks on the proposed frame of government that had commenced shortly after the document was signed and would continue until New Yorkers met in convention to ratify the plan. Later, the eighty-five essays were combined into a single collection, The Federalist, that has endured as the best commentary on the Constitution.*

In the following excerpts from Federalist 65, 68, 70, 71, and 72, Publius—in this case, Alexander Hamilton—discusses the Constitutional arrangements for the executive branch, some of which differed sharply from the provisions at that time for the executive at the state level. Discussing impeachments, presidential selection, unity in the executive, and eligibility for reelection, Publius focuses both on safeguards against a concentration of power in the executive and on provisions to insure the "energy" in the executive necessary for effective administration. An earlier essay—Federalist No. 51, authored by James Madison—had famously described the American system of separation of powers as one in which "ambition" would be made to counteract "ambition." The key to separation of powers, then, was not perfecting the delineation of power among the three departments but rather in giving each department "a will of its own." Hamilton elaborates this argument, explaining how the presidents would come to have their own will, that is, how they would be shaped by the office toward becoming willing to use their constitutional powers to both defend the executive department and to pursue their own programs.

SOURCE: *The Federalist* No. 65 [7 March 1788]; No. 68 [12 March 1788]; No. 70 [15 March 1788]; No. 71 [18 March 1788]; No. 72 [19 March 1788]; *Founders Online,* National Archives, https://goo.gl/RK1NM8; https://goo.gl/N1UBJ7; https://goo.gl/mQmQ7b; https://goo.gl/wA5rvW; https://goo.gl/hKRQjj.

The Federalist, No. 65

The remaining powers, which the plan of the Constitution allots to the Senate, in a distinct capacity, are comprised in their participation with the Executive in the appointment to offices, and in their judicial character as a court for the trial of impeachments....

A well-constructed court for the trial of impeachments, is an object not more to be desired than difficult to be obtained in a government wholly elective. The subjects of its jurisdiction are those offenses which proceed from the misconduct of public men, or in other words from the abuse or violation of some public trust. They are of a nature which may with peculiar propriety be denominated POLITICAL, as they relate chiefly to injuries done immediately to the society itself. The prosecution of them, for this reason, will seldom fail to agitate the passions of the whole community, and to divide it into parties, more or less friendly or inimical, to the accused. In many cases, it will connect itself with the pre-existing factions, and will enlist all the animosities, partialities, influence, and interest on one side, or on the other; and in such cases there will always be the greatest danger, that the decision will be regulated more by the comparative strength of parties than by the real demonstrations of innocence or guilt.

The delicacy and magnitude of a trust, which so deeply concerns the political reputation and existence of every man engaged in the administration of public affairs, speak for themselves. The difficulty of placing it rightly in a government resting entirely on the basis of periodical elections will as readily be perceived, when it is considered that the most conspicuous characters in it will, from that circumstance, be too often the leaders, or the tools of the most cunning or the most numerous faction; and on this account can hardly be expected to possess the requisite neutrality towards those, whose conduct may be the subject of scrutiny.

The Convention, it appears, thought the Senate the most fit depositary of this important trust. Those who can best discern the intrinsic difficulty of the thing will be least hasty in condemning that opinion; and will be most inclined to allow due weight to the arguments which may be supposed to have produced it.

What it may be asked is the true spirit of the institution itself? Is it not designed as a method of NATIONAL INQUEST into the conduct of public men? If this be the design of it, who can so properly be the inquisitor for the nation, as the representatives of the nation themselves? ... [T]he practice of impeachments, [is regarded] as a bridle in the hands of the legislative body upon the executive servants of the government. Is not this the true light in which it ought to be regarded?

Where else, than in the Senate could have been found a tribunal sufficiently dignified, or sufficiently independent? What other body would be likely to feel *confidence enough in its own situation,* to preserve unawed and uninfluenced the necessary impartiality between an *individual* accused, and the *representatives of the people, his accusers?*

Could the Supreme Court have been relied upon as answering this description? It is much to be doubted whether the members of that tribunal would, at all times, be endowed with so eminent a portion of fortitude, as would be called for in the execution of so difficult a task; and it is still more to be doubted, whether they would possess the degree of credit and authority, which might, on certain occasions, be indispensable, towards reconciling the people to a decision, that should happen to clash with an accusation brought by their immediate representatives. A deficiency in the first would be fatal to the accused; in the last, dangerous to the public tranquility. The hazard in both these respects could only be avoided, if at all, by rendering that tribunal more numerous than would consist with a reasonable attention to economy. The necessity of a numerous court for the trial of impeachments is equally dictated by the nature of the proceeding. This can never be tied down by such strict rules, either in the delineation of the offence by the prosecutors, or in the construction of it by the judges, as in common cases serve to limit the discretion of courts in favor of personal security. There will be no jury to stand between the judges, who are to pronounce the sentence of the law and the party who is to receive or suffer it. The awful discretion, which a court of impeachments must necessarily have, to doom to honor or to infamy the most confidential and the most distinguished characters of the community, forbids the commitment of the trust to a small number of persons.

These considerations seem alone sufficient to authorize a conclusion, that the Supreme Court would have been an improper substitute for the Senate, as a court of impeachments. There remains a further consideration which will not a little strengthen this conclusion. It is this—The punishment, which may be the consequence of conviction upon impeachment, is not to terminate the chastisement of the offender. After having been sentenced to a perpetual ostracism from the esteem and confidence, and honors and emoluments of his country; he will still be liable to prosecution and punishment in the ordinary course of law. Would it be proper that the persons, who disposed of his fame and his most valuable rights as a citizen in one trial, should in another trial, for the same offence, be also the disposers of his life and his fortune?

Would there not be the greatest reason to apprehend, that error in the first sentence would be the parent of error in the second sentence? That the strong bias of one decision would be apt to overrule the influence of any new lights, which might be brought to vary the complexion of another decision? Those, who know anything of human nature, will not hesitate to answer these questions in the affirmative; and will be at no loss to perceive, that by making the same persons judges in both cases, those who might happen to be the objects of prosecution would in a great measure be deprived of the double security, intended them by a double trial. The loss of life and estate would often be virtually included in a sentence, which, in its terms, imported nothing more than dismission from a present, and disqualification for a future office. It may be said, that the intervention of a jury, in the second instance, would obviate the danger. But juries are frequently influenced by the opinions of judges. They are sometimes induced to find special verdicts which refer the main question to the decision of the court. Who would be willing to stake his life and his estate upon the verdict of a jury, acting under the auspices of judges, who had predetermined his guilt?

Would it have been an improvement of the plan, to have united the Supreme Court with the Senate, in the formation of the court of impeachments? This Union would certainly have been attended with several advantages; but would they have not have been overbalanced by the single disadvantages, already stated, arising from the agency of the same judges in the double prosecution to which the offender would be liable? To a certain extent, the benefits of that union will be obtained from making the Chief Justice of the Supreme Court the President of the court of impeachments, as is proposed to be done in the plan of the Convention; while the inconveniences of an entire incorporation of the former into the latter will be substantially avoided. This was perhaps the prudent mean....

The Federalist, No. 68

The mode of appointment of the chief magistrate of the United States is almost the only part of the system, of any consequence, which has escaped without severe censure, or which has received the slightest mark of approbation from its opponents. The most plausible of these, who has appeared in print, has even deigned to admit, that the election of the president is pretty well guarded. I venture somewhat further; and hesitate not to affirm, that if the manner of it be not perfect, it is at least excellent....

It was desirable, that the sense of the people should operate in the choice of the person to whom so important a trust was to be confided. This end will be answered by committing the right of making it, not to any pre-established body, but to men, chosen by the people for the special purpose, and at the particular conjuncture.

It was equally desirable, that the immediate election should be made by men most capable of analyzing the qualities adapted to the station, and acting under circumstances favorable to deliberation and to a judicious combination of all the reasons and inducements, which were proper to govern their choice. A small number of persons, selected by their fellow citizens from the general mass, will be most likely to possess the information and discernment requisite to so complicated an investigation.

It was also peculiarly desirable, to afford as little opportunity as possible to tumult and disorder. This evil was not least to be dreaded in the election of a magistrate, who was to have so important an agency in the administration of the government, as the President of the United States. But the precautions which have been so happily concerted in the system under consideration, promise an effectual security against the mischief. The choice of *several* to form an intermediate body of electors, will be much less apt to convulse the community, with any extraordinary or violent movements, than the choice of one who was himself to be the final object of the public wishes. And as the electors, chosen in each state, are to assemble and vote in the state, in which they are chosen, this detached and divided situation will expose them much less to heats and ferments, which might be communicated from them to the people, than if they were all to be convened at one time, in one place.

Nothing was more to be desired, than that every practicable obstacle should be opposed to cabal, intrigue and corruption. These most deadly adversaries of republican government might naturally have been expected to make their approaches from more than one quarter, but chiefly from the desire in foreign powers to gain an improper ascendant in our councils. How could they better gratify this, than by raising a creature of their own to the chief magistracy of the union? But the convention have guarded against all danger of this sort with the most provident and judicious attention. They have not made the appointment of the president to depend on any pre-existing bodies of men who might be tampered with beforehand to prostitute their votes; but they have referred it in the first instance to an immediate act of the people of America, to be exerted in the choice of persons for the temporary and sole purpose of making the appointment. And they have excluded from eligibility to this trust all those who from situation might be suspected of too great devotion to the president in office. No senator, representative, or other person holding a place of trust or profit under the United States, can be of the number of the electors. Thus, without corrupting the body of the people, the immediate agents in the election will at least enter upon the task, free from any sinister bypass. Their transient existence and their detached situation, already taken notice of, afford a satisfactory prospect of their continuing so, to the conclusion of it. The business of corruption, when it is to embrace so considerable a number of men, requires time, as well as means. Nor would it be found easy suddenly to embark them, dispersed as they would be over thirteen states, in any combinations, founded upon motives, which though they could not properly be denominated corrupt, might yet be of a nature to mislead them from their duty.

Another and no less important desideratum was, that the executive should be independent for his continuance in office on all, but the people themselves. He might otherwise be tempted to sacrifice his duty to his complaisance for[1] those whose favor was necessary to the duration of his official consequence. This advantage will also be secured, by making his reelection to depend on a special body of representatives, deputed by the society for the single purpose of making the important choice.

All these advantages will be happily combined in the plan devised by the convention; which is, that the people of each state shall choose a number of persons as electors, equal to the number of senators and representatives of such state in the national government, who shall assemble within the state and vote for some fit person as president. Their votes, thus given, are to be transmitted to the seat of the national government, and the person who may happen to have a majority of the whole number of votes will be president. But as a majority of the votes might not always happen to center on one man and as it might be unsafe to permit less than a majority to be conclusive, it is provided, that in such a contingency, the House of Representatives shall select out of the candidates, who shall have the five highest numbers of votes, the man who in their opinion may be best qualified for the office.

This process of election affords a moral certainty, that the office of president, will seldom fall to the lot of any man, who is not in an eminent degree endowed with the requisite qualifications. Talents for low intrigue and the little arts of popularity may alone suffice to elevate a man to the first honors in a single state; but it will require other talents and a different kind of merit

---

[1] desire to please

to establish him in the esteem and confidence of the whole union, or of so considerable a portion of it as would be necessary to make him a successful candidate for the distinguished office of President of the United States. It will not be too strong to say, that there will be a constant probability of seeing the station filled by characters preeminent for ability and virtue. And this will be thought no inconsiderable recommendation of the Constitution, by those, who are able to estimate the share, which the executive in every government must necessarily have in its good or ill administration. Though we cannot acquiesce in the political heresy of the poet who says—

For forms of government let fools contest—
That which is best administered is best.[2]

—yet we may safely pronounce, that the true test of a good government is its aptitude and tendency to produce a good administration.

The Federalist, No. 70

There is an idea, which is not without its advocates, that a vigorous executive is inconsistent with the genius of republican government. The enlightened well-wishers to this species of government must at least hope that the supposition is destitute of foundation; since they can never admit its truth, without at the same time admitting the condemnation of their own principles. Energy in the executive is a leading character in the definition of good government. It is essential to the protection of the community against foreign attacks: it is not less essential to the steady administration of the laws, to the protection of property against those irregular and high handed combinations, which sometimes interrupt the ordinary course of justice to the security of liberty against the enterprises and assaults of ambition, of faction and of anarchy. Every man the least conversant in Roman story knows how often that republic was obliged to take refuge in the absolute power of a single man, under the formidable title of dictator, as well against the intrigues of ambitious individuals, who aspired to the tyranny, and seditions of whole classes of the community, whose conduct threatened the existence of all government, as against the invasions of external enemies, who menaced the conquest and destruction of Rome.

There can be no need however to multiply arguments or examples on this head. A feeble executive implies a feeble execution of the government.

---

[2] Alexander Pope, *Essay on Man*, Book VI.

A feeble execution is but another phrase for a bad execution: And a government ill executed, whatever it may be in theory, must be in practice a bad government.

Taking it for granted, therefore, that all men of sense will agree in the necessity of an energetic executive; it will only remain to inquire, what are the ingredients which constitute this energy—how far can they be combined with those other ingredients which constitute safety in the republican sense? And how far does this combination characterize the plan, which has been reported by the convention?

The ingredients, which constitute energy in the executive, are first unity, secondly duration, thirdly an adequate provision for its support, fourthly competent powers.

The circumstances which constitute safety in the republican sense are, first, a due dependence on the people, secondly a due responsibility.

Those politicians and statesmen, who have been the most celebrated for the soundness of their principles, and for the justness of their views, have declared in favor of a single executive and a numerous legislature. They have with great propriety considered energy as the most necessary qualification of the former and have regarded this as most applicable to power in a single hand; while they have with equal propriety considered the latter as best adapted to deliberation and wisdom, and best calculated to conciliate the confidence of the people and to secure their privileges and interests.

That unity is conductive to energy will not be disputed. Decision, activity, secrecy, and dispatch will generally characterize the proceedings of one man, in a much more eminent degree, than the proceedings of any greater number; and in proportion as the number is increased, these qualities will be diminished.

This unity may be destroyed in two ways; either by vesting the power in two or more magistrates of equal dignity and authority; or by vesting it ostensibly in one man, subject in whole or in part to the control and cooperation of others, in the capacity of counsellors to him. Of the first the two consuls of Rome[3] may serve as an example; of the last we shall find examples in the constitutions of several of the states. New York and New Jersey, if I recollect right, are the only states, which have entrusted the executive authority wholly

---

[3] In the ancient Roman Republic, the office of chief magistrate was invested in two consuls who were nominated by the Senate and elected in a popular assembly for one-year concurrent terms. Each consul held the power of veto over the other's decisions.

to single men. Both these methods of destroying the unity of the executive have their partisans; but the votaries of an executive council are the most numerous. They are both liable, if not equal, to similar objections; and may in most lights be examined in conjunction.

The experience of other nations will afford little instruction on this head. As far however as it teaches anything, it teaches us not to be enamoured of plurality in the executive. We have seen that the Achaeans on an experiment of two Praetors, were induced to abolish one.[4] The Roman history records many instances of mischiefs to the republic from the dissension between the consuls, and between the military tribunes, who were at times substituted to the consuls. But it gives us no specimens of any peculiar advantages derived to the state, from the circumstances of the plurality of those magistrates. That the dissension between them were not more frequent, or more fatal, is matter of astonishment; until we advert to the singular position in which the republic was almost continually placed and to the prudent policy pointed out by the circumstances of that state, and pursued by the councils, of making a division of the government between them. The Patricians engaged in a perpetual struggle with the Plebeians[5] for the preservation of their ancient authorities and dignities; the consuls, who were generally chosen out of the former body, were commonly united by the personal interest they had in the defence of the privileges of their order. In addition to this motive of union, after the arms of the republic had considerably expanded the bounds of the empire, it became an established custom with the consuls to divide the administration between themselves by lot; one of them remaining at Rome to govern the city and its environs; the other taking the command in the more distant provinces. This expedient must no doubt have had great influence in preventing those collisions and rivalships, which might otherwise have embroiled the peace of the republic.

But quitting the dim light of historical research, and attaching ourselves purely to the dictates of reason and good sense, we shall discover much greater cause to reject than to approve the idea of plurality in the executive, under any modification whatever.

Wherever two or more persons are engaged in any common enterprise or pursuit, there is always danger of difference of opinion. If it be a public trust

---

[4] Hamilton refers to the chief magistrates of Achaean League, a confederacy of Greek city-states. Publius had reviewed the ancient Greeks' attempts to form confederated republics in *Federalist* 18.

[5] Patricians were members of a hereditary noble class; plebeians were commoners.

or office in which they are clothed with equal dignity and authority, there is peculiar danger of personal emulation and even animosity. From either and especially from all these causes, the most bitter dissensions are apt to spring. Whenever these happen, they lessen the respectability, weaken the authority, and distract the plans and operations of those whom they divide. If they should unfortunately assail the supreme executive magistracy of a country, consisting of a plurality of persons, they might impede or frustrate the most important measures of the government, in the most critical emergencies of the state. And what is still worse, they might split the community into the most violent and irreconcilable factions, adhering differently to the different individuals who composed the magistracy.

Men often oppose a thing merely because they have had no agency in planning it, or because it may have been planned by those whom they dislike. But if they have been consulted and have happened to disapprove, opposition then becomes in their estimation an indispensable duty of self-love. They seem to think themselves bound in honor, and by all the motives of personal infallibility to defeat the success of what has been resolved upon, contrary to their sentiments. Men of upright, benevolent tempers have too many opportunities of remarking with horror, to what desperate lengths this disposition is sometimes carried, and how often the great interests of society are sacrificed to the vanity, to the conceit and to the obstinacy of individuals, who have credit enough to make their passions and their caprices interesting to mankind. Perhaps the question now before the public may in its consequences afford melancholy proofs of the effects of this despicable frailty, or rather detestable vice in the human characters. . . .

Upon the principles of a free government, inconveniences from the source just mentioned must necessarily be submitted to in the formation of the legislature; but it is unnecessary and therefore unwise to introduce them into the constitution of the executive. It is here too that they may be most pernicious. In the legislature, promptitude of decision is oftener an evil than a benefit. The differences of opinion, and the jarrings of parties in that department of the government, though they may sometimes obstruct salutary plans, yet often promote deliberations and circumspection; and serve to check excesses in the majority. When a resolution too is once taken, the opposition must be at an end. That resolution is a law, and resistance to it is punishable. But no favorable circumstances palliate or atone for the disadvantages of dissension in the executive department. Here they are pure and unmixed. There is no point at which they cease to operate. They serve to embarrass and weaken the execution of the plan or measure, to which they relate, from the first step to the final conclusion of it. They constantly counteract those qualities in the executive, which are most necessary ingredients in its composition, vigor and expedition, and this without any counterbalancing good. In the conduct of war, in which the energy of the executive is the bulwark of the national security, everything would be to be apprehended from its plurality.

It must be confessed that these observations apply with principal weight to the first case supposed, that is to a plurality of magistrates of equal dignity and authority; a scheme the advocates for which are not likely to form a numerous sect: But they apply, though not with equal, yet with considerable weight, to the project of a council, whose concurrence is made constitutionally necessary to the operations of the ostensible executive. An artful cabal in that council would be able to distract and to enervate the whole system of administration. If no such cabal should exist, the mere diversity of views and opinions would alone be sufficient to tincture the exercise of the executive authority with a spirit of habitual feebleness and dilatoriness.

But one of the weightiest objections to a plurality in the executive, and which lies as much against the last as the first plan, is that it tends to conceal faults, and destroy responsibility. Responsibility is of two kinds, to censure and to punishment. The first is the most important of the two; especially in an elective office. Man, in public trust, will much oftener act in such a manner as to render him unworthy of being any longer trusted, than in such a manner as to make him obnoxious to legal punishment. But the multiplication of the executive adds to the difficulty of detection in either case. It often becomes impossible, amidst mutual accusations, to determine on whom the blame or the punishment of a pernicious measure, or series of pernicious measures ought really to fall. It is shifted from one to another with so much dexterity, and under such plausible appearances, that the public opinion is left in suspense about the real author. The circumstances which may have led to any national miscarriage or misfortune are sometimes so complicated, that where there are a number of actors who may have had different degrees and kinds of agency, though we may clearly see upon the whole that there has been mismanagement, yet it may be impracticable to pronounce to whose account the evil which may have been incurred is truly chargeable. . . .

"I was overruled by my council. The council were so divided in their opinions, that it was impossible to obtain any better resolution on the point." These and similar pretexts are constantly at hand, whether true or false. And who is there that will either take the trouble or incur the odium of a strict scrutiny into the secret springs of the transaction? Should there be found a citizen zealous enough to undertake the unpromising task, if there happen to be a collusion between the parties concerned, how easy is it to clothe the circumstances with so much ambiguity, as to render it uncertain what was the precise conduct of any of those parties?

In the single instance in which the governor of this state is coupled with a council, that is in the appointment to offices, we have seen the mischiefs of it in the view now under consideration. Scandalous appointments to important offices have been made. Some cases indeed have been so flagrant that ALL PARTIES have agreed in the impropriety of the thing. When enquiry has been made, the blame has been laid by the governor on the members of the council; who on their part have charged it upon his nomination: While the people remain altogether at a loss to determine by whose influence their interests have been committed to hands so unqualified, and so manifestly improper. In tenderness,[6] I forbear to descend to particulars.

It is evident from these considerations, that the plurality of the executive tends to deprive the people of the two greatest securities they can have for the faithful exercise of any delegated power; first, the restraints of public opinion, which lose their efficacy as well on account of the division of the censure attendant on bad measures among a number, as on account of the uncertainty on whom it ought to fall; and secondly, the opportunity of discovering with facility and clearness the misconduct of the persons they trust, in order either to their removal from office, or to their actual punishment, in cases which admit of it.

In England the King is a perpetual magistrate; and it is a maxim, which has obtained for the sake of the public peace, that he is unaccountable for his administration, and his person sacred. Nothing therefore can be wiser in that kingdom than to annex to the king a constitutional council, who may be responsible to the nation for the advice they give. Without this there would be no responsibility whatever in the executive department; an idea inadmissible in a free government. But even there the king is not bound by the resolutions of his council, though they are answerable for the advice they give. He is the absolute master of his own conduct, in the exercise of his office; and may observe or disregard the council given to him at his sole discretion.

But in a republic, where every magistrate ought to be personally responsible for his behaviour in office, the reason which in the British constitution dictates the propriety of a council not only ceases to apply, but turns against the institution. In the monarchy of Great Britain, it furnishes a substitute for

---

[6] wishing to be kind or tactful

the prohibited responsibility of the chief magistrate; which serves in some degree as a hostage to the national justice for his good behavior. In the American republic it would serve to destroy, or would greatly diminish the intended and necessary responsibility of the chief magistrate himself.

The idea of a council to the executive, which has so generally obtained in the state constitutions, has been derived from that maxim of republican jealousy, which considers power as safer in the hands of a number of men than of a single man. If the maxim should be admitted to be applicable to the case, I should contend that the advantage on that side would not counterbalance the numerous disadvantages on the opposite side. But I do not think the rule at all applicable to the executive power. I clearly concur in opinion in this particular with a writer whom the celebrated Junius pronounces to be "deep, solid and ingenious,"[7] that, "the executive power is more confined when it is one:" That it is far more safe there should be a single object for the jealousy and watchfulness of the people; and in a word that all multiplication of the executive is rather dangerous than friendly to liberty.

A little consideration will satisfy us, that the species of security sought for in the multiplication of the executive is unattainable. Numbers must be so great as to render combination difficult; or they are rather a source of danger than of security. The united credit and influence of several individuals must be more formidable to liberty than the credit and influence of either of them separately. When power therefore is placed in the hands of so small a number of men, as to admit of their interests and views being easily combined in a common enterprise, by an artful leader, it becomes more liable to abuse and more dangerous when abused, than if it be lodged in the hands of one man; who from the very circumstance of his being alone will be more narrowly watched and more readily suspected, and who cannot unite so great a mass of influence as when he is associated with others. The Decemvirs of Rome,[8] whose name denotes their number, were more to be dreaded in their usurpation than any ONE of them would have been. No person would think of proposing an executive much more numerous than that body[;] from six to a dozen have been suggested for the number of the council. The extreme

---

[7] Junius was the pseudonym of a popular British polemicist. The writer Junius commended was Jean Louis de Lolme (1740–1806), a Genevan and British political theorist who wrote *The Constitution of England* (1771).

[8] Publius refers to two commissions of ten men appointed by the Roman Senate in the 5th century BC and tasked to design a written law code. The second commission became tyrannical and were ousted by popular insurrection.

of these numbers is not too great for an easy combination; and from such a combination America would have more to fear, than from the ambition of any single individual. A council to a magistrate, who is himself responsible for what he does, are generally nothing better than a clog upon his good intentions; are often the instruments and accomplices of his bad, and are almost always a cloak to his faults.

I forbear to dwell upon the subject of expense; though it be evident that if the council should be numerous enough to answer the principal end, aimed at by the institution, the salaries of the members, who must be drawn from their homes to reside at the seat of government, would form an item in the catalogue of public expenditures, too serious to be incurred for an object of equivocal[9] utility.

I will only add, that prior to the appearance of the Constitution, I rarely met with an intelligent man from any of the states, who did not admit as the result of experience, that the UNITY of the Executive of this state was one of the best of the distinguishing features of our Constitution.

The Federalist, No. 71

DURATION in office has been mentioned as the second requisite to the energy of the executive authority. This has relation to two objects: To the personal firmness of the Executive Magistrate in the employment of his constitutional powers; and to the stability of the system of administration which may have been adopted under his auspices. With regard to the first, it must be evident, that the longer the duration of office, the greater will be the probability of obtaining so important an advantage. It is a general principle of human nature, that a man will be interested in whatever he possesses, in proportion to the firmness or precariousness of the tenure, by which he holds it; will be less attached to what he holds by a momentary or uncertain title, than to what he enjoys by a durable or certain title; and of course will be willing to risk more for the sake of the one, than for the sake of the other. This remark is not less applicable to a political privilege, or honor, or trust, than to any article of ordinary property. The inference from it is, that a man, acting in the capacity of Chief Magistrate, under a consciousness, that in a very short time he *must* lay down his office, will be apt to feel himself too little interested in it, to hazard any material censure or perplexity, from the independent exertion of his powers, or from encountering the ill-humors,

---

[9] uncertain

however transient, which may happen to prevail either in a considerable part of the society itself, or even in a predominant faction in the legislative body. If the case should only be, that he *might* lay it down, unless continued by a new choice; and if he should be desirous of being continued, his wishes conspiring with his fears would tend still more powerfully to corrupt his integrity, or debase his fortitude. In either case feebleness and irresolution must be the characteristics of the station....

There are some, who would be inclined to regard the servile pliancy of the executive to a prevailing current, either in the community, or in the legislature, as its best recommendation. But such men entertain very crude notions, as well of the purposes of which government was instituted, as of the true means by which the public happiness may be promoted. The republican principle demands, that the deliberate sense of the community should govern the conduct of those to whom they entrust the management of their affairs; but it does not require an unqualified complaisance to every sudden breeze of passion, or to every transient impulse which the people may receive from the arts of men, who flatter their prejudices to betray their interests. It is a just observation, that the people commonly intend the PUBLIC GOOD. This often applies to their very errors. But their good sense would despise the adulator,[10] who should pretend that they always reason right about the means of promoting it. They know from experience, that they sometimes err; and the wonder is, that they so seldom err as they do; beset as they continually are by the wiles of parasites and sycophants, by the snares of the ambitious, the avaricious, the desperate; by the artifices of men, who possess their confidence more than they deserve it, and of those who seek to possess, rather than to deserve it. When occasions present themselves in which the interests of the people are at variance with their inclinations, it is the duty of the persons whom they have appointed to be the guardians of those interests, to withstand the temporary delusion, in order to give them time and opportunity for more cool and sedate reflection....

But however inclined we might be to insist upon an unbounded complaisance in the executive to the inclinations of the people, we can with no propriety contend for a like compliance to the humors of the legislature. The latter may sometimes stand in opposition to the former; and at other times the people may be entirely neutral. In either supposition, it is certainly desirable that the executive should be in a situation to dare to act his own opinion with vigor and decision.

---

[10] flatterer

The same rule, which teaches the propriety of a partition between the various branches of power, teaches us likewise that this partition ought to be so contrived as to render the one independent of the other. To what purpose separate the executive, or the judiciary, from the legislative, if both the executive and the judiciary are so constituted as to be at the absolute devotion of[11] the legislative? ... It is one thing to be subordinate to the laws, and another to be dependent on the legislative body. ... The tendency of the legislative authority to absorb every other, has been fully displayed and illustrated by examples, in some preceding numbers. In governments purely republican, this tendency is almost irresistible. The representatives of the people, in a popular assembly, seem sometimes to fancy that they are the people themselves; and betray strong symptoms of impatience and disgust at the least sign of opposition from any quarter; as if the exercise of its rights by either the executive or judiciary, were a breach of their privilege and an outrage to their dignity. They often appear disposed to exert an imperious control over the other departments; and as they commonly have the people on their side, they always act with such momentum as to make it very difficult for the other members of the government to maintain the balance of the Constitution.

It may perhaps be asked how the shortness of the duration in office can affect the independence of the executive on the legislature, unless the one were possessed of the power of appointing or displacing the other? One answer to this enquiry may be drawn from the principle already remarked, that is from the slender interest a man is apt to take in a short lived advantage, and the little inducement it affords him to expose himself on account of it to any considerable inconvenience or hazard. Another answer, perhaps more obvious, though not more conclusive, will result from the consideration of the influence of the legislative body over the people, which might be employed to prevent the re-election of a man, who by an upright resistance to any sinister project of that body, should have made himself obnoxious to its resentment.

It may be asked also whether a duration of four years would answer the end proposed, and if it would not, whether a less period which would at least be recommended by greater security against ambitious designs, would not for that reason be preferable to a longer period, which was at the same time too short for the purpose of inspiring the desired firmness and independence of the magistrate?

It cannot be affirmed, that a duration of four years or any other limited

---

[11] completely subordinate to

duration would completely answer the end proposed; but it would contribute towards it in a degree which would have a material influence upon the
spirit and character of the government. Between the commencement and
termination of such a period there would be a considerable interval, in which
the prospect of annihilation would be sufficiently remote not to have an
improper effect upon the conduct of a man endued with a tolerable portion
of fortitude; and in which he might reasonably promise himself, that there
would be time enough, before it arrived, to make the community sensible
of the propriety of the measures he might incline to pursue. Though it be
probable, that as he approached the moment when the public were by a new
election to signify their sense of his conduct, his confidence and with it, his
firmness would decline; yet both the one and the other would derive support
from the opportunities, which his previous continuance in the station had
afforded him of establishing himself in the esteem and good will of his constituents. He might then hazard with safety, in proportion to the proofs he
had given of his wisdom and integrity, and to the title he had acquired to the
respect and attachment of his fellow citizens. As on the one hand, a duration
of four years will contribute to the firmness of the executive in a sufficient
degree to render it a very valuable ingredient in the composition; so on the
other, it is not long enough to justify any alarm for the public liberty....

The Federalist, No. 72

The administration of government, in its largest sense, comprehends all the
operations of the body politic, whether legislative, executive, or judicial, but
in its most usual and perhaps in its most precise signification, it is limited to
executive details, and falls peculiarly within the province of the executive
department. The actual conduct of foreign negotiations, the preparatory
plans of finance, the application and disbursement of the public monies,
in conformity to the general appropriations of the legislature, the arrangement of the army and navy, the direction of the operations of war; these and
other matters of a like nature constitute what seems to be most properly
understood by the administration of government. The persons therefore, to
whose immediate management these different matters are committed, ought
to be considered as the assistants or deputies of the chief magistrate; and,
on this account, they ought to derive their offices from his appointment, at
least from his nomination, and ought to be subject to his superintendence.
This view of the subject will at once suggest to us the intimate connection
between the duration of the executive magistrate in office, and the stability

of the system of administration. To reverse and undo what has been done by a predecessor is very often considered by a successor, as the best proof he can give of his own capacity and desert; and, in addition to this propensity, where the alteration been the result of public choice, the person substituted is warranted in supposing, that the dismission of his predecessor has proceeded from a dislike to his measures, and that the less he resembles him the more he will recommend himself to the favor of his constituents. These considerations, and the influence of personal confidences and attachments, would be likely to induce every new president to promote a change of men to fill the subordinate stations; and these causes together could not fail to occasion a disgraceful and ruinous mutability in the administration of the government.

With a positive duration of considerable extent, I connect the circumstance of re-eligibility. The first is necessary to give to the officer himself the inclination and the resolution to act his part well, and to the community time and leisure to observe the tendency of his measures, and thence to form an experimental estimate of their merits. The last is necessary to enable the people, when they see reason to approve of his conduct, to continue him in the station, in order to prolong the utility of his talents and virtues, and to secure to the government, the advantage of permanency in a wise system of administration.

Nothing appears more plausible at first sight, nor more ill founded upon close inspection, than a scheme, which in relation to the present point has had some respectable advocates—I mean that of continuing the chief magistrate in office for a certain time, and then excluding him from it, either for a limited period, or for ever after. This exclusion whether temporary or perpetual would have nearly the same effects; and these effects would be for the most part rather pernicious than salutary.

One ill effect of the exclusion would be a diminution of the inducements to good behavior. There are few men who would not feel much less zeal in the discharge of a duty, when they were conscious that the advantages of the station, with which it was connected, must be relinquished at a determinate period, than when they were permitted to entertain a hope of *obtaining* by *meriting* a continuance of them. This position will not be disputed, so long as it is admitted that the desire of reward is one of the strongest incentives of human conduct, or that the best security for the fidelity of mankind is to make their interest coincide with their duty. Even the love of fame, the ruling passion of the noblest minds, which would prompt a man to plan and undertake extensive and arduous enterprises for the public benefit, requiring considerable time to mature and perfect them, if he could flatter himself with the prospect of being allowed to finish what he had begun, would on the contrary deter him from the undertaking, when he foresaw that he must quit the scene, before he could accomplish the work, and must commit that, together with his own reputation, to hands which might be unequal or unfriendly to the task. The most to be expected from the generality of men, in such a situation, is the negative merit of not doing harm instead of the positive merit of doing good.

Another ill effect of the exclusion would be the temptation to sordid views, to peculation,[12] and in some instances, [to] usurpation. An avaricious man, who might happen to fill the offices, looking forward to a time when he must at all events yield up the emoluments[13] he enjoyed, would feel a propensity, not easy to be resisted by such a man, to make the best use of the opportunity he enjoyed, while it lasted; and might not scruple to have recourse to the most corrupt expedients to make the harvest as abundant as it was transitory; though the same man probably, with a different prospect before him, might content himself with the regular perquisites of his station, and might even be unwilling to risk the consequences of an abuse of his opportunities. He avarice might be a guard upon his avarice. Add to this, that the same man might be vain or ambitious as well avaricious. And if he could expect to prolong his honors, by his good conduct, he might hesitate to sacrifice his appetite for them to his appetite for gain. But with the prospect before him of approaching and inevitable annihilation, his avarice would be likely to get the victory over this caution, his vanity or his ambition.

An ambitious man too, when he found himself seated on the summit of his country's honors, when he looked forward to the time at which he must descend from the exalted eminence forever; and reflected that no exertion or merit on his part could save him from the unwelcome reverse: Such a man, in such a situation, would be much more violently tempted to embrace a favorable conjuncture for attempting to prolongation of his power, at every personal hazard, than if he had the probability of answering the same end by doing his duty.

Would it promote the peace of the community, or the stability of the government, to have half a dozen men who had had credit enough to be raised to seat of the supreme magistracy, wandering among the people like disconnected ghosts, and sighing for a place which they destined never more to possess?

---

[12] embezzling public funds
[13] salary or other advantages of office

A third ill effect of the exclusion would be the depriving community of the advantage of the experience gained by the chief magistrate in the exercise of his office. That experience is the parent of wisdom is an adage, the truth of which is recognized by the wisest as well as the simplest of mankind. What more desirable or more essential than this quality in the governors of nations? Where more desirable or more essential than in the first magistrate of a nation? Can it be wise to put this desirable and essential quality under the ban of the Constitution; and to declare that the moment is acquired, its possessor shall be compelled to abandon the station in which it was acquired, and to which it is adapted? This nevertheless is the precise import of all those regulations, which exclude men from serving their country, by the choice of their fellow citizens, after they have, by a course of service fitted themselves for doing it with a greater degree of utility.

A fourth ill effect of the exclusion would be the banishing men from stations, in which in certain emergencies of the state their presence might be of the greatest moment to the public interest or safety. There is no nation which has not at one period or another experienced an absolute necessity of the services of particular men, in particular situations, perhaps it would not be too strong to say, to the preservation of its political existence. How unwise therefore must be every self-denying ordinance, as serves to prohibit a nation from making use of its own citizens, in the manner best suited to its exigencies and circumstances! Without supposing the personal essentiality of the man, it is evident that a change of the chief magistrate, at the breaking out of a war, or at any similar crisis, for another even of equal merit, would at all times be detrimental to the community; inasmuch as it would substitute inexperience to experience, and would tend to unhinge and set afloat the already settled train of the administration.

A fifth ill effect of the exclusion would be, that it would operate as a constitutional interdiction of stability in the administration. *By necessitating* a change of men, in the first office in the nation, it would necessitate a mutability of measures. It is not generally to be expected, that men will vary; and measures remain uniform. The contrary is the usual course of things. And we need not to be apprehensive there will be too much stability, while there is even the option of changing; nor need we desire to prohibit the people from continuing their confidence, where they think it may be safely placed, and where by constancy on their part, they may obviate the fatal inconveniences of fluctuating councils and a variable policy.

These are some of the disadvantages, which would flow from the principle of exclusion. They apply most forcibly to the scheme of a perpetual exclusion;

but when we consider that even a partial exclusion would always render the re-admission of the person a remote and precarious object, the observations which have been made will apply nearly as fully to one case as to the other.

What are the advantages promised to counterbalance these disadvantages? They are represented to be 1st. Greater independence in the magistrate; 2nd. Greater security to the people. Unless the exclusion be perpetual there will be no pretense to infer the first advantage. But even in that case, may he have no object beyond his present station to which he may sacrifice his independence? May he have no connections, no friends, for whom he may sacrifice it? May he not be less willing, by a firm conduct, to make personal enemies, when he acts under the impression, that a time is fast approaching, on the arrival of which he not only MAY, but MUST be exposed to their resentments, upon an equal, perhaps upon an inferior footing? It is not an easy point to determine whether his independence would be most promoted or impaired by such an arrangement.

As to the second supposed advantage, there is still greater reason to entertain doubts concerning it. If the exclusion were to be perpetual, a man of irregular ambition, of whom alone there could be reason in any case to entertain apprehensions, would with infinite reluctance yield to the necessity of taking his leave forever of a post, in which his passion for power and pre-eminence had acquired the force of habit. And if he had been fortunate or adroit enough to conciliate the good will of people he might induce them to consider as a very odious and unjustifiable restraint upon themselves, a provision which was calculated to debar them of the right of giving a fresh proof of their attachment to a favorite. There may be conceived circumstances, in which this disgust of the people, seconding the thwarted ambition of such a favorite, might occasion greater danger to liberty, than could ever reasonably be dreaded from the possibility of a perpetuation in office, by the voluntary suffrages of the community, exercising a constitutional privilege.

There is an excess of refinement in the idea of disabling the people to continue in office men, who had entitled themselves, in their opinion, to approbation and confidence; the advantages of which are at best speculative and equivocal; and are over-balanced by disadvantages for more certain and decisive.

Cato No. 4

January 3, 1788

B ecause the opponents of the Constitution did not agree in their objections, they were not as organized as its advocates. However, most anti-Federalists focused their criticisms on the absence of a bill of rights and on Congress. In particular, they argued that Congress's powers were undefined, that Congress was too small, and that it would be composed of elites who would not represent ordinary people. The vast majority of anti-Federalist writing did not focus on the presidency. "Cato," of New York, is an exception. (Like many of those engaged in the debate over ratification, this author wrote under a penname. While scholars have not conclusively determined who Cato was, a leading contender has long been George Clinton, the first and longest tenured governor of New York State.) Cato warned that the elective nature of the presidency would enhance the president's formal powers under the Constitution. Because the president would be able to appoint ministers, he would be able to create a court of elites who would then dominate ordinary people. Moreover, Cato worries that the length of the president's term of office, combined with the absence of a term limit, would make the president even more powerful. Notice also that Cato predicts the scenario that happened in 1824, when the selection of the president was thrown into the House—no candidate having won a majority in the Electoral College—and the House chose the person who did not win the most Electoral College votes.

SOURCE: *The New York Journal*, January 3, 1788.

... I shall begin with observations on the executive branch of this new system; and though it is not the first in order, as arranged therein, yet being the *chief*, is perhaps entitled by the rules of rank to the first consideration. The executive power as described in the 2d article, consists of a president and vice-president, who are to hold their offices during the term of four years; the same article has marked the manner and time of their election, and established the qualifications of the president; it also provides against the removal, death, or inability of the president and vice-president—regulates the salary of the president, delineates his duties and powers; and lastly, declares the causes for which the president and vice-president shall be removed from office.

Notwithstanding the great learning and abilities of the gentlemen who composed the convention, it may be here remarked with deference, that the construction of the first paragraph of the first section of the second article, is vague and inexplicit, and leaves the mind in doubt, as to the election of a president and vice-president, after the expiration of the election for the first term of four years—in every other case, the election of these great officers is expressly provided for; but there is no explicit provision for their election in case of the expiration of their offices, subsequent to the election which is to set this political machine in motion—no certain and express terms as in your state constitution, that *statedly* once in every four years, and as often as these offices shall become vacant, by expiration or otherwise, as is therein expressed, an election shall be held as follows, etc.—this inexplicitness perhaps may lead to an establishment for life....

...It is remarked by Montesquieu, in treating of republics, that in *all magistracies, the greatness of the power must be compensated by the brevity of the duration; and that a longer time than a year, would be dangerous.* It is therefore obvious to the least intelligent mind, to account why, great power in the hands of a magistrate, and that power connected, with a considerable duration, may be dangerous to the liberties of a republic—the deposit of vast trusts in the hands of a single magistrate, enables him in their exercise, to create a numerous train of dependents—this tempts his *ambition*, which in a republican magistrate is also remarked, *to be pernicious* and the duration of his office for any considerable time favors his views, give him the means and time to perfect and execute his designs—*he therefore fancies that he may be great and glorious by oppressing his fellow citizens, and raising himself to permanent grandeur on the ruins of his country.*—And here it may be necessary to compare the vast and important powers of the president, together with his continuance in office with the foregoing doctrine—his eminent magisterial situation will attach many adherents to him, and he will be surrounded by expectants and courtiers—his power of nomination and influence on all appointments—the strong posts in each state comprised within his superintendence, and garrisoned by troops under his direction—his control over the army, militia, and navy—the unrestrained power of granting pardons for treason, which may be used to screen from punishment, those whom he had secretly instigated to commit the crime, and thereby prevent a discovery of his own guilt—his duration in office for four years: these, and various other principles evidently prove the truth of the position—that if the president is possessed of ambition, he has power and time sufficient to ruin his country.

Though the president, during the sitting of the legislature, is assisted by the senate, yet he is without a constitutional council in their recess—he will therefore be unsupported by proper information and advice, and will generally be directed by minions and favorites, or a council of state will grow out of the principal officers of the great departments, the most dangerous council in a free country.

The ten miles square, which is to become the seat of government, will of course be the place of residence for the president and the great officers of state—the same observation of a great man will apply to the court of a president possessing the powers of a monarch, that is observed of that of a monarch—*ambition with idleness—baseness with pride—the thirst of riches without labour—aversion to truth—flattery—treason—perfidy—violation of engagements—contempt of civil duties—hope from the magistrate's weakness; but above all, the perpetual ridicule of virtue*—these, he remarks, are the characteristics by which the courts in all ages have been distinguished.[1]

The language and manners of this court will be what distinguishes them from the rest of the community, not what assimilates them to it, and in being remarked for a behavior that shews they are not *meanly born*, and in adulation to people of fortune and power.

The establishment of a vice-president is as unnecessary as it is dangerous. This officer, for want of other employment, is made president of the senate, thereby blending the executive and legislative powers, besides always giving to some one state, from which he is to come, an unjust pre-eminence.

It is a maxim in republics, that the representative of the people should be of their immediate choice; but by the manner in which the president is chosen he arrives to this office at the fourth or fifth hand, nor does the highest vote, in the way he is elected, determine the choice—for it is only necessary that he should be taken from the highest of five, who may have a plurality of votes.[2]

---

[1] Cato imperfectly quotes Montesquieu, *Spirit of the Laws*, Book III, which lists the vices typical of a monarch's courtiers. Rather than "hope from the magistrate's weakness," Montesquieu notes the "fear of a prince's virtue [and] hope from his [moral] weakness."

[2] Cato is referring to the contingency election in the House, whereby the House chooses from the top five candidates in the event no candidate receives an Electoral College majority. The Twelfth Amendment reduces this number to three.

Compare your past opinions and sentiments with the present proposed establishment, and you will find, that if you adopt it, that it will lead you into a system which you heretofore reprobated as odious. Every American whig, not long since, bore his emphatic testimony against a monarchical government, though limited, because of the dangerous inequality that it created among citizens as relative to their rights and property; and wherein does this president, invested with his powers and prerogatives, essentially differ from the king of Great-Britain ... [?] [T]he direct prerogatives of the president, as springing from his political character, are among the following:—It is necessary, in order to distinguish him from the rest of the community, and enable him to keep, and maintain his court, that the compensation for his services; or in other words, his revenue should be such as to enable him to appear with the splendor of a prince; he has the power of receiving ambassadors from, and a great influence on their appointments to foreign courts; as also to make treaties, leagues, and alliances with foreign states, assisted by the senate, which when made, become the supreme law of the land: he is a constituent part of the legislative power; for every bill which shall pass the house of representatives and senate, is to be presented to him for approbation; if he approves of it, he is to sign it, if he disapproves, he is to return it with objections, which in many cases will amount to a complete negative; and in this view he will have a great share in the power of making peace, coining money, etc. and all the various objects of legislation, expressed or implied in this Constitution: for though it may be asserted that the king of Great-Britain has the express power of making peace or war, yet he never thinks it prudent so to do without the advice of his parliament from whom he is to derive his support, and therefore these powers, in both president and king, are substantially the same: he is the generalissimo of the nation, and of course, has the command and control of the army, navy, and militia; he is the general conservator of the peace of the union—he may pardon all offences, except in cases of impeachment, and the principal fountain of all offices and employments. Will not the exercise of these powers therefore tend either to the establishment of a vile and arbitrary aristocracy, or monarchy? The safety of the people in a republic depends on the share or proportion they have in the government; but experience ought to teach you, that when a man is at the head of an elective government invested with great powers, and interested in his re-election, in what circle appointments will be made; by which means *an imperfect aristocracy* bordering on monarchy may be established.

You must, however, my countrymen, beware, that the advocates of this new system do not deceive you, by a fallacious resemblance between it and your own state government, which you so much prize; and if you examine, you will perceive that the chief of this state, is your immediate choice, controlled and checked by a just and full representation of the people, divested of the prerogative of influencing war and peace, making treaties, receiving and sending embassies, and commanding standing armies and navies, which belong to the power of the confederation, and will be convinced that this government is no more like a true picture of your own, that an Angel of darkness resembles an Angel of light.

Cato.

DOCUMENT 3

Remarks on the Removal Power

Representative James Madison

Speech in Congress, June 16, 1789 and Letter to Edmund Pendleton, June 21, 1789

T*he Constitution is clear about how heads of departments are created: the president appoints them, subject to the advice and consent of the Senate. But the Constitution says nothing about how department heads are removed. Must the president seek the advice and consent of the Senate to remove a department head, or does the president have this power alone? Or does the Constitution leave this power to Congress to delegate as it pleases? Or is there some other constitutional device, like impeachment, for removals?*

This question arose in the first Congress even before there were political parties. In the House, James Madison led the coalition that argued that the Constitution vested this power in the president alone. Notice how he justifies that power in the following speech on the House floor and in his account in the letter to fellow Virginian Edmund Pendleton (1721–1803). In addition to the argument about the principle of responsibility, or accountability, Madison points to the difference between the Vesting Clauses of Articles One and Two to make his case.

SOURCE: James Madison, Speech on the Removal Power of the President, [16 June] 1789, *Founders Online*, National Archives, https://goo.gl/o2MFpz; "From James Madison to Edmund Pendleton, 21 June 1789," *Founders Online*, National Archives, https://goo.gl/dzrYqB.

Speech in Congress, June 16, 1789

The Committee of the Whole took up the bill establishing a department of foreign affairs. Smith (South Carolina) and others wished to strike out the clause declaring the secretary "to be removable from office by the President of the United States."

MR. MADISON. If the construction of the Constitution is to be left to its natural course with respect to the executive powers of this government,

I own that the insertion of this sentiment ["to be removable from office by the President of the United States"] in law may not be of material importance, though if it is nothing more than a mere declaration of a clear grant made by the Constitution, it can do no harm; but if it relates to a doubtful part of the Constitution, I suppose an exposition of the Constitution may come with as much propriety from the legislature as any other department of government. If the power naturally belongs to the government, and the constitution is undecided as to the body which is to exercise it, it is likely that it is submitted to the discretion of the legislature, and the question will depend upon its own merits.

I am clearly of opinion with the gentleman from South-Carolina (Mr. Smith,) . . . that we ought in this and every other case to adhere to the Constitution, so far as it will serve as a guide to us, and that we ought not to be swayed in our decisions by the splendor of the character of the present chief magistrate, but to consider it with respect to the merit of men who, in the ordinary course of things, may be supposed to fill the chair. I believe the power here declared is a high one, and in some respects a dangerous one; but in order to come to a right decision on this point, we must consider both sides of the question: The possible abuses which may spring from a single will of the first magistrate, and the abuse which may spring from the combined will of the executive and the senatorial qualification.

When we consider that the first magistrate is to be appointed at present by the suffrages of three millions of people, and in all human probability in a few years time by double that number, it is not to be presumed that a vicious or bad character will be selected. If the government of any country on the face of the earth was ever effectually guarded against the election of ambitious or designing characters to the first office of the state, I think it may with truth be said to be the case under the Constitution of the United States. With all the infirmities incident to a popular election, corrected by the particular mode of conducting it, as directed under the present system, I think we may fairly calculate, that the instances will be very rare in which an unworthy man will receive that mark of the public confidence which is required to designate the President of the United States. Where the people are disposed to give so great an elevation to one of their fellow citizens, I own that I am not afraid to place my confidence in him; especially when I know he is impeachable for any crime or misdemeanor, before the Senate, at all times; and that at all events he is impeachable before the community at large every four years, and liable to be displaced if his conduct shall have given umbrage during the time he has been in office. Under these circumstances, although the trust is a high one, and in some degree perhaps a dangerous one, I am not sure but it will be safer here than placed where some gentlemen suppose it ought to be.

It is evidently the intention of the Constitution that the first magistrate should be responsible for the executive department; so far therefore as we do not make the officers who are to aid him in the duties of that department responsible to him, he is not responsible to his country. Again, is there no danger that an officer when he is appointed by the concurrence of the Senate, and has friends in that body, may choose rather to risk his establishment on the favor of that branch, than rest it upon the discharge of his duties to the satisfaction [of] the executive branch, which is constitutionally authorized to inspect and control his conduct? And if it should happen that the officers connect themselves with the Senate, they may mutually support each other, and for want of efficacy reduce the power of the president to a mere vapor, in which case his responsibility would be annihilated, and the expectation of it unjust. The high executive officers, joined in cabal with the Senate, would lay the foundation of discord, and end in an assumption of the executive power, only to be removed by a revolution in the government. I believe no principle is more clearly laid down in the Constitution than that of responsibility. After premising this, I will proceed to an investigation of the merits of the question upon constitutional ground.

I have since the subject was last before the House, examined the Constitution with attention, and I acknowledge that it does not perfectly correspond with the ideas I entertained of it from the first glance. I am inclined to think that a free and systematic interpretation of the plan of government, will leave us less at liberty to abate the responsibility than gentlemen imagine. I have already acknowledged, that the powers of the government must remain as apportioned by the Constitution. But it may be contended, that where the Constitution is silent it becomes a subject of legislative discretion; perhaps, in the opinion of some, an argument in favor of the clause may be successfully brought forward on this ground: I however leave it for the present untouched.

By a strict examination of the Constitution on what appears to be its true principles, and considering the great departments of government in the relation they have to each other, I have my doubts whether we are not absolutely tied down to the construction declared in the bill. In the first section of the first article, it is said, that all legislative powers herein granted shall be vested in a Congress of the United States. In the second article it is affirmed, that the executive power shall be vested in a President of the United States of America. In the third article it is declared, that the judicial power of the United States shall be vested in one supreme court, and in such inferior courts as

Congress may from time to time ordain and establish. I suppose it will be readily admitted, that so far as the Constitution has separated the power of these great departments, it would be improper to combine them together, and so far as it has left any particular department in the entire possession of the powers incident to that department, I conceive we ought not to qualify them farther than they are qualified by the Constitution. The legislative powers are vested in Congress, and are to be exercised by them uncontrolled by any other department, except the Constitution has qualified it otherwise. The Constitution has qualified the legislative power by authorizing the president to object to any act it may pass, requiring, in this case two-thirds of both houses to concur in making a law; but still the absolute legislative power is vested in Congress with this qualification alone.

The Constitution affirms, that the executive power shall be vested in the president: Are there exceptions to this proposition? Yes, there are. The Constitution says that, in appointing to office, the Senate shall be associated with the president, unless in the case of inferior officers, when the law shall otherwise direct. Have we a right to extend this exception? I believe not. If the Constitution has invested all executive power in the president, I venture to assert, that the legislature has no right to diminish or modify his executive authority.

The question now resolves itself into this, Is the power of displacing [an appointed official] an executive power? I conceive that if any power whatsoever is in its nature executive it is the power of appointing, overseeing, and controlling those who execute the laws. If the Constitution had not qualified the power of the president in appointing to office, by associating the Senate with him in that business, would it not be clear that he would have the right by virtue of his executive power to make such appointments? Should we be authorized, in defiance of that clause in the Constitution—"The executive power shall be vested in a president," to unite the Senate with the president in the appointment to office? I conceive not. If it is admitted we should not be authorized to do this, I think it may be disputed whether we have a right to associate them in removing persons from office, the one power being as much of an executive nature as the other, and the first only is authorized by being excepted out of the general rule established by the Constitution, in these words, "the executive power shall be vested in the president."

The judicial power is vested in a supreme court, but will gentlemen say the judicial power can be placed elsewhere, unless the Constitution has made an exception? The Constitution justifies the Senate in exercising a judiciary power in determining on impeachments: But can the judicial power be farther blended with the powers of that body? They cannot. I therefore say it is incontrovertible, if neither the legislative nor judicial powers are subjected to qualifications, other than those demanded in the Constitution, that the executive powers are equally unabateable as either of the other; and inasmuch as the power of removal is of an executive nature, and not affected by any constitutional exception, it is beyond the reach of the legislative body.

If this is the true construction of this instrument, the clause in the bill is nothing more than explanatory of the meaning of the Constitution, and therefore not liable to any particular objection on that account. If the Constitution is silent, and it is a power the legislature have a right to confer, it will appear to the world, if we strike out the clause, as if we doubted the propriety of vesting it in the President of the United States. I therefore think it best to retain it in the bill.

Letter to Edmund Pendleton, June 21, 1789

... For some time past I have been obliged to content myself with enclosing you the newspapers. In general they give, tho' frequently erroneous and sometimes perverted, yet on the whole, fuller accounts of what is going forward than could be put into a letter. The papers now covered contain a sketch of a very interesting discussion which consumed [a] great part of the past week. The Constitution has omitted to declare expressly by what authority removals from office are to be made. Out of this silence four constructive doctrines have arisen.

1. That the power of removal may be disposed of by the legislative discretion. To this it is objected that the legislature might then confer it on themselves, or even on the House of Representatives which could not possibly have been intended by the Constitution.

2. That the power of removal can only be exercised in the mode of impeachment. To this the objection is that it would make officers of every description hold their places during good behavior, which could have still less been intended.

3. That the power of removal is incident to the power of appointment. To this the objections are that it would require the constant session of the Senate, that it extends the mixture of legislative and executive power, that it destroys the responsibility of the president, by enabling a subordinate executive officer to entrench himself behind a party in the Senate, and destroys the utility of the Senate in their legislative and judicial characters, by involving them too much in the heats and cabals inseparable from questions of a

personal nature; in fine that it transfers the trust in fact from the president
who being at all times impeachable as well as every fourth year eligible by
the people at large, may be deemed the most responsible member of the government, to the Senate who from the nature of that institution, is and was
meant after the judiciary and in some respects without that exception to be
the most unresponsible[1] branch of the Government.

4. That the executive power being in general terms vested in the president,
all power of an executive nature, not particularly taken away must belong
to that department, that the power of appointment only being expressly
taken away, the power of removal so far as it is of an executive nature must
be reserved. In support of this construction it is urged that exceptions to
general positions are to be taken strictly, and that the axiom relating to the
separation of the legislative and executive functions ought to be favored. To
this are objected the principle on which the third construction is founded,
and the danger of creating too much influence in the executive magistrate.

The last opinion has prevailed, but is subject to various modifications, by
the power of the legislature to limit the duration of laws creating offices, or
the duration of the appointments for filling them, and by the power over the
salaries and appropriations. In truth the legislative power is of such a nature
that it scarcely can be restrained either by the Constitution or by itself. And
if the federal government should lose its proper equilibrium within itself, I
am persuaded that the effect will proceed from the encroachments of the
legislative department. If the possibility of encroachments on the part of the
executive or the Senate were to be compared, I should pronounce the danger
to lie rather in the latter than the former. The mixture of legislative, executive
and judiciary authorities lodged in that body, justifies such an inference; at
the same [time] I am fully in the opinion, that the numerous and immediate
representatives of the people, composing the other House, will decidedly
predominate in the Government.

. . .

---

[1] unresponsive to or least swayed by current public opinion

Helvidius–Pacificus Debate on Neutrality Proclamation

Alexander Hamilton and James Madison

June–August 1793

J ust as the Constitution is silent on the process for removing an executive official, it likewise does not state how to terminate a treaty. Does the president hold the power, or must the president seek the Senate's advice and consent as he does for ratifying a treaty in the first place? This question emerged in 1793 in the context of heated partisan debate about foreign policy. England and France were at war again, and the United States had signed a mutual defense treaty with France in 1778. After Washington issued his Proclamation of Neutrality, Alexander Hamilton took the pen name Pacificus to defend Washington against critics. Pacificus's defense of executive power was so broad that Thomas Jefferson urged James Madison to write a response: "For god's sake, my dear Sir, take up your pen, select the most striking heresies, and cut him to pieces in the face of the public." Madison took the pen name Helvidius to argue that Pacificus's broad reading of the executive power was not the true reading of the Constitution. Notice the place of the Vesting Clause in Hamilton's argument.

SOURCE: "Pacificus No. I, [29 June 1793]," *Founders Online*, National Archives, https://goo.gl/bkwub2; "Helvidius" Number 1, [24 August] 1793," *Founders Online*, National Archives, https://goo.gl/R5Dpr2.

Pacificus No. 1, June 29, 1793

... The objections which have been raised against the Proclamation of Neutrality lately issued by the President have been urged in a spirit of acrimony and invective, which demonstrates, that more was in view than merely a free discussion of an important public measure; that the discussion covers a design of weakening the confidence of the People in the author of the measure; in order to remove or lessen a powerful obstacle to the success of an opposition to the government ....

The objections in question fall under three heads—

1. That the Proclamation was without authority
2. That it was contrary to our treaties with France
3. That it was contrary to the gratitude, which is due from this to that country, for the succors rendered us in our own Revolution
4. That it was out of time & unnecessary.

In order to judge of the solidity of the first of these objection[s], it is necessary to examine what is the nature and design of a proclamation of neutrality.

The true nature & design of such an act is—to *make known* to the powers at war and to the Citizens of the Country, whose Government does the Act, that such a country is in the condition of a Nation at Peace with the belligerent parties, and under no obligations of treaty, to become an *associate in the war* with either of them; that this being its situation its intention is to observe a conduct conformable with it and to perform towards each the duties of neutrality; and as a consequence of this state of things, to give warning to all within its jurisdiction to abstain from acts that shall contravene those duties, under the penalties which the laws of the land (of which the law of Nations is a part) annexes to acts of contravention.

This, and no more, is conceived to be the true import of a Proclamation of Neutrality.

It does not imply, that the Nation which makes the declaration will forbear to perform to any of the warring Powers any stipulations in Treaties which can be performed without rendering it an *associate* or *party* in the war. It therefore does not imply in our case, that the United States will not make those distinctions, between the present belligerent powers, which are stipulated in the 17th and 22d articles of our Treaty with France; because these distinctions are not incompatible with a state of neutrality; they will in no shape render the United States an *associate* or *party* in the war. This must be evident, when it is considered, that even to furnish *determinate* succors, of a certain number of Ships or troops, to a Power at War, in consequence of *antecedent treaties having no particular reference to the existing war*, is not inconsistent with neutrality; a position well established by the doctrines of writers and the practice of Nations.

But no special aids, succors or favors having relation to war, not positively and precisely stipulated by some treaty of the above description, can be afforded to either party, without a breach of neutrality.

In stating that the Proclamation of Neutrality does not imply the nonperformance of any stipulations of treaties which are not of a nature to make the Nation an associate or party in the war, it is conceded that an execution of the clause of Guarantee contained in the 11th article of our of Alliance with France would be contrary to the sense and spirit of the proclamation; because it would engage use with our whole force as an *associate* or *auxiliary* in the war; it would be much more than the cause of a definite limited succor, previously ascertained.

It follows that the proclamation is virtually a manifestation of the sense of the Government that the United States are, *under the circumstances of the case, not bound* to execute the clause of Guarantee.

If this be a just view of the true force and import of the proclamation, it will remain to see whether the President in issuing it acted within his proper sphere, or stepped beyond the bounds of his constitutional authority and duty.

It will not be disputed .... that a Proclamation of Neutrality, where a nation is at liberty to keep out of a war in which other nations are engaged and means so to do, is a *usual* and a *proper* measure. *Its main object and effect are to prevent the Nation being immediately responsible for acts done by its citizens, without the privity*[1] *or connivance of the Government, in contravention of the principles of neutrality.*

An object this [is] of the greatest importance to a country whose true interest lies in the preservation of peace.

The inquiry then is—what department of the government of the United States is the proper one to make a declaration of neutrality in the cases in which the engagements of the nation permit and its interests require such a declaration.

A correct and well-informed mind will discern at once that it can belong neither to the legislative nor judicial department and, of course, must belong to the executive.

The legislative department is not the *organ* of intercourse between the United States and foreign nations. It is charged neither with *making* nor *interpreting* treaties. It is therefore not naturally that organ of the government which is to pronounce the existing condition of the nation, with regard to foreign powers, or to admonish the citizens of their obligations and duties as founded upon that condition of things. Still less is it charged with enforcing the execution and observance of these obligations and those duties.

It is equally obvious that the act in question is foreign to the judiciary

---

[1] secret knowledge

department of the government. The province of that department is to decide litigations in particular cases. It is indeed charged with the interpretation of treaties; but it exercises this function only in the litigated cases; that is where contending parties bring before it a specific controversy. It has no concern with pronouncing upon the external political relations of treaties between government and government.

It must then of necessity belong to the executive department to exercise the function in question—when a proper case for the exercise of it occurs.

It appears to be connected with that department in various capacities, as the *organ* of intercourse between the nation and foreign nations—as the interpreter of the national treaties in those cases in which the judiciary is not competent, that is in the cases between government and government—as that power, which is charged with the execution of the laws, of which treaties form a part—as that power which is charged with the command and application of the public force.

This view of the subject is so natural and obvious—so analogous to general theory and practice—that no doubt can be entertained of its justness, unless such doubt can be deduced from particular provisions of the Constitution of the United States.

Let us see then if cause for such doubt is to be found in that constitution.

The second Article of the Constitution of the United States, section 1st, established this general proposition, that "The executive power shall be vested in a President of the United States of America."

The same article in a succeeding section proceeds to designate particular cases of Executive Power. It declares among other things that the President shall be Commander in Chief of the army and navy of the United States and of the militia of the several states when called into the actual service of the United States, that he shall have power by and with the advice of the Senate to make treaties; that it shall be his duty to receive ambassadors and other public Ministers and to take care that the laws be faithfully executed.

It would not consist with the rules of sound construction to consider this enumeration of particular authorities as derogating from the more comprehensive grant contained in the general clause, further than as it may be coupled with express restrictions or qualifications; as in regard to the cooperation of the Senate in the appointment of Officers and the making of treaties; which are qualifications of the general executive powers of appointing officers and making treaties: Because the difficulty of a complete and perfect specification of all the cases of executive authority would naturally dictate the use of general terms—and would render it improbable that a specification of certain particulars was designed as a substitute for those terms, when antecedently used. The different mode of expression employed in the Constitution in regard to the two powers, the Legislative and the Executive, serves to confirm this inference. In the article which grants the legislative powers of the Government the expressions are—"*All Legislative powers herein granted shall be vested in a Congress of the United States;*" in that which grants the Executive Power the expressions are, as already quoted: the Executive Power shall be vested in a President of the United States of America."

The enumeration ought rather therefore to be considered as intended by way of greater caution, to specify and regulate the principal articles implied in the definition of Executive Power; leaving the rest to flow from the general grant of that power, interpreted in conformity to other parts [of] the Constitution and to the principles of free government.

The general doctrine then of our Constitution is, that the EXECUTIVE POWER of the nation is vested in the president; subject only to the *exceptions* and *qualifications* which are expressed in the instrument.

Two of these have been already noticed—the participation of the Senate in the appointment of officers and the making of treaties. A third remains to be mentioned: the right of the Legislature "to declare war and grant letters of marque and reprisal."

With these exceptions, the Executive Power of the Union is completely lodged in the President. This mode of construing the Constitution has indeed been recognized by Congress in formal acts, upon full consideration and debate. The power of removal from office is an important instance.[2]

And since upon general principles for reasons already given, the issuing of a proclamation of neutrality is merely an Executive Act; since also the general executive power of the Union is vested in the president, the conclusion is, that the step, which has been taken by him, is liable to no just exception on the score of authority.

It may be observed that this inference would be just if the power of declaring war had [not] been vested in the Legislature, but that [this] power naturally includes the right of judging whether the nation is under obligations to make war or not.

The answer to this is, that however true it may be, that the right of the Legislature to declare war includes the right of judging whether the Nation be under obligations to make war or not—it will not follow that the Executive

---

[2] See Document 3.

is in any case excluded from a similar right of judgment, in the execution of its own functions.

If the Legislature have a right to make war on the one hand—it is on the other the duty of the Executive to preserve peace till war is declared; and in fulfilling that duty, it must necessarily possess a right of judging what is the nature of the obligations which the treaties of the country impose on the Government; and when in pursuance of this right it has concluded that there is nothing in them inconsistent with a *state* of neutrality, it becomes both its province and its duty to enforce the laws incident to that state of the nation. The Executive is charged with the execution of all laws, the laws of nations as well as the municipal law, which recognizes and adopts those laws. It is consequently bound, by faithfully executing the laws of neutrality, when that is the state of the nation, to avoid giving a cause of war to foreign Powers.

This is the direct and proper end of the proclamation of neutrality. It declares to the United States their situation with regard to the Powers at war and makes known to the Community that the laws incident to that situation will be enforced. In doing this, it conforms to an established usage of Nations, the operation of which as before remarked is to obviate a responsibility on the part of the whole Society, for secret and unknown violations of the rights of any of the warring parties by its citizens.

Those who object to the proclamation will readily admit that it is the right and duty of the Executive to judge of, or to interpret, those articles of our treaties which give to France particular privileges, in order to the enforcement of those privileges: But the necessary consequence of this is, that the Executive must judge what are the proper bounds of those privileges—what rights are given to other nations by our treaties with them—what rights the law of Nature and Nations gives and our treaties permit, in respect to those nations with whom we have no treaties; in fine what are the reciprocal rights and obligations of the United States and of all and each of the powers at war.

The right of the Executive to receive ambassadors and other public Ministers may serve to illustrate the relative duties of the Executive and Legislative departments. This right includes that of judging, in the case of a revolution of government in a foreign country, whether the new rulers are competent organs of the National Will and ought to [be] recognized or not: And where a treaty antecedently exists between the United States and such nation that right involves the power of giving operation or not to such treaty. For until the new Government is *acknowledged,* the treaties between the nations, as far at least as regards *public* rights, are of course suspended.

This power of determining virtually in the case supposed upon the operation of national treaties as a consequence, of the power to receive ambassadors and other public Ministers, is an important instance of the right of the Executive to decide the obligations of the nation with regard to foreign nations. To apply it to the case of France, if there had been a treaty of alliance *offensive* [and] defensive between the United States and that country, the unqualified acknowledgement of the new Government would have put the United States in a condition to become an associate in the war in which France was engaged—and would have laid the Legislature under an obligation, if required, and there was otherwise no valid excuse, of exercising its power of declaring war.

This serves as an example of the right of the Executive, in certain cases, to determine the condition of the Nation, though it may consequentially affect the proper or improper exercise of the power of the Legislature to declare war. The Executive indeed cannot control the exercise of that power further than by the exercise of its general right of objecting to all acts of the Legislature; liable to being overruled by two thirds of both houses of Congress. The Legislature is free to perform its own duties according to its own duties according to its own sense of them—though the Executive in the exercise of its constitutional powers, may establish an antecedent state of things which ought to weigh in the legislative decisions. From the division of the Executive Power there results, in reference to it, a *concurrent* authority, in the distributed cases.

Hence in the case stated, though treaties can only be made by the President and Senate, their activity may be continued or suspended by the President alone.

No objection has been made to the President's having acknowledged the Republic of France, by the reception of its Minister, without having consulted the Senate; though that body is connected with him in the making of treaties, and though the consequence of his act of reception is to give operation to the treaties heretofore made with that country: But he is censured for having declared the United States to be in a state of peace & neutrality, with regard to the Powers at War; because the right of *changing* that state & *declaring war* belongs to the Legislature.

It deserves to be remarked, that as the participation of the Senate in the making of treaties and the power of the Legislature to declare war are exceptions out of the general "Executive Power" vested in the President, they are to be construed strictly—and ought to be extended no further than is essential to their execution.

While therefore the Legislature can alone declare war, can alone actually transfer the nation from a state of peace to a state of war—it belongs to the "Executive Power" to do whatever else the laws of nations cooperating with the treaties of the country enjoin, in the intercourse of the United States with foreign Powers.

In this distribution of powers the wisdom of our Constitution is manifested. It is the province and duty of the Executive to preserve to the nation the blessings of peace. The Legislature alone can interrupt those blessings, by placing the nation in a state of war.

But though it has been thought advisable to vindicate the authority of the Executive on this broad and comprehensive ground—it was not absolutely necessary to do so. That clause of the Constitution which makes it his duty to "take care that the laws be faithfully executed" might alone have been relied upon, and this simple process of argument pursued.

The President is the constitutional Executor of the laws. Our treaties and the laws of nations form a part of the law of the land. He who is to execute the laws must first judge for himself of their meaning. In order to the observance of that conduct, which the laws of nations combined with our treaties prescribed to this country, in reference to the present war in Europe, it was necessary for the President to judge for himself whether there was anything in our treaties incompatible with an adherence to neutrality. Having judged that there was not, he had a right, and if in his opinion the interests of the nation required it, it was his duty, as Executor of the laws, to proclaim the neutrality of the nation, to exhort all persons to observe it, and to warn them of the penalties which would attend its nonobservance.

The Proclamation has been represented as enacting some new law. This is a view of it entirely erroneous. It only proclaims a *fact* with regard to the existing state of the nation, informs the citizens of what the laws previously established require of them in that state, and warns them that these laws will be put in execution against the infractors of them.

Helvidius Number 1, August 24, 1793

Several pieces with the signature of PACIFICUS were lately published, which have been read with singular pleasure and applause, by the foreigners and degenerate citizens among us, who hate our republican government, and the French revolution; whilst the publication seems to have been too little regarded, or too much despised by the steady friends to both.

Had the doctrines inculcated by the writer, with the natural consequences from them, been nakedly presented to the public, this treatment might have been proper. Their true character would then have struck every eye, and been rejected by the feelings of every heart. But they offer themselves to the reader in the dress of an elaborate dissertation; they are mingled with a few truths that may serve them as a passport to credulity; and they are introduced with professions of anxiety for the preservation of peace, for the welfare of the government, and for the respect due to the present head of the executive, that may prove a snare to patriotism.

In these disguises, they have appeared to claim the attention I propose to bestow on them; with a view to show, from the publication itself, that under color of vindicating an important public act, of a chief magistrate, who enjoys the confidence and love of his country, principles are advanced which strike at the vitals of its Constitution, as well as its honor and true interest.

As it is not improbable that attempts may be made to apply insinuations, which are seldom spared when particular purposes are to be answered, to the author of the ensuing observations it may not be improper to premise, that he is a friend to the Constitution, that he wishes for the preservation of peace, and that the present chief magistrate has not a fellow-citizen who is penetrated with deeper respect for his merits, or feels a purer solicitude for his glory.

This declaration is made with no view of courting a more favorable ear to what may be said than it deserves. The sole purpose of it is, to obviate imputations which might weaken the impressions of truth; and which are the more likely to be resorted to, in proportion as solid and fair arguments may be wanting.

The substance of the first piece, sifted from its inconsistencies and its vague expressions, may be thrown into the following propositions:

That the powers of declaring war and making treaties are, in their nature, executive powers;

That being particularly vested by the Constitution in other departments, they are to be considered as exceptions out of the general grant to the executive department;

That being, as exceptions, to be construed strictly, the powers not strictly within them, remain with the executive;

That the executive consequently, as the organ of intercourse with foreign nations, and the interpreter and executor of treaties, and the law of nations, is authorized, to expound all articles of treaties, those involving questions of war and peace, as well as others; to judge of the obligations of the United

States to make war or not, under any *casus federis*[3] or eventual operation of the contract, relating to war; and, to pronounce the state of things resulting from the obligations of the United States, as understood by the executive;

That in particular the executive had authority to judge whether in the case of the mutual guaranty between the United States and France, the former were bound by it to engage in the war;

That the executive has, in pursuance of that authority, decided that the United States are not bound; And,

That its proclamation of the 22d of April last, is to be taken as the effect and expression of that decision.

The basis of the reasoning is, we perceive, the extraordinary doctrine, that the powers of making war and treaties, are in their nature executive; and therefore comprehended in the general grant of executive power, where not specially and strictly excepted out of the grant.

Let us examine this doctrine; and that we may avoid the possibility of misstating the writer, it shall be laid down in his own words: a precaution the more necessary, as scarce anything else could outweigh the improbability, that so extravagant a tenet should be hazarded, at so early a day, in the face of the public.

His words are: "Two of these (exceptions and qualifications to the executive powers) have been already noticed—the participation of the Senate in the *appointment of officers*, and the *making of treaties*. A *third* remains to be mentioned—the right of the legislature to *declare war, and grant letters of marque and reprisal*."

Again: "It deserves to be remarked, that as the participation of the Senate in the *making treaties*, and the power of the legislature to *declare war*, are *exceptions* out of the general *executive power*, vested in the President, they are to be construed *strictly*, and ought to be extended no farther than is essential to their execution."

If there be any countenance to these positions, it must be found either first, in the writers, of authority, on public law; or second, in the quality and operation of the powers to make war and treaties; or third, in the Constitution of the United States.

It would be of little use to enter far into the first source of information, not only because our own reason and our own Constitution, are the best guides; but because a just analysis and discrimination of the powers of government, according to their executive, legislative, and judiciary qualities are

---

[3] a "case for alliance"

not to expected in the works of the most received jurists, who wrote before a critical attention was paid to those objects, and with their eyes too much on monarchical governments, where all powers are confounded in the sovereignty of the prince. It will be found however, I believe, that all of them, particularly Wolfius, Burlamaqui and Vattel,[4] speak of the powers to declare war, to conclude peace, and to form alliances, as among the highest acts of the sovereignty; of which the legislative power must at least be an integral and preeminent part.

Writers, such as Locke and Montesquieu,[5] who have discussed more particularly the principles of liberty and the structure of government, lie under the same disadvantage, of having written before these subjects were illuminated by the events and discussions which distinguish a very recent period. Both of them too are evidently warped by a regard to the particular government of England, to which one of them owed allegiance; and the other professed an admiration bordering on idolatry. Montesquieu, however, has rather distinguished himself by enforcing the reasons and the importance of avoiding a confusion of the several powers of government, than by enumerating and defining the powers which belong to each particular class. And Locke, notwithstanding the early date of his work on civil government, and the example of his own government before his eyes, admits that the particular powers in question, which, after some of the writers on public law he calls *federative*, are really *distinct* from the *executive*, though almost always united with it, and *hardly to be separated into distinct hands.* Had he not lived under a monarchy, in which these powers were united; or had he written by the lamp which truth now presents to lawgivers, the last observation would probably never have dropt from his pen. But let us quit a field of research which is more likely to perplex than to decide, and bring the question to other tests of which it will be more easy to judge.

2. If we consult for a moment, the nature and operation of the two powers to declare war and make treaties, it will be impossible not to see that they can

---

[4] Christian Wolff (1679–1754), Jean-Jacques Burlamaqui (1694–1748) and Emmerich de Vattel (1714–1767) were Enlightenment writers who had published works on international law.

[5] John Locke (1632–1704) was an English philosopher whose *Two Treatises of Government* (1689) made the case for the right of revolution and for the necessity of a fundamental constitution. Charles-Louis de Secondat, baron de La Brède et de Montesquieu (1689–1755) was a French philosopher whose *Spirit of the Laws* (1748) was influential among Americans for its recommendations regarding separation of powers.

never fall within a proper definition of executive powers. The natural province of the executive magistrate is to execute laws, as that of the legislature is to make laws. All his acts therefore, properly executive, must presuppose the existence of the laws to be executed. A treaty is not an execution of laws: it does not presuppose the existence of laws. It is, on the contrary, to have itself the force of a *law*, and to be carried into *execution*, like all *other laws*, by the *executive magistrate*. To say then that the power of making treaties which are confessedly laws, belongs naturally to the department which is to execute laws, is to say, that the executive department naturally includes a legislative power. In theory, this is an absurdity—in practice a tyranny.

The power to declare war is subject to similar reasoning. A declaration that there shall be war, is not an execution of laws: it does not suppose pre-existing laws to be executed: it is not in any respect, an act merely executive. It is, on the contrary, one of the most deliberative acts that can be performed; and when performed, has the effect of *repealing* all the *laws* operating in a state of peace, so far as they are inconsistent with a state of war: and of *enacting as a rule for the executive*, a *new code* adapted to the relation between the society and its foreign enemy. In like manner, a conclusion of peace *annuls* all the *laws* peculiar to a state of war, and *revives* the general laws incident to a state of peace.

These remarks will be strengthened by adding that treaties, particularly treaties of peace, have sometime the effect of changing not only the external laws of the society, but operate also on the internal code, which is purely municipal, and to which the legislative authority of the country is of itself competent and complete.

From this view of the subject it must be evident, that although the executive may be a convenient organ of preliminary communications with foreign governments, on the subjects of treaty or war; and the proper agent for carrying into execution the final determinations of the competent authority; yet it can have no pretensions from the nature of the powers in question compared with the nature of the executive trust, to that essential agency which gives validity to such determinations.

It must be further evident that, if these powers be not in their nature purely legislative, they partake so much more of that, than of any other quality, that under a constitution leaving them to result to their most natural department, the legislature to be noted is, without a rival in its claim.

Another important inference to be noted is, that the powers of making war and treaty being substantially of a legislative, not an executive nature, the rule of interpreting exceptions strictly, must narrow instead of enlarging executive pretensions on those subjects.

3. It remains to be enquired whether there be any thing in the Constitution itself which shows that the powers of making war and peace are considered as of an executive nature, and as comprehended within a general grant of executive power.

It will not be pretended that this appears from any *direct* position to be found in the instrument.

If it were *deducible* from any particular expressions it may be presumed that the publication would have saved us the trouble of the research.

Does the doctrine then result from the actual distribution of powers among the several branches of the government? Or from any fair analogy between the powers of war and treaty and the enumerated powers vested in the executive alone?

Let us examine.

In the general distribution of powers, we find that of declaring war expressly vested in the Congress, where every other legislative power is declared to be vested, and without any other qualification than what is common to every other legislative act. The constitutional idea of this power would seem then clearly to be, that it is of a legislative and not an executive nature.

This conclusion becomes irresistible, when it is recollected, that the Constitution cannot be supposed to have placed either any power legislative in its nature, entirely among executive powers, or any power executive in its nature, entirely among legislative powers, without charging the Constitution, with that kind of intermixture and consolidation of different powers, which would violate a fundamental principle in the organization of free governments. If it were not unnecessary to enlarge on this topic here, it could be shown, that the Constitution was originally vindicated, and has been constantly expounded, with a disavowal of any such intermixture.

The power of treaties is vested jointly in the President and in the Senate, which is a branch of the legislature. From this arrangement merely, there can be no inference that would necessarily exclude the power from the executive class: since the senate is joined with the President in another power, that of appointing to offices, which as far as relate to executive offices at least, is considered as of an executive nature. Yet on the other hand, there are sufficient indications that the power of treaties is regarded by the constitution as materially different from mere executive power, and as having more affinity to the legislative than to the executive character.

One circumstance indicating this, is the constitutional regulation under which the Senate give their consent in the case of treaties. In all other cases the consent of the body is expressed by a majority of voices. In this particular case, a concurrence of two thirds at least is made necessary, as a substitute or compensation for the other branch of the legislature, which on certain occasions, could not be conveniently a party to the transaction.

But the conclusive circumstance is, that treaties when formed according to the constitutional mode, are confessedly to have the force and operation of laws, and are to be a rule for the courts in the controversies between man and man, as much as any other laws. They are even emphatically declared by the Constitution to be "the supreme law of the land."

So far the argument from the Constitution is precisely in opposition to the doctrine. As little will be gained in its favor from a comparison of the two powers, with those particularly vested in the President alone.

As there are but few it will be most satisfactory to review them one by one.

"The President shall be commander in chief of the army and navy of the United States, and of the militia when called into actual service of the United States."

There can be no relation worth examining between this power and the general power of making treaties. And instead of being analogous to the power of declaring war, it affords a striking illustration of the incompatibility of the two powers in the same hands. Those who are to *conduct a war* cannot in the nature of things, be proper or safe judges, whether *a war ought* to be *commenced, continued,* or *concluded.* They are barred from the latter functions by a great principle in free government, analogous to that which separates the sword from the purse, or the power of executing from the power of enacting laws....

"He shall take care that the laws shall be faithfully executed and shall commission all officers of the United States." To see the laws faithfully executed constitutes the essence of the executive authority. But what relation has it to the power of making treaties and war, that is, of determining what the *laws shall be* with regard to other nations? No other certainly than what subsists between the power of executing and enacting laws; no other consequently, than what forbids a coalition of the powers in the same department....

It may be proper however to take notice of the power of removal from office, which appears to have been adjudged to the President by the laws establishing the executive departments; and which the writer has endeavored to press into his service. To justify any favorable inference from this case, it must be shown, that the powers of war and treaties are of a kindred nature to the power of removal, or at least are equally within a grant of executive power. Nothing of this sort has been attempted, nor probably will be attempted. Nothing can in truth be clearer, than that no analogy, or shade of analogy, can be traced between a power in the supreme officer responsible for the faithful execution of the laws, to displace a subaltern officer employed in the execution of the laws; and a power to make treaties, and to declare war, such as these have been found to be in their nature, their operation, and their consequences.

Thus it appears that by whatever standard we try this doctrine, it must be condemned as no less vicious in theory that it would be dangerous in practice. It is countenanced neither by the writers on law; nor by the nature of the powers themselves; nor by any general arrangements or particular expressions, or plausible analogies, to be found in the Constitution.

Whence then can the writer have borrowed it?

There is but one answer to this question.

The power of making treaties and the power of declaring war, are *royal prerogatives* in the *British government*, and are accordingly treated as executive prerogatives by *British commentators*.

We shall be the more confirmed in the necessity of this solution of the problem, by looking back to the era of the Constitution, and satisfying ourselves that the writer could not have been misled by the doctrines maintained by our own commentators on our own government. That I may not ramble beyond prescribed limits, I shall content myself with an extract from a work which entered into a systematic explanation and defence of the Constitution, and to which there has frequently been ascribed some influence in conciliating the public assent to the government in the form proposed. Three circumstances conspire in giving weight to this contemporary exposition. It was made at a time when no application to *persons* or *measures* could bias; The opinion given was not transiently mentioned, but formally and critically elucidated; It related to a point in the Constitution which must consequently have been viewed as of importance in the public mind. The passage relates to the power of making treaties; that of declaring war, being arranged with such obvious propriety among the legislative powers, as to be passed over without particular discussion.

"Tho' several writers on the subject of government place that power (of *making treaties*) in the class of *Executive authorities*, yet this is *evidently* an *arbitrary disposition*. For if we attend *carefully*, to its operation, it will be found to partake *more* of the *legislative* than of the *executive* character, though it does not seem strictly to fall within the definition of either of them. The essence of the legislative authority, is to enact laws; or in other words, to prescribe rules for the regulation of the society. While the execution of the laws and the employment of the common strength, either for this purpose, or for the common defense, seem to comprise *all* functions of the *Executive magistrate.* The power of making treaties is *plainly* neither the one nor the other. It relates neither to the execution of the subsisting laws, nor to the enaction of new ones, and still less to an exertion of the common strength. Its objects are contracts with foreign nations, which have the *force of law,* but derive it from the obligations of good faith. They are not rules prescribed by the sovereign to the subject, but agreements between sovereign and sovereign. The power in question seems therefore to form a distinct department, and to belong properly neither to the legislative nor to the executive. The qualities else-where detailed as indispensable in the management of foreign *negotiations,* point out the executive as the most fit agent in those transactions: whilst the vast importance of the trust, and the operation of treaties as *Laws,* plead strongly for the participation of the whole or a part of the *legislative body* in the office of making them."[6]

It will not fail to be remarked on this commentary, that whatever doubts may be started as to the correctness of its reasoning against the legislative nature of the power to make treaties: it is clear, *consistent* and *confident,* in deciding that the power is *plainly* and *evidently* not an *executive power.*

---

[6] *Federalist* No. 75, written by Hamilton.

Proclamation on the Whiskey Rebellion

President George Washington

August 7, 1794

*F*ollowing the model of the British crown, George Washington issued proclamations, even though the Constitution does not use the word. Today, presidents
still issue proclamations and other unilateral orders, such as executive orders;
the main difference is that executive orders apply to employees of the executive
branch and proclamations apply to the wider citizenry. Under British practice,
kings could issue a proclamation to announce the enforcement of a law but not to
make new law. Making law was the job of Parliament. In the twenty-first century,
however, it has become increasingly hard to determine the difference between
enforcing the law and making a new one.

In the example below, Washington issued a proclamation warning citizens of
Western Pennsylvania to comply with the laws (and pay their taxes). Famously,
Washington himself led a force of over 10,000 men to put down the Whiskey
Rebellion and to demonstrate the power of the young national government. Notice
also that Washington complied with a law passed by Congress. In 1792, Congress
passed the Militia Act, which required in cases of rebellion that before the president could use force, the president would have to certify that the courts of justice
could not meet the threat and then announce a warning by way of proclamation.

SOURCE: President George Washington, Proclamation, 7 August 1794, *Founders Online*,
National Archives, https://goo.gl/yu6KcC.

Proclamation Calling Out the Militia to Occupy
the Western Counties of Pennsylvania

[Philadelphia, 7 Aug. 1794]

Whereas combinations to defeat the execution of the laws laying duties
upon Spirits distilled within the United States and upon stills, have from
the time of the commencement of those laws existed in some of the western
parts of Pennsylvania;

And whereas the said combinations, proceeding in a manner subversive equally of the just authority of government and of the rights of individuals have hitherto effected their dangerous and criminal purpose; by the influence of certain irregular meetings whose proceedings have tended to encourage and uphold the spirit of opposition, by misrepresentations of the laws calculated to render them odious, by endeavors to deter those who might be so disposed from accepting offices under them, through fear of public resentment and of injury to person and property, and to compel those who had accepted such offices by actual violence to surrender or forbear the execution of them; by circulating vindictive menaces against all those who should otherwise directly or indirectly aid in the execution of the said laws, or who, yielding to the dictates of conscience and to a sense of obligation should themselves comply therewith, by actually injuring and destroying the property of persons who were understood to have so compiled; by inflicting cruel and humiliating punishments upon private citizens for no other cause than that of appearing to be friends of the laws; by intercepting the public officers on the high ways, abusing, assaulting and otherwise ill treating them; by going to their houses in the night, gaining admittance by force, taking away their papers and committing other outrages; employing for these unwarrantable purposes the agency of armed banditti, disguised in such a manner as for the most part to escape discovery:

And whereas the endeavors of the legislature to obviate objections to the said laws, by lowering the duties and by other alterations conducive to the convenience of those whom they immediately affect (though they have given satisfaction in other quarters) and the endeavors of the executive officers to conciliate a compliance with the laws, by explanations, by forbearance and even by particular accommodations founded on the suggestion of local considerations, have been disappointed of their effect by the machinations of persons whose industry to excite resistance has increased with every appearance of a disposition among the people to relax in their opposition and the acquiesce in the laws: insomuch that many persons in the said western parts of Pennsylvania have at length been hardy enough to perpetrate acts which I am advised amount to treason, being overt acts of levying war against the United States; the said persons having on the sixteenth and seventeenth of July last past proceeded in arms (on the second day amounting to several hundreds) to the house of John Neville Inspector of the Revenue for the fourth survey of the District of Pennsylvania, having repeatedly attacked the said house with the persons therein, wounding some of them, having seized David Lenox, Marshal of the District of Pennsylvania, who previous thereto had been fired upon, while in the execution of his duty, by a party of armed men detaining him for some time prisoner, till for the preservation of his life and the obtaining of his liberty he found it necessary to enter into stipulations to forbear the execution of certain official duties touching processes issuing out of a Count of the United States—and having finally obliged the said Inspector of the Revenue and the said marshal from considerations of personal safety to fly from that part of the Country, in order by a circuitous route to proceed to the seat of Government; avowing as the motives of these outrageous proceedings an intention to prevent by force of arms the execution of the said laws, to oblige the said Inspector of the Revenue to renounce his said office, to withstand by open violence the lawful authority of the Government of the United States, and to compel thereby an alteration in the measures of the legislature and a repeal of the laws aforesaid.

And whereas by a law of the United States entitled "An Act to provide for calling forth the militia to execute the laws of the Union, suppress insurrection, and repel invasions," it is enacted

that whenever the laws of the United States shall be opposed or the execution thereof obstructed in any state by combinations too powerful to be suppressed by the ordinary course of judicial proceedings or by the powers vested in the marshals by that act, the same being notified by an associate justice of the district judge, it shall be lawful for the President of the United States to call forth the militia of such state to suppress such combinations and to cause the laws to be duly executed. And if the militia of a state where such combinations may happen shall refuse or be insufficient to suppress the same it shall be lawful for the president if the legislature of the United States shall not be in session to call forth and employ such numbers of the militia of any other state or states most convenient thereto, as may be necessary, and the use of the militia so to be called forth may be continued, if necessary, until the expiration of thirty days after the commencement of the ensuing session: provided always that whenever it may be necessary in the judgment of the president to use the military force hereby directed to be called forth, the President shall forthwith and previous thereto, by Proclamation, command such insurgents to disperse and retire peaceably to their respective abodes within a limited time.

And whereas James Wilson an associate justice on the fourth instant by writing under his hand did, from evidence which had been laid before him,

notify to me that "in the counties of Washington and Alleghany in Pennsylvania laws of the United States are opposed, and the execution thereof
obstructed by combinations too powerful to be suppressed by the ordinary
course of judicial proceedings or by the powers vested in the marshal of that
district;"

And whereas it is in my judgment necessary under the circumstances of
the case to take measures for calling forth the militias in order to suppress
the combinations aforesaid and to cause the laws to be duly executed, and
I have accordingly determined so to do, feeling the deepest regret for the
occasion, but withal the most solemn conviction, that the essential interests
of the union demand it, that the very existence of government and the fundamental principles of social order are materially involved in the issue, and that
the patriotism and firmness of all good citizens are seriously called upon, as
occasion may require, to aid in the effectual suppression of so fatal a spirit;

Wherefore, and in pursuance of the proviso above recited, I George Washington, President of the United States, do hereby command all persons, being
insurgents as aforesaid and all others whom it may concern on or before the
first day of September next to disperse and retire peaceably to their respective abodes. And I do moreover warn all persons whomsoever against aiding,
abetting or comforting the perpetrators of the aforesaid treasonable acts: and
do require all officers and other citizens according to their respective duties
and the laws of the land to exert their utmost endeavors to prevent and suppress such dangerous proceedings.

In testimony whereof I have caused the Seal of the United States of America to be affixed to these presents, and signed the same with my hand. Done
at the City of Philadelphia the seventh day of August one thousand seven
hundred and ninety-four, and of the Independence of the United States of
America, the nineteenth.

George Washington

First Inaugural Address

President Thomas Jefferson

March 4, 1801

Thomas Jefferson was the first president to preside over a transfer of power from one party to another. But he was also the first president to use the inaugural address as an opportunity to declare "the essential principles" by which his administration would be governed, for neither Washington nor Adams used the inauguration to declare a new set of political principles. Jefferson lists these principles in the fourth paragraph but only after proclaiming in the second paragraph that Americans were both Republicans and Federalists, that is, that they all shared the same principles. In the fifth paragraph, Jefferson suggests that the president alone sees the "whole ground," thus anticipating claims by later presidents that the president alone represents the whole nation.

SOURCE: Thomas Jefferson, First Inaugural Address, 4 March 1801, *Founders Online*, National Archives, https://goo.gl/B616RD.

Friends & Fellow Citizens,

Called upon to undertake the duties of the first executive office of our country, I avail myself of the presence of that portion of my fellow citizens which is here assembled to express my grateful thanks for the favor with which they have been pleased to look towards me, to declare a sincere consciousness that the task is above my talents, and that I approach it with those anxious and awful presentiments which the greatness of the charge, and the weakness of my powers so justly inspire. A rising nation, spread over a wide and fruitful land, traversing all the seas with the rich productions of their industry, engaged in commerce with nations who feel power and forget right, advancing rapidly to destinies beyond the reach of mortal eye; when I contemplate these transcendent objects, and see the honor, the happiness, and the hopes of this beloved country committed to the issue and auspices of this day, I shrink from the contemplation and humble myself before the magnitude of the undertaking. Utterly indeed should I despair, did not the presence of many, whom I here see, remind me, that, in the other high authorities provided by our Constitution, I shall find resources of wisdom, of virtue, and of zeal, on which to rely under all difficulties. To you, then, gentlemen, who are charged with the sovereign functions of legislation, and to those associated with you, I look with encouragement for that guidance and support which may enable us to steer with safety the vessel in which we are all embarked, amidst the conflicting elements of a troubled world.

During the contest of opinion through which we have passed, the animation of discussions and of exertions has sometimes worn an aspect which might impose on strangers unused to think freely, and to speak and to write what they think; but this being now decided by the voice of the nation, announced according to the rules of the Constitution[,] all will of course arrange themselves under the will of the law, and unite in common efforts for the common good. All too will bear in mind this sacred principle, that though the will of the majority is in all cases to prevail, that will, to be rightful, must be reasonable; that the minority possess their equal rights, which equal laws must protect, and to violate would be oppression. Let us then, fellow citizens, unite with one heart and one mind, let us restore to social intercourse that harmony and affection without which liberty, and even life itself, are but dreary things. And let us reflect that having banished from our land that religious intolerance under which mankind so long bled and suffered, we have yet gained little if we countenance a political intolerance, as despotic, as wicked, and capable of as bitter and bloody persecutions. During the throes and convulsions of the ancient world, during the agonizing spasms of infuriated man, seeking through blood and slaughter his long lost liberty, it was not wonderful that the agitation of the billows should reach even this distant and peaceful shore; that this should be more felt and feared by some and less by others; and should divide opinions as to measures of safety; but every difference of opinion is not a difference of principle. We have called by different names brethren of the same principle. We are all republicans: we are all federalists. If there be any among us who would wish to dissolve this Union, or to change its republican form, let them stand undisturbed as monuments of the safety with which error of opinion may be tolerated, where reason is left free to combat it. I know indeed that some honest men fear that a republican government cannot be strong; that this government is not strong enough. But would the honest patriot, in the full tide of successful experiment, abandon a government which has so far kept us free and firm, on the theoretic and visionary fear, that this government, the world's best hope, may, by possibility, want energy to preserve itself? I trust not. I believe this, in the contrary, the strongest government on earth. I believe it the only one, where every man, at the call of the law, would fly to the standard of the law, and would meet invasions of the public order as his own personal concern.—Sometimes it is said that man cannot be trusted with the government of himself. Can he then be trusted with the government of others? Or have we found angels, in the form of kings, to govern him? Let history answer this question.

Let us then, with courage and confidence, pursue our own federal and republican principles; our attachment to union and representative government. Kindly separated by nature and a wide ocean from the exterminating havoc of one quarter of the globe; too high minded to endure the degradations of others, possessing a chosen country, with room enough for our descendants to the thousandth and thousandth generation, entertaining a due sense of our equal right to the use of our own faculties, to the acquisition of our own industry, to honor and confidence from our fellow citizens, resulting not from birth, but from our actions and their sense of them, enlightened by a benign religion, professed indeed and practiced in various forms, yet all of them inculcating honesty, truth, temperance, gratitude and the love of man, acknowledging and adoring an overruling providence, which by all its dispensations proves that it delights in the happiness of man here, and his greater happiness hereafter; with all these blessings, what more is necessary to make us a happy and a prosperous people? Still one thing more, fellow citizens, a wise and and frugal government, which shall restrain men from injuring one another, shall leave them otherwise free to regulate their own pursuits of industry and improvement, and shall not take from the mouth of labor the bread it has earned. This is the sum of good government; and this is necessary to close the circle of our felicities.

About to enter, fellow citizens, on the exercise of duties which comprehend everything dear and valuable to you, it is proper you should understand what I deem the essential principles of our government, and consequently those which ought to shape its administration. I will compress them within the narrowest compass they will bear, stating the general principle, but not all its limitations.—Equal and exact justice to all men, of whatever state or persuasion, religious or political;—peace, commerce, and honest friendship with all nations, entangling alliances with none;—the support of the state governments in all their rights as the most competent administrations for our domestic concerns, and the surest bulwarks against anti-republican tendencies;—the preservation of the General government in its whole constitutional vigor, as the sheet anchor of our peace at home and safety abroad;—a jealous care of the right of election by the people, a mild and safe corrective of abuses which are lopped by the sword of revolution where peaceable remedies are unprovided;—absolute acquiescence in the decisions of the majority, the vital principle of republics, from which is no appeal but to force, the vital principle and immediate parent of despotism;—a well-disciplined militia, our best reliance in peace, and for the first moments of war, till regulars may relieve them;—the supremacy of the civil over the military authority;—economy in the public expense, that labor may be lightly burthened;—the honest payment of our debts and sacred preservation of the public faith;—encouragement of agriculture, and of commerce as its handmaid;—the diffusion of information, and arraignment of all abuses at the bar of the public reason;—freedom of religion, freedom of the press, and freedom of person, under the protection of the Habeas Corpus;—and trial by juries impartially selected. These principles form the bright constellation, which has gone before us and guided our steps through an age of revolution and reformation. The wisdom of our sages, and blood of our heroes have been devoted to their attainment:—they should be the creed of our political faith, the text of civic instruction, the touchstone by which to try the services of those we trust; and should we wander from them in moments of error or of alarm, let us hasten to retrace our steps, and to regain the road which alone leads to peace, liberty and safety.

I repair then, fellow citizens, to the post you have assigned me. With experience enough in subordinate offices to have seen the difficulties of this the greatest of all, I have learnt to expect that it will rarely fall to the lot of imperfect man to retire from this station with the reputation, and the favor, which bring him into it. Without pretensions to that high confidence you reposed in our first and greatest revolutionary character, whose pre-eminent services had entitled him to the first place in his country's love, and destined for him the fairest page in the volume of faithful history, I ask so much confidence only as may give firmness and effect to the legal administration of your affairs. I shall often go wrong through defect of judgement. When right, I shall often be thought wrong by those whose positions will not command a view of the whole ground. I ask your indulgence for my own errors, which will never be intentional; and your support against the errors of others, who may condemn what they would not if seen in all its parts. The approbation implied by your suffrage, is a great consolation to me for the past; and my future solicitude will be, to retain the good opinion of those who have bestowed it in advance, to conciliate that of others by doing them all the good in my power, and to be instrumental to the happiness and freedom of all.

Relying then on the patronage of your good will, I advance with obedience to the work, ready to retire from it whenever you become sensible how much better choices it is in your power to make. And may that infinite power, which rules the destinies of the universe, lead our councils to what is best, and give them a favorable issue for your peace and prosperity.

Letter to Elias Shipman and Others

President Thomas Jefferson

July 12, 1801

O nce in office, Jefferson had to decide what to do about the Federalist office-holders in the executive branch. Initially, he announced that only midnight appointments—appointments made by John Adams after Adams knew that he lost the election of 1800—and those who had abused their office would lose their appointments; no man would be removed for his beliefs alone. But Jefferson soon changed course and announced a broader removal policy aimed at restoring a proper proportion of Republicans. This partisan defense of removals provoked an outcry from Federalists, including a group of merchants in New Haven, Connecticut, who sent a letter to Jefferson complaining about Jefferson's removal of the customs collector in New Haven. In reply to the New Haven merchants, Jefferson published an open letter arguing that the administration must reflect the will of nation as it was revealed in the presidential election. Jefferson's defense of the removal power thus went beyond Madison's by emphasizing the partisan nature of presidential accountability.

SOURCE: From Thomas Jefferson to the New Haven Merchants, 12 July 1801, *Founders Online*, National Archives, https://goo.gl/tAqQ9y.

Gentlemen:

I have received the remonstrance you were pleased to address to me, on the appointment of Samuel Bishop to the office of Collector of New Haven, lately vacated by the death of David Austin; the right of our fellow citizens to represent to the public functionaries their opinion, on proceedings interesting to them, is unquestionably a constitutional right, often useful, sometimes necessary, and will always be respectfully acknowledged by me.

Of the various Executive duties, no one excites more anxious concern than that of placing the interests of our fellow citizens in the hands of honest men, with understandings sufficient for their station. No duty, at the same time, is more difficult to fulfill. The knowledge of characters possessed by a single individual is of necessity limited. To seek out the best through the whole Union, we must resort to other information, which, from the best men, acting disinterestedly and with the purest motives, is sometimes incorrect.

... The removal, as it is called, of Mr. Goodrich, forms another subject of complaint.[1] Declarations by myself in favor of *political tolerance*, exhortations to *harmony* and affection in social intercourse, and to respect for the *equal rights* of the minority, have, on certain occasions, been quoted and misconstrued into assurances that the tenure of offices was to be undisturbed;[2] but could candor apply such a construction? It is not indeed in the remonstrance that we find it: but it leads to the explanations which that calls for.

When it is considered that, during the late administration, those who were not of a particular sect of politics were excluded from all office; when, by a steady pursuit of this measure, nearly the whole offices of the United States were monopolized by that sect; when the public sentiment at length declared itself, and burst open the doors of honor and confidence to those whose opinions they more approved; was it to be imagined that this monopoly of the office was still to be continued in the hands of the minority? Does it violate their *equal rights* to assert some rights in the majority also? Is it *political intolerance* to claim a proportionate share in the direction of the public affairs? Can they not *harmonize* in society unless they have every thing in their own hands? If the will of the nation, manifested by their various elections, calls for an administration of government according with the opinion of those elected; if, for the fulfilment of that will, displacements are necessary, with whom can they so justly begin as with persons appointed in the last moments of an administration, not for its own aid, but to begin a career at the same time with their successors, by whom they had never been approved, and who could scarcely expect from them a cordial co-operation? Mr. Goodrich was one of these. Was it proper for him to place himself in office, without knowing whether those, whose agent he was to be, would have confidence in his agency? Can the preference of another, as the successor to Mr. Austin, be candidly called a removal of Mr. Goodrich? If a due participation of office is a matter of right, how are vacancies to be obtained? Those by death are few, by resignation none. Can any other mode then, but the removal, be proposed?

This is a painful office, but it is made my duty, and I meet it as such. I proceed in the operation with deliberation and enquiry, that it may injure the

---

[1] Elizur Goodrich was customs collector at the port of New Haven.
[2] Jefferson endorsed all of these ideas in his First Inaugural Address (Document 6), which proclaimed, "We are all Republicans, we are all Federalists."

best men least, and effect the purposes of justice and public utility with the least private distress: that [this enquiry into and decision to remove office-holders] may be thrown, as much as possible on delinquency, on oppression, on intolerance, on antirevolutionary adherence to our enemies.

The Remonstrance laments "that a change in the administration must produce a change in the subordinate officers:" in the other words, that it should be deemed necessary for all officers to think with their principal. But on whom does this imputation bear? On those who have excluded from office every shade of opinion which was not theirs? Or on those who have been so excluded? I lament sincerely that unessential differences of opinion should ever have been deemed sufficient to interdict half the society from the rights and the blessings of self-government; to proscribe them as unworthy of every trust. It would have been to me a circumstance of great relief had I found a moderate participation of office in the hands of the majority. I would gladly have left to time and accident to raise them to their just share. But their total exclusion calls for prompter correctives. I shall correct the procedure, but, that done, return with joy to that state of things when the only questions concerning a candidate shall be, is he honest? Is he capable? Is he faithful to the Constitution? I tender you the homage of my high respect.

TH: Jefferson

Resolution Rejecting the 12th Amendment

Delaware General Assembly

1804

Jefferson famously called his election the Revolution of 1800, but, as his critics pointed out, that revolution took 36 ballots in the US House of Representatives to break the deadlock between Jefferson and his running mate Aaron Burr. Because the Framers did not anticipate the rise of national parties, the Constitution did not require members of the Electoral College to designate whom they intended to be president and whom they intended to be vice-president. In fact, they assumed that most presidential electors would choose someone from their home states with one of the choices, and a national consensus would emerge around the second choices of the electors. But when the parties organized around a national slate of candidates, this logic was overturned. In 1800, Jefferson defeated Adams but tied his own running mate, because Republicans forgot to cast aside one of the Burr ballots.

The Twelfth Amendment fixed this problem by requiring candidates to distinguish between the president and vice-president on their ballots. This was a step toward acknowledging the two-party system. But it also made it more likely that presidents would represent a majority of the Electoral College. Under the original Constitution, the House would choose from the top five candidates in the event that none received an Electoral College majority. The Twelfth Amendment lowered this number to three. Because the House vote is by state delegation rather than by individual member, this was a blow to the small states.

As the objections from Delaware illustrate, Federalists believed that the amendment would make the president too powerful, and it would provide too great an advantage for the most populous states. Thus, the opponents of the Twelfth Amendment perceived that the innovation would invite presidential claims of representing a national majority.

SOURCE: Journal of the House of Representatives of the State of Delaware, 1804, 26–27. Courtesy of the Delaware Public Archives.

First, Because at all times innovations of the Constitution are dangerous, but more especially when the changes are dictated by party spirit, are designed for temporary purposes, and calculated to accomplish personal views.

Second, Because as representatives of a small state, we are sensible that in the nature of things, every change in the Constitution will be in favor of the large states who will never be disposed to allow, and will always have the means to prevent a variation favorable to the interests of the small states.

Third, Because in fact, the proposed amendment does reduce the power and weight of the small states, in the case provided by the Constitution, for the choice of President by the House of Representatives, by limiting the selection to three instead of five candidates, having the greatest number of electoral votes.

Fourth, Because the present mode of election gives to the small states a control and weight in the election for President and Vice-President, which are destroyed by the contemplated amendment.

Fifth, Because it is the true and permanent interest of a free people, among whom the relations of majority and minority must ever be fluctuating, to maintain the just weight and respectability of the minority by every proper provision, not impeaching the principle that the majority ought to govern; and we consider the present mode of election as calculated to repress the natural intolerance of a majority, and to secure some consideration and forbearance in relation to the minority.

Sixth, Because we view the existing provision in the Constitution as among the wisest of its regulations. History furnishes many examples of nations and particularly of republics, in their delirious devotion to individuals being ready to sacrifice their liberties and their dearest rights to the personal aggrandizement of their idol. The existing regulation furnishes some check to this human infirmity, by the occasional power given to a few to negative the will of the majority, as to one man, leaving them every other qualified citizen in the country for the range of their selection.

Letter to the New Jersey Legislature

President Thomas Jefferson

December 10, 1807

W*hen George Washington retired after two terms, he set an important example of a president who would voluntarily turn over power without seeking it. When Jefferson announced that he would retire after his second term, he continued the precedent set by Washington. But Jefferson went further than Washington by explaining his decision as one of principle rather than one of personal preference. Washington, by comparison, had emphasized his longing for private life.*

Since 1787, Jefferson had favored a term limit for the presidency. Here, Jefferson warns that the absence of such a limit would allow the presidency to degenerate into a lifetime appointment. Near the end, he also inserts a subtle insult to Washington and other executives in world history.

He also connects his retirement to principles announced in his First Inaugural Address (Document 6), especially to his faith in Americans to risk their lives and fortune to defend the country against threats to liberty.

SOURCE: From Thomas Jefferson to New Jersey Legislature, 10 December 1807, *Founders Online*, National Archives, https://goo.gl/aSpKJ2.

To the Representatives of the people of New Jersey in their legislature.

The sentiments, fellow citizens, which you are pleased to express in your address of the 4th. inst.[1] of attachment and esteem for the general government, and of confidence and approbation of those who direct its councils, cannot but be pleasing to the friends of union generally, and give a new claim on those who direct the public affairs, for every thing which zeal can effect for the good of their country.

It is indeed to be deplored that, distant as we are from the storms and

---

[1] abbreviation for "instant," meaning "of the present month"

convulsions which agitate the European world, the pursuit of honest neutrality, beyond the reach of reproach, has been insufficient to secure to us the certain enjoyment of peace with those whose interests, as well as ours would be promoted by it. What will be the issue of present misunderstandings cannot as yet be foreseen; but the measures adopted for their settlement have been sincerely directed to maintain the rights, the honor and the peace of our country. Should they fail, the ardor of our citizens to obey the summons of their country, and the offer, which you attest, of their lives and fortunes in its support, are worthy of their patriotism, and are pledges of our safety.

The suppression of the late conspiracy by the hand of the people, up-lifted to destroy it wherever it reared its head, manifests their fitness for self-government, and the power of a nation of which every individual feels that his own will is a part of the public authority.

The effect of the public contributions in reducing the national debt, and liberating our resources from the canker of interest, has been so far salutary; and encourages us to continue the same course; or, if necessarily interrupted, to resume it as soon as practicable.

I perceive with sincere pleasure that my conduct in the chief magistracy has so far met with your approbation, that my continuance in that office, after its present term, would be acceptable to you. But that I should lay down my charge at a proper period, is as much a duty, as to have borne it faithfully. If some termination to the services of the chief magistrate be not fixed by the Constitution, or supplied by practice, his office, nominally for years, will, in fact, become for life; and history shows how easily that degenerates into an inheritance. Believing that a representative government, responsible at short periods of election, is that which produces the greatest sum of happiness to mankind, I feel it a duty to do no act which shall essentially impair that principle; and I should unwillingly be the person who, disregarding the sound precedent set by an illustrious predecessor, should furnish the first example of prolongation beyond the second term of office.

Truth also obliges me to add that I am sensible of that decline which advancing years bring on; and feeling their physical, I ought not to doubt their mental effect. Happy [am I], if I am the first to perceive and to obey this admonition of nature, and to solicit a retreat from cares too great for the wearied faculties of age.

Declining a re-election on grounds which cannot but be approved, I am sincerely thankful for the approbation which the Legislature of New Jersey are pleased to manifest of the principles and measures pursued in the management of their affairs: and should I be so fortunate as to carry into retirement the equal approbation and good will of my fellow citizens generally, it will be the comfort of my future days, and will close a service of forty years with the only reward it ever wished.

TH: Jefferson

Letter to John B. Colvin

Thomas Jefferson

September 20, 1810

*J*efferson's letter to John B. Colvin is one of the most important statements by a president about what the English philosopher John Locke called the prerogative power. According to Locke, the prerogative power is the power to act "without the prescription of the law, and sometimes even against it," for the public good. Jefferson wrote his letter in response to Colvin's question whether sometimes officers in high trust had to act beyond the law. Colvin had also notified Jefferson that he was writing the memoirs for General James Wilkinson who had violated the law in order to put down the Burr Conspiracy, so it is likely that Jefferson knew his words would find their way to print. The Conspiracy was and remains somewhat hazy with respect to all of the facts, but it turned on some scheme by Aaron Burr to either incite an insurrection among enslaved persons in Louisiana and or start a new republic in present day Texas. Burr was captured and tried for treason. Somewhere along the way, Burr was denied key rights of the accused. Because the Burr Conspiracy was a controversial event in Jefferson's second term, it is also likely that Jefferson chose his words with great care.

Jefferson's answer begins with several examples that are meant to lead to an easy answer: when necessary for self-preservation, the unwritten law of survival must be paramount to the written law. But Jefferson complicates his answer with a "hypothetical," which no longer seems to be about self-preservation. Having thus prepared the way with these examples, Jefferson answers Colvin's question about Wilkinson and Burr. Importantly, Jefferson never asserts a constitutional basis for the prerogative. Rather, he requires that the officer come clean and accept judgment by Congress or the people after the fact.

SOURCE: Thomas Jefferson to John B. Colvin, 20 September 1810, *Founders Online*, National Archives, https://goo.gl/RkC7ak.

Your favor of the 14th has been duly received, and I have to thank you for the many obliging things respecting myself which are said in it. If I have left in the breasts of my fellow citizens a sentiment of satisfaction with my conduct in the transaction of their business it will soften the pillow of my repose thro' the residue of life.

The question you propose, whether circumstances do not sometimes occur which make it a duty in officers of high trust to assume authorities beyond the law, is easy of solution in principle, but sometimes embarrassing in practice. A strict observance of the written laws is doubtless *one* of the high duties of a good citizen: but it is not *the highest*. The laws of necessity, of self-preservation, of saving our country when in danger, are of higher obligation. To lose our country by a scrupulous adherence to written law, would be to lose the law itself, with life, liberty, property and all those who are enjoying them with us; thus absurdly sacrificing the end to the means. When, in the battle of Germantown, General Washington's army was annoyed from Chew's house, he did not hesitate to plant his cannon against it, altho' the property of a citizen.[1] When he besieged Yorktown, he levelled the suburbs, feeling that the laws of property must be postponed to the safety of the nation. While that army was before Yorktown, the Governor of Virginia took horses, carriages, provisions and even men, by force, to enable that army to stay together till it could master the public enemy; and he was justified. A ship at sea in distress for provisions meets another having abundance, yet refusing a supply; the law of self-preservation authorizes the distressed to take a supply by force. In all these cases the unwritten laws of necessity, of self-preservation, and of the public safety control the written laws of *meum* and *tuum*.[2] Farther to exemplify the principle I will state an hypothetical case. Suppose it had been made known to the Executive of the union in the autumn of 1805, that we might have the Floridas for a reasonable sum, that that sum had not indeed been so appropriated by law, but that Congress were to meet within three weeks, and might appropriate it on the first or second day of their session.[3] Ought he, for so great an advantage to his country, to have risked himself by transcending the law, and making the purchase? The public advantage offered, in this supposed case was indeed immense: but a reverence for law, and the probability that the advantage might still be *legally*

---

[1] The Battle of Germantown occurred in October, 1777, in Pennsylvania.

[2] the laws of private property, or "mine and thine"

[3] When the United States acquired the Louisiana Purchase, it believed that the deal included West Florida, which extended from Baton Rouge into most of the Panhandle. Spain, who held East Florida (the rest of Florida), claimed that it had not ceded West Florida to France and so France could not have sold it to the US.

accomplished by a delay of only three weeks, were powerful reasons against hazarding the act.—But supposed it foreseen that a John Randolph[4] would find means to protract the proceeding on it by Congress until the ensuing spring, by which time new circumstances would change the mind of the other party. Ought the Executive, in that case, and with that foreknowledge, to have secured the good to his country, and to have trusted to their justice for the transgression of the law? I think he ought, and that the act would have been approved.—

After the affair of the Chesapeake, we thought war a very possible result.[5] Our magazines were illy provided with some necessary articles, nor had any appropriations been made for their purchase. We ventured however to provide them and to place our country in safety, and stating the case to Congress, they sanctioned the act.

To proceed to the conspiracy of Burr, and particularly to General Wilkinson's situation in New Orleans.[6] In judging this case we are bound to consider the state of the information, correct and incorrect, which he then possessed. He expected Burr and his band from above, a British fleet from below, and he knew there was a formidable conspiracy within the city. Under these circumstances, was he justifiable[:]

1. In seizing notorious conspirators? On this there can be but two opinions; one, of the guilty and their accomplices; the other, that of all honest men.

2. In sending them to the seat of government when the written law gave them a right to trial in the territory? The danger of their rescue, of their continuing their machinations, the tardiness and weakness of the law, apathy of the judges, active patronage of the whole tribe of lawyers, unknown disposition of the juries, an hourly expectation of the enemy, salvation of the city, and of the Union itself, which would have been convulsed to its center, had that conspiracy succeeded, all these constituted a law of necessity and self-preservation, and rendered the *salus populi* supreme over the written law.[7]

---

[4] John Randolph was an influential Representative from Virginia. He led a group of Jeffersonian Republicans, called the "Quids," who opposed Jefferson on the grounds that the Louisiana Purchase had violated Jefferson's own principle of a strict construction of the Constitution.

[5] In June, 1807, the USS *Chesapeake* was attacked by a British ship while patrolling off the coast of Virginia.

[6] General James Wilkinson (1757–1825) was the governor of the Louisiana Territory who eventually captured Burr.

[7] the safety or welfare of the people

The officer who is called to act on this superior ground, does indeed risk himself on the justice of the controlling powers of the Constitution, and his station makes it his duty to incur the risk. But those controlling powers, and his fellow citizens generally, are bound to judge according to the circumstances under which he acted. They are not to transfer the information of this place or moment to the time and place of his action: but to put themselves into his situation. We knew here that there never was danger of a British fleet from below, and that Burr's band was crushed before it reached the Mississippi. But Gen. Wilkinson's information was very different, and he could act on no other.

From these examples and principles, you may see what I think on the question proposed. They do not go to the case of persons charged with petty duties, where consequences are trifling, and time allowed for a legal course, nor to authorize them to take such cases out of the written law. In these the example of overleaping the law is of greater evil than a strict adherence to its imperfect provisions. It is incumbent on those only who accept of great charges, to risk themselves on great occasions, when the safety of the nation, or some of its very high interests are at stake. An officer is bound to obey orders: yet he would be a bad one who should do it in cases for which they were not intended, and which involved the most important consequences. The line of discrimination between cases may be difficult; but the good officer is bound to draw it at his own peril, and throw himself on the justice of his country and the rectitude of his motives.

I have indulged freer views on this question on your assurances that they are for your own eye only, and that they will not get into the hands of news-writers. I met their scurrilities without concern while in pursuit of the great interests with which I was charged, but in my present retirement no duty forbids my wish for quiet.

Accept the assurances of my esteem and respect,

TH: Jefferson

First Annual Message

President Andrew Jackson

December 8, 1829

A ndrew Jackson was elected in 1828 by an electoral coalition still angry about the results of the election of 1824. In that election, Jackson had earned a plurality of Electoral College votes but not a majority, and the election went to the House of Representatives under the Twelfth Amendment (see Document 8). Led by Henry Clay, the Kentucky delegation chose John Quincy Adams even though he was from Massachusetts and Jackson was from neighboring Tennessee. This choice prevailed in the House at large, and when Adams became president, he then named Clay as his Secretary of State. At the time, this was the office regarded as the stepping-stone to the presidency, because Jefferson, Madison, and Monroe had served as Secretary of State before becoming president. Jackson and his supporters labeled the nomination of Clay a "corrupt bargain," and they argued for reforms to presidential selection.

In his First Annual message, Jackson recommended direct election of the president as well as term limits for federal officeholders. In 1826, Congress had debated amending the Constitution with respect to presidential selection, but the advocates for change could not win the necessary supermajority. Jackson's proposals went nowhere, but they illustrate his understanding of presidential power and anticipate arguments in the twentieth century.

SOURCE: James D. Richardson, ed., *A Compilation of the Messages and Papers of the Presidents, 1789–1897.* Volume II. (Washington, D.C.: Government Printing Office, 1896), 442–43, 447–49.

Fellow-Citizens of the Senate and House of Representatives:

It affords me pleasure to tender my friendly greetings to you on the occasion of your assembling at the seat of Government to enter upon the important duties to which you have been called by the voice of our countrymen. The task devolves on me, under a provision of the Constitution, to present to you, as the Federal Legislature of twenty-four sovereign States and 12,000,000 happy people, a view of our affairs, and to propose such measures as in the discharge of my official functions have suggested themselves as necessary to promote the objects of our Union.

In communicating with you for the first time it is to me a source of unfeigned satisfaction, calling for mutual gratulation[1] and devout thanks to a benign Providence, that we are at peace with all of mankind, and that our country exhibits the most cheering evidence of general welfare and progressive improvement. Turning our eyes to other nations, our great desire is to see our brethren of the human race secured in the blessings enjoyed by ourselves, and advancing in knowledge, in freedom, and in social happiness.

Our foreign relations, although in their general character pacific and friendly, present subjects of difference between us and other powers of deep interest as well to the country at large as to many of our citizens. To effect an adjustment of these shall continue to be the object of my earnest endeavors, and notwithstanding the difficulties of the task, I do not allow myself to apprehend unfavorable results. Blessed as our country is with everything which constitutes national strength, she is fully adequate to the maintenance of all her interests. In discharging the responsible trust confided to the Executive in this respect it is my settled purpose to ask nothing that is not clearly right and to submit to nothing that is wrong; and I flatter myself that, supported by the other branches of government and by the intelligence and patriotism of the people, we shall be able, under the protection of Providence, to cause all our just rights to be respected . . . .

I consider it one of the most urgent of my duties to bring to your attention the propriety of amending that part of our Constitution which relates to the election of President and Vice-President. Our system of government was by its framers deemed an experiment, and they therefore consistently provided a mode of remedying its defects.

To the people belongs the right of electing their Chief Magistrate; it was never designed that their choice should in any case be defeated, either by the intervention of electoral colleges or by the agency confided, under certain contingencies, to the House of Representatives. Experience proves that in proportion as agents to execute the will of the people are multiplied there is danger of their wishes being frustrated. Some may be unfaithful; all are liable to err. So far, therefore, as the people can with convenience speak, it is safer for them to express their own will.

The number of aspirants to the Presidency and the diversity of the interests

---

[1] happiness and/or satisfaction at one's circumstance

which may influence their claims leave little reason to expect a choice in the first instance, and in that event the election must devolve on the House of Representatives, where it is obvious the will of the people may not be always ascertained, or, if ascertained, may not be regarded. From the mode of voting by States the choice is made by twenty-four votes, and it may often occur that one of these will be controlled by an individual Representative. Honors and offices are at the disposal of the successful candidate. Repeated ballotings may make it apparent that a single individual holds the cast in his hand. May he not be tempted to name his reward? But even without corruption, supposing the probity of the Representative to be proof against the powerful motives by which it may be assailed, the will of the people is still constantly liable to be misrepresented. One may err from ignorance of the wishes of his constituents; another from a conviction that it is his duty to be governed by his own judgement of the fitness of the candidates; finally, although all were inflexibly honest, all accurately informed of the wishes of their constituents, yet under the present mode of election a minority may often elect a President, and when this happens it may reasonably be expected that efforts will be made on the part of the majority to rectify this injurious operation of their institutions. But although no evil of this character should result from such a perversion of the first principle of our system - *that the majority is to govern* - it must be very certain that a President elected by a minority cannot enjoy the confidence necessary to the successful discharge of his duties.

In this as in all other matters of public concern, policy requires that as few impediments as possible should exist to the free operation of the public will. Let us, then, endeavor so to amend our system that the office of Chief Magistrate may not be conferred upon any citizen but in pursuance of a fair expression of the will of the majority.

I would therefore recommend such an amendment of the Constitution as may remove all intermediate agency in the elections of the President and Vice-President. The mode may be so regulated as to preserve to each State its present relative weight in the election, and a failure in the first attempt may be provided for by confining the second to a choice between the two highest candidates. In connection with such an amendment it would seem advisable to limit the service of Chief Magistrate to a single term of either four or six years. If, however, it should not be adopted, it is worthy of consideration whether a provision disqualifying for office the Representatives in Congress on whom such an election may have devolved would not be proper.

While members of Congress can be constitutionally appointed to offices of trust and profit it will be the practice, even under the most conscientious adherence to duty, to select them for such stations as they are believed to be better qualified to fill than other citizens; but the purity of our government would doubtless be promoted by their exclusion from all appointments in the gift of the President, in whose election they may have been officially concerned. The nature of the judicial office and the necessity of securing in the cabinet and in diplomatic stations of the highest rank the best talents and political experience should, perhaps, except these from the exclusion.

There are, perhaps, few men who can for any great length of time enjoy office and power without being more or less under the influence of feelings unfavorable to the faithful discharge of their public duties. Their integrity may be proof against improper considerations immediately addressed to themselves, but they are apt to acquire a habit of looking with indifference upon the public interests and of tolerating conduct from which an unpracticed man would revolt. Office is considered as a species of property, and government rather as a means of promoting individual interests than as an instrument created solely for the service of the people. Corruption in some and in others a perversion of correct feelings and principles divert government from its legitimate ends and make it an engine for the support of the few at the expense of the many. The duties of all public officers are, or at least admit of being made, so plain and simple that men of intelligence may readily qualify themselves for their performance; and I cannot [but] believe that more is lost by the long continuance of men in office than is generally to be gained by their experience. I submit, therefore, to your consideration whether the efficiency of the government would not be promoted and official industry and integrity better secured by a general extension of the law which limits appointments to four years.[2]

In a country where offices are created solely for the benefit of the people no one man has any more intrinsic right to official station than another. Offices were not established to give support to particular men at the public expense. No individual wrong is, therefore, done by removal, since neither appointment to nor continuance in office is matter of right. The incumbent became an officer with a view to public benefits, and when these require his removal they are not to be sacrificed to private interests. It is the people, and they alone, who have a right to complain when a bad officer is substituted for a good one. He who is removed has the same means of obtaining a living that are enjoyed by the millions who never held office. The proposed limitation

---

[2] See *Federalist* Nos. 57 and 72 (Document 1) for the case against term limits for the House and president.

would destroy the idea of property now so generally connected with official station, and although individual distress may be sometimes produced, it would, by promoting that rotation which constitutes a leading principle in the republican creed, give healthful action to the system.

Speeches on the Removal Power

Senator Henry Clay
December 26, 1833 and March 7, 1834

Perhaps the most divisive policy issue of Jackson's presidency was the Second Bank of the United States. To set a political trap for Jackson, his opponents sought to re-charter the Bank early, before the election of 1832. Jackson vetoed it, making it the central issue of his reelection campaign, and, when he won, he declared that the people had delivered a mandate in support of his policy. Jackson then went on offense, ordering the Secretary of the Treasury William Duane to remove the Bank's deposits and distribute them among state banks more friendly to his policies. When Duane refused, Jackson removed Duane from office and replaced him with Roger Taney.

This was the first high profile removal of a department head since John Adams' presidency, and it brought to a head a simmering controversy about removals in the Jackson administration. Jackson's opponents revisited the constitutional arguments associated with removals and rejected the logic of the decision of 1789, in which Madison had successfully argued that the Constitution gives the power to the president alone. They argued that giving the president this power would interfere with Congress's ability to make the laws, law that could for example direct the Treasury Secretary to disobey the president's orders. In this speech before the Senate, Henry Clay proposes a new law that would reject the decision of 1789 and state clearly that Congress may set the terms of removal. Moreover, Clay lays the groundwork for the argument, later used in the Tenure of Office Act, requiring the president to share the power with the Senate (Document 19). Notice also that Clay's concerns were anticipated by Cato during the debate over ratification (Document 2).

SOURCE: *Register of Debates*, Senate, 23rd Congress, First Session (Washington, D.C: Gales and Seaton) 66, 834–36.

December 26, 1833

...At all events, he [President Andrew Jackson] seems to regard the issue of the election as an approbation of all constitutional opinions previously

expressed by him, no matter in what ambiguous language. I differ, sir, entirely
from the President. No such conclusions can be legitimately drawn from his
re-election. He was re-elected from his presumed merits generally, and from
the attachment and confidence of the people, and also from the unworthiness
of his competitor.[1] The people had no idea, by that exercise of their suffrage,
of expressing their approbation of all the opinions which the President held.
Can it be believed that Pennsylvania, so justly denominated the keystone
of our federal arch, which has been so steadfast in her adherence to certain
great national interests, and, among others, to that of the Bank of the United
States, intended, by supporting the re-election of the President, to reverse
all her own judgments, and to demolish all that she had built up? The truth
is, that the re-election of the President no more proves that the people had
sanctioned all the opinion previously expressed by him, than, if he had had
king's evil or a carbuncle, it would demonstrate that they intended to sanction his physical infirmity.

But the president infers his duty to remove the deposits from the Constitution and the suffrages of the American people. As to the latter source of
authority, I think it confers none. The election of a President, in itself, gives
no power, but merely designates the person who, as an officer of the Government, is to exercise power granted by the Constitution and laws. In this sense,
and in this sense only, does an election confer power. The President alleges a
right in himself to superintend the operations of the executive departments
from the Constitution and the suffrages of the people. Now, neither grants
any such right. The Constitution gives him the power, and no other power,
than to call upon the heads of each of the executive departments to give his
opinion, in writing, as to any matter connected with his department. The
issue of the election simply puts him in a condition to exercise that right. By
the laws, not by the Constitution, all the departments, with the exception of
that of the treasury, are placed under the direction of the President. And, by
various laws, specific duties of the Secretary of the Treasury (such as con-
tracting for loans, &c.) are required to be performed under the direction of
the President. This is done from greater precaution; but his power, in these
respects, is derived from the laws, and not from the Constitution. Even in
regard to those departments other than that of the treasury, in relation to
which by law, and not by the Constitution, a control is assigned to the Chief
Magistrate, duties may be required of them, by the law, beyond his control,

---

[1] Clay is being strategically coy here; in the election of 1832, he ran against Jackson
on the National Republican ticket.

and for the performance of which their heads are responsible. This is true of the State Department, that which, above all others, is most under the immediate direction of the President....

March 7, 1834

Mr. Clay rose to present four resolutions, which he said he had prepared for the consideration of the Senate. It was not his (Mr. C's) purpose now to engage in the discussion of them; but to propose that they be assigned to some convenient day, and it made the special order for that day. He wished, however, to accompany their presentation with one or two explanatory observations.

The first resolution asserted that the President, by the Constitution, is not invested with the power of removal from office at his pleasure. The second, declared that Congress is authorized by the Constitution to prescribe the tenure, terms, and conditions, of all offices established by law, where the Constitution itself has not affixed the tenure. The third, instructed the Committee on the Judiciary to inquire into the expediency of providing, by law, that removal from office shall not, in future, be made without the concurrence of the Senate; and, when that body is not in session, the power shall only be exercised provisionally, subject to the consideration of the Senate when it convenes. And the fourth directs an inquiry by the Committee on the Post Office and Post Roads, into the propriety of making provision by law for requiring the concurrence of the Senate in the appointment of all deputy postmasters, under certain restrictions.

These resolutions comprehend grave questions, of the highest importance, and which he (Mr. C) verily believed involved the just equilibrium between the several branches of the government, and the purity, if not the actual continuance, of the Government. The three first proceeded upon the assumption that the President is not clothed, by the Constitution, with the power of removal from office. That power, he was fully aware, by a vote of 34 to 20 in the House of Representatives, and by the casting vote of the Vice President, had, in the first Congress, been conceded to the chief Magistrate. Except in an incidental debate which arose in the Senate about four years ago, the propriety of that concession had never, he believed, been directly and deliberately considered. He had examined the Constitution with the utmost care and attention of which he was capable, and he felt firmly convinced that it did not grant any such power to the President. It was sustained in the first Congress as an implied or constructive power. And he felt himself authorized to pronounce that there was not another instance, among all the constructive powers, which had been controverted, of one which has so little foundation to rest upon as this power of removal at the pleasure of the President. The concession of it had been improvidently, in his opinion, made by the first Congress. It was made, probably, among other considerations, in consequence of the unbounded confidence reposed in the prudence, moderation, and wisdom, of the Father of his Country, the President of the United States [George Washington]. And it is remarkable that it was made with qualifications, which have been totally disregarded by the present Chief Magistrate.

The doctrines of the present administration, and the principles asserted by its supportersd, during the progress of the debate on the deposit question, maintain that all persons employed in the executive department of the Government, throughout all its ramifications, are bound to conform to the will of the President, no matter how contrary to their own judgement that will may be. The total number of persons, in all the various branches of the public service attached to the executive department of the Government, has been estimated at not less than forty thousand; and he presumed, from the size of the Blue Book,[2] that the estimate was rather below than above the mark. There are upwards of ten thousand deputy postmasters; and the number of persons employed in that single department, including postmasters, contractors, clerks, stage-drivers, and other carriers of the mail, is not probably short of thirty thousand. If this immense mass is to be actuated by one spirit, to obey one impulse, and to conform to the will of one man, it is not difficult to anticipate the arrival of the day when all the guaranties which we have supposed ourselves to posses for our liberties, will be utterly vain and unavailing. It has been a settled axiom in all free governments, and among all friends of civil liberty, that a standing army, in time of peace, is dangerous to the existence of freedom. A standing army is separate and distinct from the mass of society; dispersed and divided into different, and, perhaps, distant corps, stationed in their barracks or quarters. The amount of the danger arising from it can be seen, estimated, and guarded against. But what precautions can the community employ against the operations and influence of a standing army of forty thousand official incumbents? They are everywhere; in the cities and villages, at the taverns, at the cross-roads, and at every public place, mixing in the mass of society; and, if they have orders from headquarters, they will, without doubt, attempt to direct all the political movements of the country. In the possession of all the channels of

---

[2] The Blue Book is a nickname for the published directory of government employees.

intelligence, the mails and the post offices, how is it possible to resist their combined influence? Such a tremendous official corps, if a corrective be not applied, will, sooner or later, acquire the power to control and dispose of the succession of the Presidential office, as certainly as the less formidable Praetorian band of Rome[3] disposed, at will, of the imperial crown.

The object of the resolutions which he (Mr. C.) was about to present, was to invite a deliberate review of the constitutional powers of the President and of Congress; and to ascertain if the wisdom of our fathers had really rendered subservient to the will of one man, a vast power, capable of totally changing the character of the Government, and rendering it although in form a republic in fact a despotism. He hoped gentlemen who supported the executive prerogative would come to the discussion prepared to show, from the terms of the Constitution itself, that the power was granted to the President. He hoped that they would not entrench themselves behind one solitary precedent. Precedents were entitled, he admitted, to respect. They had been correctly defined to be the evidence of truth; but they were only evidence. And he did not think that a single precedent, without further examination into the Constitution, ought to be allowed to transform our free Government into a practical despotism.

If greater stability can be conferred on the tenure by which public offices are held, the functionary will be rendered less dependent on the capricious pleasure of one man. They will feel, as they ought to feel, that they have an equal right with other citizens to exercise the elective franchise, without responsibility to any man. Their continuance in office ought not to depend upon the independent manner of its exercise, but upon the ability, integrity, and fidelity, with which their official duties are performed. Filled, as most of the executive offices are, with partisans of the present administration, he (Mr. C.) could not be justly accused of any improper motive in proposing a measure which may give greater security to their abiding in them. The Constitution expressly provides for one and only one mode of removal from office—by impeachment. It may be expedient to authorize some more summary process in cases of ascertained unfitness or delinquency. The resolutions look to that object, but seek to provide a remedy against the possible prejudices, passions, or imperfections, of one man. He seriously and solemnly believed that the accomplishment of purpose contemplated by the resolutions, in some way or other, was essential to the purity and durability of the Government.

---

[3] the group of soldiers selected to serve as the body guards of the Roman emperors

With these feelings, views, and opinions, he (Mr. C.) submitted the resolutions to the Senate, and moved that they be printed, and he made the
special order of the day for the first Monday in April next. All of which was
ordered accordingly.

The resolutions thus offered were the following:

1. *Resolved*, That the Constitution of the United States does not vest in the
President power to remove at his pleasure officers under the Government of
the United States, whose offices have been established by law.

2. *Resolved*, That, in all cases of offices created by law, the tenure of holding which is not prescribed by the Constitution, Congress is authorized by
the Constitution to prescribe the tenure, terms, and conditions on which
they are to be holden [held].

3. *Resolved*, That the Committee on the Judiciary be instructed to inquire
into the expediency of providing by law that in all instances of appointment
to office by the President, by and with the advice and consent of the Senate,
other than diplomatic appointment to office by the President, by and with
the advice and consent of the Senate, other than diplomatic appointments,
the power of removal shall be exercised only in concurrence with the Senate,
and, when the Senate is not in session, that the President may suspend any
such officer, communicating his reasons for the suspension to the Senate at
its first succeeding session; and, if the Senate concur with him, the officer
shall be removed, but if it do not concur with him, the officer shall be restored
to office.

4. *Resolved*, That the Committee on the Post Office and Post Roads be
instructed to inquire into the expediency of making provision by law for the
appointment, by and with the advice and consent of the Senate, of all deputy
postmasters, whose annual emoluments exceed a prescribed amount.

After the transaction of some other business, the Senate adjourned over
to Monday.

Message to the Senate Protesting
the Censure Resolution

President Andrew Jackson

April 15, 1834

Although the Whigs controlled the Senate during Andrew Jackson's second term, they did not control the House. Impeachment was not a possibility, nor was passing laws like the one proposed by Clay in the preceding selection. In March, 1834, they took a novel course by passing a resolution of censure. The resolution charged that Jackson had assumed power beyond the laws and beyond the Constitution. Jackson is the only president to have been censured by a chamber of Congress.

Jackson responded the next month with a formal protest. He argued that a resolution of censure was not a constitutionally available path. The only path under the Constitution was the impeachment process. Jackson also defended his removal of Treasury Secretary William Duane, connecting that action to the Decision of 1789. To make that argument, Jackson provided the most muscular theory of executive power provided by a president up to that time.

SOURCE: James D. Richardson, ed., *A Compilation of the Messages and Papers of the Presidents, 1789–1897,* Volume III (Washington, D.C.: Government Printing Office, 1897), 69–93.

To the Senate of the United States:

The responsibilities of the President are numerous and weighty. He is liable to impeachment for high crimes and misdemeanors, and on due conviction to removal from office and perpetual disqualification; and notwithstanding such conviction, he may also be indicted and punished according to law. He is also liable to the private action of any party who may have been injured by his illegal mandates or instructions in the same manner and to the same extent as the humblest functionary. In addition to the responsibilities which may thus be enforced by impeachment, criminal prosecution, or suit at law, he is also accountable at the bar of public opinion for every act of his Administration. Subject only to the constraints of truth and justice, the free people of the United States have the undoubted right, as individuals or collectively, orally or in writing, at such times and in such language and form as they may think proper, to discuss his official conduct and to discuss and promulgate their opinions concerning it. Indirectly his conduct may come under review in either branch of the Legislature, or in the Senate when acting in its direct executive capacity, and so far as the executive and legislative proceedings of these bodies may require it, it may be exercised by them. These are believed to be the proper and only modes in which the President of the United States is to be held accountable for his official conduct.

Tested by these principles, the resolution of the Senate is wholly unauthorized by the Constitution, and in derogation of its entire spirit. It assumes that a single branch of the legislative department may for the purposes of public censure, and without any view to legislation or impeachment, take up, consider, or decide upon the official acts of the executive. But in no part of the Constitution is the President subjected to any such responsibility, and in no part of that instrument is any such power conferred on either branch of the Legislature....

By the Constitution "the power is vested in a President of the United States." Among the duties imposed upon him, and which he is sworn to perform, is that of "taking care that the laws be faithfully executed." Being thus made responsible for the entire action of the executive department, it was but reasonable that the power of appointing, overseeing, and controlling those who execute the laws—a power in its nature executive—should remain in his hands. It is therefore not only his right, but the Constitution makes it his duty, to "nominate, and, by and with the advice and consent of the Senate, appoint" all "officers of the United States whose appointments are not in the Constitution otherwise provided for," with a proviso that the appointment of inferior officers may be vested in the President alone, in the courts of justice, or in the heads of Departments.

The executive power vested in the Senate is neither that of "nominating" nor "appointing." It is merely a check upon the executive power of appointment. If individuals are proposed for appointment by the President [who are] by them deemed incompetent or unworthy, they may withhold their consent and the appointment can not be made. They check the action of the executive but can not in relation to those very subjects act themselves nor direct him. Selections are still made by the President, and the negative given to the Senate, without diminishing his responsibility, furnishes an additional guarantee to the country that the subordinate executive as well as the judicial offices shall be filled with worthy and competent men.

The whole executive power being vested in the President, who is responsible for its exercise, it is a necessary consequence that he should have a right to employ agents of his own choice to aid him in the performance of his duties, and to discharge them when he is no longer willing to be responsible for their acts. In strict accordance with this principle, the power of removal, which, like that of appointment, is an original executive power, is left unchecked by the Constitution in relation to all executive officers, for whose conduct the President is responsible, while it is taken from him in relation to all judicial officers, for whose acts he is not responsible. In the government from which many of the fundamental principles of our system are derived the head of the executive department originally had the power to appoint and remove at will all officers, executive and judicial. It was to take the judges out of this general power of removal, and thus make them independent of the executive, that the tenure of their offices was changed to good behavior. Nor is it conceivable why they are placed in our Constitution upon a tenure different from all other officers appointed by the executive unless it be for the same purpose.

But if there were any just ground for doubt on the face of the Constitution whether all executive officers are removable at the will of the President, it is obviated by the cotemporaneous construction of the instrument and the uniform practice under it.

The power of removal was a topic of solemn debate in the Congress of 1789 while organizing the administrative departments of the Government, and it was finally decided that the President derived from the Constitution the power of removal so far as it regards that department for whose acts he is responsible. Although the debate covered the whole ground, embracing the Treasury as well as all the other executive departments, it arose on a motion to strike out of the bill to establish a Department of Foreign Affairs, since called the Department of State, a clause declaring the Secretary "to be removable from office by the President of the United States." After that motion had been decided in the negative it was perceived that these words did not convey the sense of the House of Representatives in relation to the true source of power of removal. With the avowed object of preventing any future inference that this power was exercised by the President in virtue of a grant from Congress, when in fact that body considered it as derived from the Constitution, the words which had been the subject of debate were struck out, and in lieu thereof a clause was inserted in a provision concerning the chief clerk of the department, which declared that "whenever the said principal officer shall be removed from office by the President of the United States, or in any other case of vacancy," the chief clerk should during such vacancy have charge of the papers of the office. This change having been made for the express purpose of declaring the sense of Congress that the President derived the power of removal from the Constitution, the act as it passed has always been considered as a full expression of the sense of the Legislature on this important part of the American Constitution.

Here, then, we have the concurrent authority of President Washington, of the Senate, and the House of Representatives, numbers of whom had taken an active part in the convention which framed the Constitution and in the State conventions which adopted it, that the President derived an unqualified power of removal from that instrument itself, which is "beyond the reach of legislative authority." Upon this principle the government has now been steadily administered for about forty-five years, during which there have been numerous removals made by the President or by his direction, embracing every grade of executive officers from the heads of departments to the messengers of bureaus....

The dangerous tendency of the doctrine which denies to the President the power of supervising, directing, and controlling the Secretary of the Treasury in like manner with the other executive officers would soon be manifest in practice were the doctrine to be established. The President is the direct representative of the American people, but the Secretaries are not. If the Secretary of the Treasury be independent of the President in the execution of the laws, then is there no direct responsibility to the people in that important branch of this Government to which is committed to the care of the national finances. And it is in the power of the Bank of the United States, or any other corporation, body of men, or individuals, if a secretary should be found to accord with them in opinion or can be induced in practice to promote their views, to control through him the whole action of the Government (so far as it is exercised by his department) in defiance of the Chief Magistrate elected by the people and responsible to them....

Speech on Assuming Office of the President

President John Tyler

April 9, 1841

*A*rticle Two of the Constitution is not clear about whether the vice-president *becomes president or merely acts as president until a new president is elected. When William Henry Harrison died after only a month in office, his vice-president John Tyler wasted little time in deciding that the Constitution made him president and that he would finish Harrison's full term. To publicize and legitimate his position, Tyler shrewdly issued his own version of an inaugural address.*

Tyler's address quickly followed this move with others that stunned his Whig allies in Congress. He issued ten vetoes, including vetoes of Whig legislation on the Bank of the United States and the tariff, prompting the first resolution of impeachment of a president to be introduced in the House. Tyler was called "His Accidency" by his opponents, but his presidency was a hint of the unilateral power that twentieth century presidents would find Constitutionally justified and assert when they lacked support in Congress. His presidency was also a bitter irony for the Whigs, who, thanks to the financial Panic of 1837, had finally won the presidency. The Whig view of the presidency (Document 12) rested on a rejection of Andrew Jackson's vigorous use of the veto and removal powers (Document 13). Any lingering confusion about presidential succession was later settled by the 25th Amendment.

SOURCE: James D. Richardson, ed., *A Compilation of the Messages and Papers of the Presidents, 1789–1897.* Volume IV (Washington, D.C.: Government Printing Office, 1897), 36–39.

To the People of the United States.

Fellow-Citizens: Before my arrival at the seat of Government the painful communication was made to you by the officers presiding over the several Departments of the deeply regretted death of William Henry Harrison, late President of the United States. Upon him you had conferred your suffrages for the first office in your gift, and had selected him as your chosen instrument to correct and reform all such errors and abuses as had manifested themselves from time to time in the practical operation of the Government. While standing at the threshold of this great work he has by the dispensation of all-wise Providence been removed from amongst us, and by the provisions of the Constitution the efforts to be directed to the accomplishing of this vitally important task have devolved upon myself: This same occurrence has subjected the wisdom and sufficiency of our institutions to a new test. For the first time in our history the person elected to the Vice-Presidency of the United States, by the happening of a contingency provided for in the Constitution, has had devolved upon him the Presidential office. The spirit of faction, which is directly opposed to the spirit of a lofty patriotism, may find in this occasion for assaults upon my administration; and in succeeding, under circumstances so sudden and unexpected and to responsibilities so greatly augmented, to the administration of public affairs I shall place in the intelligence and patriotism of the people my only sure reliance. My earnest prayer shall be constantly addressed to that all-wise and all-powerful Being who made me, and by whose dispensation I am called to the high office of President of this Confederacy, understandingly to carry out the principles of that Constitution which I have sworn "to protect, preserve, and defend."

The usual opportunity which is afforded to a Chief Magistrate upon his induction to office of presenting to his countrymen an exposition of the policy which would guide [his] administration, in the form of an inaugural address, not having, under the peculiar circumstances which have brought me to the discharge of the high duties of President of the United States, been afforded to me, a brief exposition of the principles which will govern me in the general course of my administration of public affairs would seem to be due as well to myself as to you.

In regard to foreign nations, the groundwork of my policy will be justice on our part to all, submitting to injustice from none. While I shall sedulously cultivate the relations of peace and amity with one and all, it will be my most imperative duty to see that the honor of the country shall sustain no blemish. With a view to this, the condition of our military defenses will become a matter of anxious solicitude. The army, which has in other days covered itself with renown, and the navy, not inappropriately termed the right arm of the public defense, which has spread a light of glory over the American standard in all waters of the earth, should be rendered replete with efficiency.

In view of the fact, well avouched by history, that the tendency of all human institutions is to concentrate power in the hands of a single man, and that their ultimate downfall has proceeded from this cause, I deem it of the most essential importance that a complete separation should take place between the sword and the purse. No matter where or how the public moneys shall be deposited, so long as the President can exert the power of appointing and removing at his pleasure the agents selected for their custody the Commander in Chief of the Army and Navy is in fact the treasurer. A permanent and radical change should therefore be decreed. The patronage incident to the Presidential office, already great, is constantly increasing. Such increase is destined to keep pace with the growth of our population, until, without a figure of speech, an army of officeholders may be spread over the land. The unrestrained power exerted by a selfishly ambitious man in order either to perpetuate his authority or to hand it over to some favorite as his successor may lead to the employment of all the means within his control to accomplish his object. The right to remove from office, while subjected to no just restraint, is inevitably destined to produce a spirit of crouching servility with the official corps, which, in order to uphold the hand which feeds them, would lead to direct and active interference in the elections, both State and Federal, thereby subjecting the course of State legislation to the dictation of the chief executive officer and making the will of that officer absolute and supreme. I will at a proper time invoke the action of Congress upon this subject, and shall readily acquiesce in the adoption of all proper measures which are calculated to arrest these evils, so full of danger in their tendency. I will remove no incumbent from office who has faithfully and honestly acquitted himself of the duties of his office, except in such cases where such officer has been guilty of an active partisanship or by secret means—the less manly, and therefore the more objectionable—has given his official influence to the purposes of party, thereby bringing the patronage of the Government in conflict with the freedom of elections. Numerous removals may become necessary under this rule. These will be made by me through no acerbity of feeling—I have had no cause to cherish or indulge unkind feelings toward any—but my conduct will be regulated by a profound sense of what is due to the country and its institutions; nor shall I neglect to apply the same unbending rule to those of my own appointment. Freedom of opinion will be tolerated, the full enjoyment of the right of suffrage will be maintained as the birthright of every American citizen; but I say emphatically to the official corps, "Thus far and no farther." I have dwelt the longer upon this subject because removals from office are likely often to arise, and I would have my countrymen to understand the principle of the executive actions.

In all public expenditures the most rigid economy should be resorted to, and, as one of its results, a public debt in time of peace be sedulously avoided. A wise and patriotic constituency will never object to the imposition of necessary burdens for useful ends, and true wisdom dictates the resort to such means in order to supply deficiencies in the revenue, rather than to those doubtful expedients which, ultimating[1] in a public debt, serve to embarrass the resources of the country and to lessen its ability to meet any great emergency which may arise. All sinecures should be abolished. The appropriations should be direct and explicit, so as to leave as limited a share of discretion to the disbursing agents as may be found compatible with the public service. A strict responsibility on the part of all the agents of the Government should be maintained and peculation or defalcations visited with immediate expulsion from office and the most condign punishment.

The public interest also demands that if any war has existed between the Government and the currency it shall cease. Measures of a financial character now having the sanction of legal enactment shall be faithfully enforced until repealed by the legislative authority. But I owe it to myself to declare that I regard existing enactments as unwise and impolitic and in a high degree oppressive. I shall promptly give my sanction to any constitutional measure which, originating in Congress, shall have for its object the restoration of a sound circulating medium, so essentially necessary to give confidence in all the transactions of life, to secure to industry its just and adequate rewards, and to reestablish the public prosperity. In deciding upon the adaptation of any such measure to the end proposed, as well as its conformity to the Constitution, I shall resort to the fathers of the great republican school for advice and instruction, to be drawn from their sage views of our system of government and the light of their ever-glorious example.

The institutions under which we live, my countrymen, secure each person in the perfect enjoyment of all his rights. The spectacle is exhibited to the world of a government deriving its powers from the consent of the governed and having imparted to it only so much power as is necessary for its successful operation. Those who are charged with its administration should carefully abstain from all attempts to enlarge the range of powers thus granted to the several departments of the Government other than by an appeal to the people for additional grants, lest by so doing they disturb that balance which the patriots and statesmen who framed the Constitution designed to established between the Federal Government and the States composing the Union. The observance of these rules is enjoined upon us by that feeling of reverence and affection which finds a place in the heart of every patriot for the preservation of union and the blessings of union—for the good of our children and

---

[1] reaching their ultimate end, or culmination

our children's children through countless generations. An opposite course could not fail to generate factions intent upon the gratification of their selfish ends, to give birth to local and sectional jealousies, and to ultimate either in breaking asunder the bonds of union or in building up a central system which would inevitably end in a bloody scepter and an iron crown.

In conclusion I beg you to be assured that I shall exert myself to carry the foregoing principles into practice during my administration of the Government, and, confiding in the protecting care of an ever watchful and overruling Providence, it shall be my first and highest duty to preserve unimpaired the free institutions under which we live and transmit them to those who shall succeed me in their full force and vigor.

John Tyler

First Inaugural Address

President Abraham Lincoln

March 4, 1861

B y the time Abraham Lincoln was elected president, parties had become accus-
tomed to issuing party platforms. Notice the importance of the Republican
Party Platform in Lincoln's address. As he puts it, some constitutional controversies
can be solved only by electoral contests, and the contest of 1860 should have settled
the question of whether Congress can exclude slavery from the territories. Because
his party won, and because his party's platform was clear on the question of slavery
in the territories, his party's victory was a victory for a particular way to settle the
controversy over the expansion of slavery (at least until the next electoral contest).
Later on, Lincoln also hints at the doctrine of departmentalism, in his assertion
that the president (and Congress, and the people themselves)—not only the Supreme
Court—have a responsibility for the proper interpretation of the Constitution.

Several states (South Carolina, Mississippi, Florida, Alabama, Georgia, Louisiana, and Texas) responded to Lincoln's electoral victory by declaring their
intention to secede from the Union during the winter of 1860–61. Although he
professed his desire for an amicable resolution to the crisis, Lincoln nevertheless
explains that the president's oath of office requires the president to use force to
preserve the Union.

SOURCE: Abraham Lincoln, First Inaugural Address, Final Version, March 1861, Abraham
Lincoln Papers (Series 1: General Correspondence, 1833 to 1916), Library of Congress, Manuscript Division, https://goo.gl/DswcBr.

Fellow citizens of the United States:

In compliance with a custom as old as government itself, I appear before
you to address you briefly, and to take, in your presence, the oath prescribed
by the Constitution of the United States, to be taken by the President "before
he enters on the execution of his office."[1]

---

[1] Article II, Section 1

I do not consider it necessary, at present, for me to discuss those matters of administration about which there is no special anxiety, or excitement.

Apprehension seems to exist among the people of the Southern States, that by the accession of a Republican administration, their property, and their peace, and personal security, are to be endangered. There has never been any reasonable cause for such apprehension. Indeed, the most ample evidence to the contrary had all the while existed, and been open to their inspection. It is found in nearly all the published speeches of him who now addresses you. I do but quote from one of those speeches when I declare that "I have no purpose, directly or indirectly, to interfere with the institution of slavery in the States where it exists. I believe I have no lawful right to do so, and I have no inclination to do so."[2] Those who nominated and elected me did so with full knowledge that I had made this, and many similar declarations, and had never recanted them. And more than this, they placed in the platform, for my acceptance, and as a law to themselves and to me, the clear and emphatic resolution which I now read:

Resolved, That the maintenance inviolate of the rights of the States, and especially the right of each State to order and control its own domestic institutions according to its own judgment exclusively, is essential to that balance of power on which the perfection and endurance of our political fabric depend; and we denounce the lawless invasion by armed force of the soil of any State or Territory, no matter under what pretext, as among the gravest of crimes.[3]

I now reiterate these sentiments: and in doing so, I only press upon the public attention the most conclusive evidence of which the case is susceptible, that the property, peace and security of no section are to be in anywise endangered by the now incoming administration. I add too, that all the protection which, consistently with the Constitution and the laws, can be given, will be cheerfully given to all the States when lawfully demanded, for whatever cause—as cheerfully to one section, as to another.

[2] See, for example, Lincoln's speech at Ottawa, Illinois, on August 21, 1858.
[3] National Republican Platform, Adopted by the National Republican Convention, held in Chicago, May 17, 1860 (Chicago Press and Tribune Office, Chicago, Illinois, 1860.) Library of Congress, Rare Book and Special Collections Division, Alfred Whital Stern Collection of Lincolniana, http://hdl.loc.gov/loc.rbc/lprbscsm.scsm0716.

There is much controversy about the delivering up of fugitives from service or labor. The clause I now read is as plainly written in the Constitution as any other of its provisions:

> No person held to service or labor in one State, under the laws thereof, escaping into another, shall, in consequence of any law or regulation therein, be discharged from such service or labor, but shall be delivered up on claim of the party to whom such service or labor may be due.

It is scarcely questioned that this provision was intended by those who made it, for the reclaiming of what we call fugitive slaves; and the intention of the law-giver is the law. All members of Congress swear their support to the whole Constitution—to this provision as much as to any other. To the proposition, then, that slaves whose cases come within the terms of the clause, "shall be delivered up," their oaths are unanimous. Now, if they would make the effort in good temper, could they not, with nearly equal unanimity, frame and pass a law, by means of which to keep good that unanimous oath?

There is some difference of opinion whether this clause should be enforced by national or by state authority; but surely that difference is not a very material one. If the slave is to be surrendered, it can be of but little consequence to him, or to others, by which authority it is done. And should any one, in any case, be content that his oath shall go unkept, on a merely unsubstantial controversy as to how it shall be kept?

Again, in any law upon this subject, ought not all the safeguards of liberty known in civilized and humane jurisprudence to be introduced, so that a free man be not, in any case, surrendered as a slave? And might it not be well, at the same time, to provide by law for the enforcement of that clause in the Constitution which guaranties that "The citizens of each State shall be entitled to all privileges and immunities of citizens in the several States?"

I take the official oath to-day, with no mental reservations, and with no purpose to construe the Constitution or laws, by any hypercritical rules. And while I do not choose now to specify particular acts of Congress as proper to be enforced, I do suggest, that it will be much safer for all, both in official and private stations, to conform to, and abide by, all those acts which stand unrepealed, than to violate any of them, trusting to find impunity in having them held to be unconstitutional.

It is seventy-two years since the first inauguration of a President under our national Constitution. During that period fifteen different and greatly distinguished citizens, have, in succession, administered the executive branch of the government. They have conducted it through many perils; and, generally, with great success. Yet, with all this scope for precedent, I now enter upon the same task for the brief constitutional term of four years, under great and peculiar difficulty. A disruption of the Federal Union heretofore only menaced, is now formidably attempted.

I hold, that in contemplation of universal law, and of the Constitution, the Union of these States is perpetual. Perpetuity is implied, if not expressed, in the fundamental law of all national governments. It is safe to assert that no government proper, ever had a provision in its organic law for its own termination. Continue to execute all the express provisions of our national Constitution, and the Union will endure forever—it being impossible to destroy it, except by some action not provided for in the instrument itself.

Again, if the United States be not a government proper, but an association of States in the nature of contract merely, can it, as a contract, be peaceably unmade, by less than all the parties who made it? One party to a contract may violate it—break it, so to speak; but does it not require all to lawfully rescind it?

Descending from these general principles, we find the proposition that, in legal contemplation, the Union is perpetual, confirmed by the history of the Union itself. The Union is much older than the Constitution. It was formed in fact, by the Articles of Association in 1774. It was matured and continued by the Declaration of Independence in 1776. It was further matured and the faith of all the then thirteen States expressly plighted and engaged that it should be perpetual, by the Articles of Confederation in 1778. And finally, in 1787, one of the declared objects for ordaining and establishing the Constitution, was "*to form a more perfect union.*"

But if destruction of the Union, by one, or by a part only, of the States, be lawfully possible, the Union is *less* perfect than before the Constitution, having lost the vital element of perpetuity.

It follows from these views that no State, upon its own mere motion, can lawfully get out of the Union,—that *resolves* and *ordinances* to that effect are legally void; and that acts of violence, within any State or States, against the authority of the United States, are insurrectionary or revolutionary, according to circumstances.

I therefore consider that, in view of the Constitution and the laws, the Union is unbroken; and, to the extent of my ability, I shall take care, as the Constitution itself expressly enjoins upon me, that the laws of the Union be faithfully executed in all the States.[4] Doing this I deem to be only a simple duty on my part; and I shall perform it, so far as practicable, unless my rightful masters, the American people, shall withhold the requisite means, or, in some authoritative manner, direct the contrary. I trust this will not be regarded as a menace, but only as the declared purpose of the Union that it *will* constitutionally defend and maintain itself.

In doing this there needs to be no bloodshed or violence; and there shall be none, unless it be forced upon the national authority. The power confided to me, will be used to hold, occupy, and possess the property, and places belonging to the government, and to collect the duties and imposts; but beyond what may be necessary for these objects, there will be no invasion—no using of forces against, or among the people anywhere. Where hostility to the United States, in any interior locality, shall be so great and so universal, as to prevent competent resident citizens from holding the Federal offices, there will be no attempt to force obnoxious strangers among the people for that object. While the strict legal right may exist in the government to enforce the exercise of these offices, the attempt to do so would be so irritating, and so nearly impracticable with all, that I deem it better to forego, for the time, the uses of such offices.

The mails, unless repelled, will continue to be furnished in all parts of the Union. So far as possible, the people everywhere shall have that sense of perfect security which is most favorable to calm thought and reflection. The course here indicated will be followed, unless current events, and experience, shall show a modification, or change, to be proper; and in every case and exigency, my best discretion will be exercised, according to circumstances actually existing, and with a view and a hope of a peaceful solution of the national troubles, and the restoration of fraternal sympathies and affections. . . .

All profess to be content in the Union, if all constitutional rights can be maintained. Is it true, then, that any right, plainly written in the Constitution, has been denied? I think not. Happily the human mind is so constituted, that no party can reach to the audacity of doing this. Think, if you can, of a single instance in which a plainly written provision of the Constitution has ever been denied. If, by the mere force of numbers, a majority should deprive a minority of any clearly written constitutional right, it might, in a moral point of view, justify revolution—certainly would, if such right were a vital one. But such is not our case. All the vital rights of minorities, and of individuals, are so plainly assured to them, by affirmations and negations, guaranties and

---

[4] Article II, Section 3.

prohibitions, in the Constitution, that controversies never arise concerning them. But no organic law can ever be framed with a provision specifically applicable to every question which may occur in practical administration. No foresight can anticipate, nor any document of reasonable length contain express provisions for all possible questions. Shall fugitives from labor be surrendered by national or by State authority? The Constitution does not expressly say. May Congress prohibit slavery in the territories? The Constitution does not expressly say. Must Congress protect slavery in the territories? The Constitution does not expressly say.

From questions of this class spring all our constitutional controversies, and we divide upon them into majorities and minorities. If the minority will not acquiesce, the majority must, or the government must cease. There is no other alternative; for continuing the government is acquiescence on one side or the other. If a minority, in such case, will secede rather than acquiesce, they make a precedent which, in turn, will divide and ruin them; for a minority of their own will secede from them, whenever a majority refuses to be controlled by such minority. For instance, why may not any portion of a new confederacy, a year or two hence, arbitrarily secede again, precisely as portions of the present Union now claim to secede from it. All who cherish disunion sentiments, are now being educated to the exact temper of doing this. Is there such perfect identity of interests among the States to compose a new Union, as to produce harmony only, and prevent renewed secession?

Plainly, the central idea of secession is the essence of anarchy. A majority, held in restraint by constitutional checks, and limitations, and always changing easily, with deliberate changes of popular opinions and sentiments, is the only true sovereign of a free people. Whoever rejects it, does, of necessity, fly to anarchy or to despotism. Unanimity is impossible; the rule of a minority, as a permanent arrangement, is wholly inadmissible; so that, rejecting the majority principle, anarchy, or despotism in some form, as all that is left.

I do not forget the position assumed by some, that constitutional questions are to be decided by the Supreme Court; nor do I deny that such decisions must be binding in any case, upon the parties to a suit, as to the object of that suit, while they are also entitled to very high respect and consideration, in all parallel cases, by all other departments of the government. And while it is obviously possible that such decision may be erroneous in any given case, still the evil effect following it, being limited to that particular case, with the chance that it may be overruled, and never become a precedent for other cases, can better be borne than could the evils of a different practice. At the same time the candid citizen must confess that if the policy of the

government, upon vital questions, affecting the whole people, is to be irrevocably fixed by decisions of the Supreme Court, the instant they are made, in
ordinary litigation between parties, in personal actions, the people will have
ceased, to be their own rulers, having, to that extent, practically resigned
their government, into the hands of that eminent tribunal. Nor is there, in
this view, any assault upon the court, or the judges. It is a duty, from which
they may not shrink, to decide cases properly brought before them; and it is
no fault of theirs, if others seek to turn their decisions to political purposes.

One section of our country believes slavery is *right*, and ought to be
extended, while the other believes it is *wrong*, and ought not to be extended.
This is the only substantial dispute. The fugitive slave clause of the Constitution, and the law for the suppression of the foreign slave trade, are each as well
enforced, perhaps, as any law can ever be in a community where the moral
sense of the people imperfectly supports the law itself. The great body of the
people abide by the dry legal obligation in both cases, and a few break over in
each. This, I think, cannot be perfectly cured; and it would be worse in both
cases *after* the separation of the sections, than before. The foreign slave trade,
now imperfectly suppressed, would be ultimately revived without restriction,
in one section; while fugitive slaves, now only partially surrendered, would
not be surrendered at all, by the other.

Physically speaking, we cannot separate from each other. We cannot
remove our respective sections from each other, nor build an impassable
wall between them. A husband and wife may be divorced, and go out of the
presence, and beyond the reach of each other; but the different parts of our
country cannot do this. They cannot but remain face to face; and intercourse,
either amicable or hostile, must continue between them. Is it possible then
to make that intercourse more advantageous, or more satisfactory, *after* separation than *before*? Can aliens make treaties easier than friends can make
laws? Can treaties be more faithfully enforced between aliens, than laws can
among friends? Suppose you go to war, you cannot fight always; and when,
after much loss on both sides, and no gain on either, you cease fighting, the
identical old questions, as terms of intercourse, are again upon you.

This country, with its institutions, belongs to the people who inhabit
it. Whenever they shall grow weary of the existing government, they can
exercise their *constitutional* right of amending it, or their *revolutionary* right
to dismember, or overthrow it. I can not be ignorant of the fact that many
worthy, and patriotic citizens are desirous of having the national constitution amended. While I make no recommendation of amendments, I fully
recognize the rightful authority of the people over the whole subject, to be

exercised in either of the modes prescribed in the instrument itself; and I should, under existing circumstances, favor, rather than oppose, a fair opportunity being afforded the people to act upon it.

I will venture to add that, to me, the convention mode seems preferable, in that it allows amendments to originate with the people themselves, instead of only permitting them to take, or reject, propositions, originated by others, nor especially chosen for the purpose, and which might not be precisely such, as they would wish to either accept or refuse. I understand a proposed amendment to the Constitution—which amendment, however, I have not seen, has passed Congress, to the effect that the federal government, shall never interfere with the domestic institutions of the States, including that of persons held to service. To avoid misconstruction of what I have said, I depart from my purpose not to speak of particular amendments, so far as to say that, holding such a provision to now be implied constitutional law, I have no objection to its being made express, and irrevocable.

The Chief Magistrate derives all his authority from the people, and they have conferred none upon him to fix terms for the separation of the States. The people themselves can do this also if they choose; but the executive, as such, has nothing to do with it. His duty is to administer the present government, as it came to his hands, and to transmit it, unimpaired by him, to his successor.

Why should there not be a patient confidence in the ultimate justice of the people? Is there any better, or equal hope, in the world? In our present differences, is either party without faith of being in the right? If the Almighty Ruler of nations, with his eternal truth and justice, be on your side of the North, or on yours of the South, that truth, and that justice, will surely prevail, by the judgement of this great tribunal, the American people.

By the frame of the government under which we live, this same people have wisely given their public servants but little power for mischief; and have, with equal wisdom, provided for the return of that little to their own hands at very short intervals.

While the people retain their virtue, and vigilance, no administration, by any extreme of wickedness or folly, can very seriously injure the government, in the short space of four years.

My countrymen, one and all, think calmly and *well*, upon this whole subject. Nothing valuable can be lost by taking time. If there be an object to *hurry* any of you, in hot haste, to a step which you would never take *deliberately*, that object will be frustrated by taking time; but no good object can be frustrated by it. Such of you as are now dissatisfied, still have the old Constitution unimpaired, and, on the sensitive point, the laws of your own framing under it; while the new administration will have no immediate power, if it would, to change either. If it were admitted that you who are dissatisfied, hold the right side in the dispute, there still is no single good reason for precipitate action. Intelligence, patriotism, Christianity, and a firm reliance on Him, who has never yet forsaken this favored land, are still competent to adjust, in the best way, all our present difficulty.

In *your* hands, my dissatisfied fellow countrymen, and not in *mine*, is the momentous issue of civil war. The government will not assail *you*. You can have no conflict, without being yourselves the aggressors. *You* have no oath registered in Heaven to destroy the government, while *I* shall have the most solemn one to "preserve, protect, and defend" it.

I am loth to close. We are not enemies, but friends. We must not be enemies. Though passion may have strained, it must not break our bonds of affection. The mystic chords of memory, stretching from every battle-field, and patriot grave, to every living heart and hearthstone, all over this broad land, will yet swell the chorus of the Union, when again touched, as surely they will be, by the better angels of our nature.

Message to Congress in Special Session

President Abraham Lincoln

July 4, 1861

A*fter the Confederate attack on Fort Sumter, Lincoln took measures aimed at a military response including calling forth militia, blockading Confederate ports, and adding to the Army and Navy. Lincoln also authorized the suspension of habeas corpus in Maryland along train lines connecting Washington to Philadelphia. In Ex parte Merryman (1861), Chief Justice Roger Taney ruled in a circuit court that Lincoln lacked the power to suspend habeas corpus because the power could only be exercised by Congress. For Taney, the location of the Suspension Clause in Article One of the Constitution signified that the power was meant to be legislative not executive.*

Lincoln called Congress into special session, and, in a special message, he reported his actions since the Sumter attack. In the passage below, Lincoln defends himself against Taney's charge that he violated the Constitution. Lincoln makes two arguments, that the Constitution must have provided for occasions when Congress was out of session, and the president's oath of office authorizes the president to violate one law in order to preserve all of the laws.

SOURCE: Abraham Lincoln, Abraham Lincoln papers: Series 1. General Correspondence.—1916: Abraham Lincoln, May–June 1861 Message to Congress, July 4, 1861, Second Printed Draft, with Changes in Lincoln's Hand. May, 1861. Library of Congress, Manuscript Division, https://goo.gl/JFmNqx.

Fellow-citizens of the Senate and House of Representatives:

... It is thus seen that the assault upon, and reduction of, Fort Sumter, was, in no sense, a matter of self defense on the part of the assailants. They well knew that the garrison in the Fort could, by no possibility, commit aggression upon them. They knew—they were expressly notified—that the giving of bread to the few brave and hungry men of the garrison, was all which would on that occasion be attempted, unless themselves, by resisting so much, should provoke more. They knew that this desired to keep the garrison in the Fort, not to assail them, but merely to maintain visible possession, and thus to preserve the Union from actual, and immediate dissolution—trusting, as herein-before stated, to time, discussion, and the ballot-box, for final adjustment; and they assailed, and reduced the Fort, for precisely the reverse object—to drive out the visible authority of the Federal Union, and thus force it to immediate dissolution.

That this was their object, the Executive well understood; and having said to them in the inaugural address, "You can have no conflict without being yourselves the aggressors,"[1] he took pains, not only to keep this declaration good, but also to keep the case so free from the power of ingenious sophistry, as that the world should not be able to misunderstand it. By the affair at Fort Sumter, with its surrounding circumstances, that point was reached. Then, and thereby, the assailants of the government, began the conflict of arms, without a gun in sight, or in expectancy, to return their fire, save only the few in the Fort, sent to the harbor, years before, for their own protection and still ready to give that protection, in whatever was lawful. In this act, discarding all else, they have forced upon the country, the distinct issue: "immediate dissolution, or blood."

And this issue embraces more than the fate of these United States. It presents to the whole family of man, the question, whether a constitutional republic, or a democracy—a government of the people, by the same people—can, or cannot, maintain its territorial integrity, against its own domestic foes. It presents the question, whether discontented individuals, too few in numbers to control administration, according to organic law, in any case, can always, upon the pretense made in this case, or on any other pretenses, or arbitrarily, without any pretense, break up their government, and thus practically put an end to free government upon the earth. It forces us to ask: "Is there, in all republics, this inherent, and fatal weakness?" "Must a government, of necessity, be too *strong* for the liberties of its own people, or *too weak* to maintain its own existence?"

So viewing the issue, no choice was left but to call out the war power of the government; and so to resist force, employed for its destruction, by force, for its preservation....

Soon after the first call for militia, it was considered a duty to authorize the Commanding General, in proper cases, according to his discretion, to suspend the privilege of the writ of habeas corpus; or, in other words, to arrest, and detain, without resort to the ordinary processes and forms of

---

[1] See Document 15

law, such individuals as he might deem dangerous to the public safety. This authority has purposely been exercised but very sparingly. Nevertheless, the legality and propriety of what has been done under it, are questioned; and the attention of the country has been called to the proposition that one who is sworn to "take care that the laws be faithfully executed," should not himself violate them. Of course, some consideration was given to the questions of power, and propriety, before this matter was acted upon. The whole of the laws which required to be faithfully executed, were being resisted, and failing of execution, in nearly one-third of the States. Must they be allowed to finally fail of execution, even had it been perfectly clear, that by the use of the means necessary to their execution, some single law, made in such extreme tenderness of the citizen's liberty, that practically, it relieves more of the guilty, than of the innocent, should, to a very limited extent, be violated? To state the question more directly, are all the laws, *but one*, to go unexecuted, and the government itself go to pieces, lest that one be violated? Even in such a case, would not the official oath be broken, if the government should be overthrown, when it was believed that disregarding the single law, would tend to preserve it? But it was not believed that this question was presented. It was not believed that any law was violated. The provision of the Constitution that "The privilege of the writ of habeas corpus, shall not be suspended unless when, in cases of rebellion or invasion, the public safety may require it," is equivalent to a provision—is a provision—that such privilege may be suspended when, in cases of rebellion, or in invasion, the public safety *does* require it. It was decided that we have a case of rebellion, and that the public safety does require a qualified suspension of the privilege of the writ which was authorized to be made. Now it is insisted that Congress, and not the Executive, is vested with this power. But the Constitution itself, is silent as to which, or who, is to exercise the power; and as the provision was plainly made for a dangerous emergency, it cannot be believed the framers of the instrument intended, that in every case, the danger should run its course, until Congress could be called together; the very assembling of which might be prevented, as was intended in this case, by the rebellion.

No more extended argument is now offered; as an option, at some length will probably be presented by the Attorney General. Whether there shall be any legislation upon the subject, and if any, what, is submitted entirely to the better judgement of Congress....

Letter to Albert G. Hodges

President Abraham Lincoln

April 4, 1864

I n this letter to newspaper editor Albert Hodges, Lincoln explains his actions
with respect to slavery and the Constitution. Lincoln specifically justifies the
Emancipation Proclamation on grounds of military necessity, not his moral opposition to slavery. As he did in a special message of July 4, 1861 (Document 16),
Lincoln points to the oath of office as a source of authority to preserve the nation.

Unlike Thomas Jefferson, who did not defend the Louisiana Purchase as constitutional, Lincoln reads the Constitution to be different during times of emergency. Lincoln's letter to Hodges should be compared to Jefferson's letter to Colvin
(Document 10). Whereas Lincoln grounds the source of his authority in the president's oath of office, Jefferson refrains from making a constitutional argument
to support his answer to Colvin that there are occasions when an officer in high
trust must go beyond the law. Later presidents will appeal to both examples (Document 35).

SOURCE: Abraham Lincoln, Abraham Lincoln papers: Series 1. General Correspondence.
1833 to 1916: Abraham Lincoln to Albert G. Hodges, April 4, 1864. Library of Congress,
Manuscript Division, https://goo.gl/dpkx2e.

My dear Sir: You ask me to put in writing the substance of what I verbally said
the other day, in your presence, to Governor Bramlette and Senator Dixon.[1]
It was about as follows:

"I am naturally anti-slavery. If slavery is not wrong, nothing is wrong. I

---

[1] Governor Thomas E. Bramlette, (1817–1875) served as the governor of Kentucky
from 1863–1867. A Union Democrat, he supported the war and President Lincoln
until the army began recruiting black men to serve. Archibald Dixon (1802–1876)
served as senator from Kentucky from 1852–1855, and remained active in the state's
politics through the Civil War era, advocating for policies that were both pro-slavery
and pro-Union.

can not remember when I did not so think, and feel. And yet I have never understood that the Presidency conferred upon me an unrestricted right to act officially upon this judgement and feeling. It was in the oath I took that I would, to the best of my ability, preserve, protect, and defend the Constitution of the United States. I could not take the office without taking the oath. Nor was it my view that I might take an oath to get power, and break the oath in using the power. I understood, too, that in ordinary civil administration this oath even forbade me to practically indulge my primary abstract judgement on the moral question of slavery. I had publicly declared this many times, and in many ways. And I aver that, to this day, I have done no official act in mere deference to my primary abstract judgement on the moral question of slavery. I did understand however, that my oath to preserve the Constitution to the best of my ability, imposed upon me the duty of preserving, by every indispensable means, that government—that nation—of which that constitution was the organic law. Was it possible to lose the nation, and yet preserve the Constitution? By general law life *and* limb must be protected; yet often a limb must be amputated to save a life; but a life is never wisely given to save a limb. I felt that measures, otherwise unconstitutional, might become lawful, by becoming indispensable to the preservation of the Constitution, through the preservation of the nation. Right or wrong, I assumed this ground, and now avow it. I could not feel that, to the best of my ability, I had even tried to preserve the Constitution, if, to save slavery, or any minor matter, I should permit the wreck of government, country, and Constitution all together. When, early in the war, Gen. Fremont[2] attempted military emancipation, I forbade it, because I did not then think it an indispensable necessity. When a little later, Gen. Cameron,[3] then Secretary of War, suggested the arming of the blacks, I objected, because I did not yet think it an indispensable necessity. When, still later, Gen. Hunter[4] attempted military emancipation, I again forbade it, because I did not yet think the indispensable necessity had come. When, in March, and May, and July 1862 I made

---

[2] John Charles Fremont (1813–1890) served as a Union general in the West; Lincoln not only superceded his emancipation order, he relieved Fremont of command as a result of it.

[3] Simon Cameron (1799–1889) served as United States Secretary of War under Lincoln at the start of the Civil War, a post at which he failed abysmally; he was forced to resign under a cloud of corruption charges that resulted in a congressional censure.

[4] David Hunter (1802–1886), an outspoken abolitionist, served as a Union general. In May 1862, as commander of the Department of the South, he issued General Order No. 11, emancipating the slaves in Georgia, South Carolina, and Florida.

earnest, and successive appeals to the border states to favor compensated emancipation, I believed that the indispensable necessity for military emancipation, and arming the blacks would come, unless averted by that measure. They declined the proposition; and I was, in my best judgment, driven to the alternative of either surrendering the Union, and with it, the Constitution, or of laying [a] strong hand upon the colored element. I chose the latter. In choosing it, I hoped for greater gain than loss; but of this, I was not entirely confident. More than a year of trial now shows no loss by it in our foreign relations, none in our home popular sentiment, none in our white military force,—no loss by it any how or anywhere. On the contrary, it shows a gain of quite a hundred and thirty thousand soldiers, seamen, and laborers. These are palpable facts, about which, as facts, there can be no caviling. We have the men; and we could not have had them without the measure.

"And now let any Union man who complains of the measure, test himself by writing down in one line that he is for subduing the rebellion by force of arms; and in the next, that he is for taking these hundred and thirty thousand men from the Union side, and placing them where they would be but for the measure he condemns. If he cannot face his case so stated, it is only because he cannot face the truth."

I add a word which was not in the verbal conversation. In telling this tale I attempt no compliment to my own sagacity. I claim not to have controlled events, but confess plainly that events have controlled me. Now, at the end of three years' struggle the nation's condition is not what either party, or any man devised, or expected. God alone can claim it. Whither it is tending seems plain. If God now wills the removal of a great wrong, and wills also that we of the North as well as you of the South, shall pay fairly for our complicity in that wrong, impartial history will find therein new cause to attest and revere the justice and goodness of God.

Yours truly,
A. Lincoln

Ex parte Milligan

Associate Justice David Davis

December 1866

I n late 1864, Lambdin Milligan, an outspoken "Copperhead" Northern Demo-crat (that is, one who advocated reaching a negotiated settlement with the Con-federacy, even at the cost of Union), was arrested in Indiana for conspiracy against the United States. Having been identified as a leader in a secret organization that aimed to subvert the war effort by encouraging resistance to the draft and by freeing Confederate prisoners, Milligan was tried by a military tribunal in India-napolis and sentenced to death. Although his guilty verdict came only two weeks after his arrest, his execution was scheduled for May, 19, 1865. Lee surrendered at Appomattox on April 9, 1865. Milligan challenged his conviction in court, and the Supreme Court ultimately decided in Milligan's favor. All nine Justices agreed that Milligan's conviction by military tribunal was unlawful, but four of the nine argued in a separate opinion that the problem was not the tribunals themselves but the fact that Congress had not authorized them. In the opinion below, Justice David Davis argued instead that the key factor was that the civil courts of jus-tice in Indiana had never closed. Because the military was using tribunals under Lincoln's authority, this case is an important early example of the Supreme Court challenging the power of the president as Commander in Chief during wartime. Note, however, that the decision was given after the War had ended.

SOURCE: *Cases Argued and Adjudged in the Supreme Court of the United States, December Term, 1866.* Volume IV. (New York and Albany: Banks and Brothers, Law Publishers, 1889), 107–30.

Mr. Justice Davis delivered the opinion of the court....

The controlling question in the case is this: Upon the *facts* stated in Milligan's petition, and the exhibits filed, had the military commission mentioned in it *jurisdiction*, legally, to try and sentence him? Milligan, not a resident of one of the rebellious states, or a prisoner of war, but a citizen of Indiana for twenty years past, and never in the military or naval service, is, while at his home, arrested by the military power of the United States, imprisoned, and, on certain criminal charges preferred against him, tried, convicted, and sentenced to be hanged by a military commander of the military district of Indiana. Had this tribunal the *legal* power and authority to try and punish this man?

No graver question was ever considered by this court, nor one which more nearly concerns the rights of the whole people; for it is the birthright of every American citizen when charged with crime, to be tried and punished according to law. The power of punishment is alone [the means through] which the laws have provided for that purpose, and if they are ineffectual, there is an immunity from punishment, no matter how great an offender the individual may be, or how much his crimes may have shocked the sense of justice of the country, or endangered its safety. By the protection of the law human rights are secured; withdraw that protection, and they are at the mercy of wicked rulers, or the clamor of an excited people. If there was law to justify this military trial, it is not our province to interfere; if there was not, it is our duty to declare the nullity of the whole proceedings. The decision of this question does not depend on argument or judicial precedents, numerous and highly illustrative as they are. These precedents inform us of the extent of the struggle to preserve liberty and to relieve those in civil life from military trials. The founders of our government were familiar with the history of that struggle; and secured in a written constitution every right which the people had wrested from power during a contest of ages. By that Constitution and the laws authorized by it this question must be determined. The provisions of that instrument on the administration of criminal justice are too plain and direct, to leave room for misconstruction or doubt of their true meaning. Those applicable to this case are found in that clause of the original Constitution which says, "That the trial of all crimes, except in case of impeachment, shall be by jury;"[1] and in the fourth, fifth, and sixth articles of the amendments. The fourth proclaims the right to be secure in person and effects against unreasonable search and seizure; and directs that a judicial warrant shall not issue "without proof of probable cause supported by oath or affirmation." The fifth declares "that no person shall be held to answer for a capital or otherwise infamous crime unless on presentment by a grand jury, except in cases arising in the land or naval forces, or in the militia, when in actual service in time of war or public danger, nor be deprived of life, liberty, or property, without due process of law." And the sixth guarantees the right of trial by jury, in such manner and with such regulations that with upright

---

[1] Article III, Section 2.

judges, impartial juries, and an able bar, the innocent will be saved and the guilty punished. It is in these words:

In all criminal prosecutions the accused shall enjoy the right to a speedy and public trial by an impartial jury of the state and district shall have been previously ascertained by law, and to be informed of the nature and cause of the accusation, to be confronted with the witnesses against him, to have compulsory process for obtaining witnesses in his favor, and to have the assistance of counsel for his defense.

These securities for personal liberty thus embodied, were such as wisdom and experience had demonstrated to be necessary for the protection of those accused of crime. And so strong was the sense of the country of their importance, and so jealous were the people that these rights, highly prized, might be denied them by implication, that when the original Constitution was proposed for adoption it encountered severe opposition; and, but for the belief that it would be so amended as to embrace them, it would never have been ratified.

Time has proven the discernment of our ancestors; for even these provisions, expressed in such plain English words, that it would seem the ingenuity of man could not evade them, are *now*, after the lapse of more than seventy years, sought to be avoided. Those great and good men foresaw that troublous times would arise, when rulers and people would become restive under restraint, and seek by sharp and decisive measures to accomplish ends deemed just and proper; and that the principles of constitutional liberty would be in peril, unless established by irrepealable law. The history of the world had taught them that what was done in the past might be attempted in the future. The Constitution of the United States is a law for rulers and people, equally in war and in peace, and covers with the shield of its protection all classes of men, at all times, and under all circumstances. No doctrine, involving more pernicious consequences, was ever invented by the wit of man than that any of its provisions can be suspended during any of the great exigencies of government. Such a doctrine leads directly to anarchy or despotism, but the theory of necessity on which it is based is false; for the government, within the Constitution, has all the powers granted to it, which are necessary to preserve its existence; as has been happily proved by the result of the great effort to throw off its just authority.

Have any of the rights guaranteed by the Constitution been violated in the case of Milligan? And if so, what are they?

Every trial involves the exercise of judicial power; and from what source did the military commission that tried him derive their authority? Certainly, no part of the judicial power of the country was conferred on them; because the Constitution expressly vests it "in one supreme court and such inferior courts as the Congress may from time to time ordain and establish,"[2] and it is not pretended that the commission was a court ordained and established by Congress. They cannot justify on the mandate of the President; because he is controlled by law, and has his appropriate sphere of duty, which is to execute, not to make, the laws; and there is "no unwritten criminal code to which resort can be had as a source of jurisdiction."[3]

But it is said that the jurisdiction is complete under the "laws and usages of war."[4]

It can serve no useful purpose to inquire what those laws and usages are, whence they originated, where found, and on whom they operate; they can never be applied to citizens in states which have upheld the authority of the government, and where the courts are open and their process unobstructed. This court has judicial knowledge that in Indiana the Federal authority was always unopposed, and its courts always open to hear criminal accusations and redress grievances; and no usage of war could sanction a military there for any offence whatever of a citizen in civil life, in nowise connected with the military service. Congress could grant no such power; and to the honor of our national legislature be it said, it has never been provoked by the state of the country even to attempt its exercise. One of the plainest constitutional provisions was, therefore, infringed when Milligan was tried by a court not ordained and established by Congress, and not composed of judges appointed during good behavior.

Why was he not delivered to the Circuit Court of Indiana to be proceeded against according to law? No reason of necessity could be urged against it;

---

[2] Article III, Section 1
[3] This line appears in an antebellum legal commentary: Alfred Conkling, *A Treatise on the Organization, Jurisdiction and Practice of the Courts of the United States* (W. A. Gould and Company, 1831), 74. Conkling (1789–1874) was a lawyer and a long-term district court judge in New York state.
[4] Possibly a reference to military historian Francis Lieber's lecture series on military ethics by that title, or to his pamphlet, *Guerrilla Parties: Considered with Reference to the Laws and Usages of War* (D. Van Nostrand, 1862). Lieber (1798–1892) was such a respected expert in the field of military ethics that President Lincoln tasked him with serving as the primary author of the army's revised code of conduct, *Instructions for the Government of Armies of the United States in the Field* (1863), known also as *General Order № 100*, or simply, the Lieber Instructions.

because Congress had declared penalties against the offences charged, pro-vided for their punishment, and directed that court to hear and determine them. And soon after this military tribunal was ended, the Circuit Court met, peacefully transacted its business, and adjourned. It needed no bayonets to protect it, and required no military aid to execute it judgements. It was held in a state, eminently distinguished for patriotism, by judges commissioned during the Rebellion, who were provided with juries, upright, intelligent, and selected by a marshal appointed by the President. The government had no right to conclude that Milligan, if guilty, would not receive in that court merited punishment; for its records disclose that it was constantly engaged in the trial of similar offences, and was never interrupted in its administration of criminal justice. If it was dangerous, in the distracted condition of affairs, to leave Milligan unrestrained of his liberty, because he "conspired against the government, afforded aid and comfort to rebels, and incited the people to insurrection,"[5] the *law* said arrest him, confine him closely, render him powerless to do further mischief; and then present his case to the grand jury of the district, with proofs of his guilt, and, if indicted, try him according to the course of the common law. If this had been done, the Constitution would have been vindicated, the law of 1863 enforced, and the securities for personal liberty preserved and defended.

Another guarantee of freedom was broken when Milligan was denied a trial by jury. The great minds of the country have differed on the correct interpretation to be given to various provisions of the Federal Constitution; and judicial decision has been often invoked to settle their true meaning; but until recently no one ever doubted that the right of trial by jury was fortified in the organic law against the power of attack. It is *now* assailed; but if ideas can be expressed in words, and language has any meaning, *this right*—one of the most valuable in a free country—is preserved to everyone accused of crime who is not attached to the army, or navy, or militia in actual service. The sixth amendment affirms that "in all criminal prosecutions the accused shall enjoy the right to a speedy and public trial by an impartial jury," language broad enough to embrace all persons and cases; but the fifth, recognizing the necessity of an indictment, or presentment, before anyone can be held to answer for high crimes, "*excepts* cases arising in the land or naval forces, or in the militia, when in actual service, in time of war or public danger;" and the framers of the Constitution, doubtless, meant to limit the right of

---

[5] Presumably a quotation from the case against Milligan.

trial by jury, in the sixth amendment, to those persons who were subject to indictment or presentment in the fifth.

The discipline necessary to the efficiency of the army and navy, required other and swifter modes of trial than are furnished by the common law courts; and, in pursuance of the power conferred by the Constitution, Congress has declared the kinds of trial, and the manner in which they shall be conducted, for offences committed while the party is in the military or naval service. Every one connected with these branches of the public service is amenable to the jurisdiction which Congress has created for their government, and, while thus serving, surrenders his right to be tried by the civil courts. *All other persons*, citizens of states where the courts are open, if charged with crime, are guaranteed the inestimable privilege of trial by jury. This privilege is a vital principle, underlying the whole administration of criminal justice; it is not held by sufferance, and cannot be frittered away on any plea of state or political necessity. When peace prevails, and the authority of the government is undisputed, there is no difficulty of preserving the safeguards of liberty; for the ordinary modes of trial are never neglected, and no one wished it otherwise; but if society is disturbed by civil commotion—if the passions of men are aroused and the restraints of law weakened, if not disregarded—these safeguards need, and should receive, the watchful care of those entrusted with the guardianship of the Constitution and laws. In no other way can we transmit to posterity unimpaired the blessings of liberty, consecrated by the sacrifices of the Revolution.

It is claimed that martial law covers with its broad mantle the proceedings of this military commission. The proposition is this: that in a time of war the commander of an armed force (if in his opinion the exigencies of the country demand it, and of which he is to judge), has the power, within the lines of his military district, to suspend all civil rights and their remedies, and subject citizens as well as soldiers to the rule of *his will*; and in the exercise of his lawful authority cannot be restrained, except by his superior officer or the President of the United States.

If this position is sound to the extent claimed, then when war exists, foreign or domestic, and the country is subdivided into military departments for mere convenience, the commander of one them can, if he chooses, within his limits, on the plea of necessity, with the approval of the Executive, substitute military force for and to the exclusion of the laws, and punish all persons, as he thinks right and proper, without fixed or certain rules.

The statement of this proposition shows its importance; for, if true, republican government is a failure, and there is an end of liberty regulated by law.

Martial law, established on such a basis, destroys every guarantee of the Constitution, and effectually renders the "military independent of and superior to the civil power"—the attempt to do which by the King of Great Britain was deemed by our fathers such an offence, that they assigned it to the world as one of the causes which impelled them to declare their independence. Civil liberty and this kind of martial law cannot endure together; the antagonism is irreconcilable; and, in the conflict, one or the other must perish.

Third Annual Message

President Andrew Johnson

December 3, 1867

H enry Clay's failed attempt in 1834 to reign in the president's power to remove executive branch officers found new life in the Reconstruction Congress when Republicans passed the Tenure of Office Act of 1867 over Andrew Johnson's veto. The law required the Senate's advice and consent for removal of several department heads including the Secretaries of State and War and the Attorney General. For certain other offices, it required the Senate's confirmation of a replacement before a removal could go into effect.

The law was part of a larger conflict between Congress and the president about the direction and control of Reconstruction. Johnson wanted terms more favorable to the South, and he was relying on unilateral executive powers to pursue his goals. For example, he issued twenty-nine vetoes in four years (four times the rate of Andrew Jackson). He also removed the military commanders of four of the five military districts in the South, targeting those who were committed to carrying out Congress's Reconstruction Acts. In this message, Johnson explains why he believes the Tenure of Office Act was unconstitutional. His later removal of Secretary of War Edwin M. Stanton (see Document 20) relied on this interpretation.

SOURCE: James D. Richardson, ed., *A Compilation of the Messages and Papers of the Presidents, 1789–1897.* Volume VI (Washington, D.C.: Government Printing Office, 1897), 558–81.

...How far the duty of the President "to preserve, protect, and defend the Constitution"[1] requires him to go in opposing an unconstitutional act of Congress is a very serious and important question, on which I have deliberated much and felt extremely anxious to reach a proper conclusion. Where an act has been passed according to the forms of the Constitution by the supreme legislative authority and is regularly enrolled among the public

---

[1] Here Johnson quotes from the presidential oath of office; see Article II, Section 1 of the Constitution.

statutes of the country, Executive resistance to it, especially in times of high party excitement, would be likely to produce violent collision between the respective adherents of the two branches of Government. This would be simply civil war, and civil war must be resorted to only as the last remedy for the worst of evils. Whatever might tend to provoke it should be most carefully avoided. A faithful and conscientious magistrate will concede very much to honest error, and something even to perverse malice, before he will endanger the public peace; and he will not adopt forcible measures, or such as might lead to force, as long as those which are peaceable remain open to him or to his constituents. It is true that cases may occur in which the Executive would be compelled to stand on its rights, and maintain them regardless of all consequences. If Congress should pass an act which is not only in palpable conflict with the Constitution, but will certainly, if carried out, produce immediate and irreparable injury to the organic structure of the Government, and if there be neither judicial remedy for the wrongs it inflicts nor power in the people to protect themselves without the official aid of their elected defender—if, for instance, the legislative department should pass an act even through all the forms of law to abolish a coordinate department of the Government—in such a case the President must take the high responsibilities of his office and save the life of the nation at all hazards. The so-called reconstruction acts, though as plainly unconstitutional as any that can be imagined, were not believed to be within that last class mentioned. The people were not wholly disarmed of the power of self-defense. In all the Northern States they still held in their hands the sacred right of the ballot, and it was safe to believe that in due time they would come to the rescue of their own institutions. . . .

It is well and publicly known that enormous frauds have been perpetrated on the Treasury and that colossal fortunes have been made at the public expense. This species of corruption has increased, is increasing, and if not diminished will soon bring us into total ruin and disgrace. The public creditors and the taxpayers are alike interested in an honest administration of the finances, and neither class will long endure the large-handed robberies of the recent past. For this discreditable state of things there are several causes. Some of the taxes are so laid as to present an irresistible temptation to evade payment. The great sums which officers may win by connivance at fraud create a pressure which is more than the virtue of many can withstand, and there can be no doubt that the open disregard of constitutional obligations avowed by some of the highest and most influential men in the country has greatly weakened the moral sense of those who serve in subordinate places.

The expenses of the United States, including interest on the public debt, are more than six times as much as they were seven years ago. To collect and disburse this vast amount requires careful supervision as well as systematic vigilance. The system, never perfected, was much disorganized by the "tenure-of-office bill," which has almost destroyed official accountability. The President may be thoroughly convinced that an officer is incapable, dishonest, or unfaithful to the Constitution, but under the law which I have named the utmost he can do is to complain to the Senate and ask the privilege of supplying his place with a better man. If the Senate be regarded as personally or politically hostile to the President, it is natural, and not altogether unreasonable, for the officer to expect that it will take his part as far as possible, restore him to his place, and give him a triumph over his Executive superior. The officer has other chances of impunity arising from accidental defects of evidence, the mode of investigating it, and the secrecy of the hearing. It is not wonderful that official malfeasance should become bold in proportion as the delinquents learn to think themselves safe. I am entirely persuaded that under such a rule the President cannot perform the great duty assigned to him of seeing the laws faithfully executed, and that it disables him most especially from enforcing that rigid accountability which is necessary to the due execution of the revenue laws.

The Constitution invests the President with authority to *decide* whether a removal should be made in any given case; the act of Congress declares in substance that he shall only *accuse* such as he supposed to be unworthy of their trust. The Constitution makes him sole *judge* in the premises, but the statute takes away his jurisdiction, transfers it to the Senate, and leaves him nothing but the odious and sometimes impracticable duty of becoming a *prosecutor*. The prosecution is to be conducted before a tribunal whose members are not, like him, responsible to the whole people, but to separate constituent bodies, and who may hear his accusation with great disfavor. The Senate is absolutely without any known standard of decision applicable to such a case. Its judgment cannot be anticipated, for it is not governed by any rule. The law does not define what shall be deemed good cause for removal. It is impossible even to conjecture what may or may not be so considered by the Senate. The nature of the subject forbids clear proof. If the charge be incapacity, what evidence will support it? Fidelity to the Constitution may be understood or misunderstood in a thousand different ways, and by violent party men, in violent party times, unfaithfulness to the Constitution may even come to be considered meritorious. If the officer be accused of dishonesty, how shall it be made out? Will it be inferred from acts unconnected with public duty, from private history, or from general reputation, or must the President await the commission of an actual misdemeanor in office? Shall he in the meantime risk the character and interest of the nation in the hands of men to whom he cannot give his confidence? Must he forbear his complaint until the mischief is done and cannot be prevented? If his zeal in the public service should impel him to anticipate the overt act, must he move at the peril of being tried himself for the offense of slandering his subordinate? In the present circumstances of the country someone must be held responsible for official delinquency of every kind. It is extremely difficult to say where that responsibility should be thrown if it be not left where it has been placed by the Constitution. But all just men will admit that the President ought to be entirely relieved from such responsibility if he cannot meet it by reason of restrictions placed by law upon his action.

The unrestricted power of removal from office is a very great one to be trusted even to a magistrate chosen by the general suffrage of the whole people and accountable directly to them for his acts. It is undoubtedly liable to abuse, and at some periods of our history perhaps has been abused. If it be thought desirable and constitutional that it should be so limited as to make the President merely a common informer against other public agents, he should at least be permitted to act in that capacity before some open tribunal, independent of party politics, ready to investigate the merits of every case, furnished with the means of taking evidence, and bound to decide according to established rules. This would guarantee the safety of the accuser when he acts in good faith, and at the same time secure the rights of the other party. I speak, of course, with all proper respect for the present Senate, but it does not seem to me that any legislative body can be so constituted as to insure its fitness for these functions.

It is not the theory of this Government that public offices are the property of those who hold them. They are given merely as a trust for the public benefit, sometimes for a fixed period, sometimes during good behavior, but generally they are liable to be terminated at the pleasure of the appointing power, which represents the collective majesty and speaks the will of the people. The forced retention in office of a single dishonest person may work great injury to the public interests. The danger to the public service comes not from the power to removed, but from the power to appoint. Therefore it was that the framers of the Constitution left the power of removal unrestricted, while they gave the Senate a right to reject all appointments which in its opinion were not fit to be made. A little reflection on this subject will probably satisfy all who have the good of the country at heart that our best course is to take the Constitution for our guide, walk in the path marked out by the founders of the Republic, and obey the rules made sacred by the observance of our great predecessors....

DOCUMENT 20

Articles of Impeachment of Andrew Johnson

House of Representatives

1868

The Constitution states that the president may be impeached and removed for "Treason, Bribery, and other high Crimes and Misdemeanors" (Article II, Section 4). Although most people today assume that "high Crimes and Misdemeanors" require that the president commit some indictable offense, the history of the phrase suggests a broader meaning. The Constitution invites debate about the scope of impeachment, and those subject to impeachment are most likely to insist on its narrowest application.

When Republicans passed the Tenure of Office Act (Document 19) they had already failed to impeach Johnson. The House Judiciary Committee had supported impeaching Johnson for undermining congressional prerogatives, arguing that it was not necessary to prove that the president had committed a specific crime. This effort failed to muster a majority in the House, and so Republicans passed the Tenure of Office Act to force Johnson to break a specific law. When Johnson removed Secretary of War Edwin M. Stanton, Republicans were able to secure a majority in the House to vote to impeach Johnson. Of the eleven articles of impeachment, nine have to do with the Tenure of Office Act and the removal of Stanton. The Tenth and Eleventh articles argue that Johnson violated more fundamental constitutional norms having to do with the presidency and separation of powers.

In the end, Republicans failed to secure the two-thirds majority in the Senate required to remove Johnson from office. There was some question about whether the law applied to current department heads. Johnson's lead attorney, William M. Evarts (1818–1901), argued in the trial that even if Johnson did violate the law, his motive was to create a legal controversy to be settled by the Supreme Court. Several senators may have been persuaded that the question regarding Stanton needed to be resolved by the federal judiciary.

SOURCE: *Supplement to the Congressional Globe Containing the Proceedings of the Senate Sitting for the Trial of Andrew Johnson, President of the United States.* 40th Congress, Second Session. (Washington, D.C.: F & J Rives & George A Bailey, 1868), 3–5.

Articles established by the House of Representatives of the Unites States

In the name of themselves and all the people of the United States, against Andrew Johnson, President of the United States, in maintenance and support of their impeachment against him for high crimes and misdemeanors.

ARTICLE I

That said Andrew Johnson, President of the Unites States, on the 21st day of February, in the year of our Lord 1868, at Washington, in the District of Columbia, unmindful of the high duties of his office, of his oath of office, and of the requirement of the Constitution that he should take care that the laws be faithfully executed, did unlawfully and in violation of the Constitution and laws of the United States issue an order in writing for the removal of Edwin M. Stanton from the office of Secretary for the Department of War, said Edwin M. Stanton having been theretofore only appointed and commissioned, by and with the advice and consent of the Senate of the United States, as such Secretary, and said Andrew Johnson, President of the United States, on the 12th day of August, in the year of our Lord 1867, and during the recess of said Senate, having suspended by his order Edwin M. Stanton from said office, and within twenty days after the first day of the next meeting of said Senate, that is to say, on the 12th day of December, in the year last aforesaid, having reported to said Senate such suspension, with the evidence and reasons for his action in the case and the name of the person designated to perform the duties of such office temporarily until the next meeting of the Senate, and said Senate there afterward, on the 13th day of January, in the year of our Lord 1868, having duly considered the evidence and reasons reported by said Andrew Johnson for said suspension, and having refused to concur in said suspension, whereby and by force of the provisions of an act entitled "An act regulating the tenure of certain civil offices" passed March 2, 1867, said Edwin M. Stanton did forthwith resume the functions of his office, whereof the said Andrew Johnson had then and there due notice, and said Edwin M. Stanton, by reason of the premises, on said 21st day of February, being lawfully entitled to hold said office of Secretary for the Department of War, which said order for the removal of said Edwin M. Stanton is in substance as follows, that is to say:

EXECUTIVE MANSION
WASHINGTON D.C., February 21st, 1868.

SIR: By virtue of the power and authority vested in me as President by the Constitution and laws of the United States, you are hereby removed from office as Secretary for the Department of War, and your functions as such will terminate upon receipt of this communication.

You will transfer to Brevet Major General Lorenzo Thomas,[11] Adjutant General of the Army, who has this day been authorized and empowered to act as Secretary of War ad interim, all records, books, papers, and other public property now in your custody and charge.

Respectfully yours, ANDREW JOHNSON.

Hon. EDWIN M. STANTON, *Washington D.C.*

Which order was unlawfully issued with intent then and there to violate the act entitled "An act regulating the tenure of certain civil offices," passed March 2nd, 1867; and, with the further intent contrary to the provisions of said act, in violation thereof, and contrary to the provisions of the Constitution of the United States, and without the advice and consent of the Senate of the United States, the said Senate then and there being in session, to remove said Edwin M. Stanton from the office of Secretary for the Department of War, the said Edwin M. Stanton being then and there Secretary of War, and being then and there in the due and lawful execution and discharge of the duties of said office, whereby said Andrew Johnson, President of the United States, did then and there commit, and was guilty of a high misdemeanor in office.

...

ARTICLE X.

That said Andrew Johnson. President of the United States, unmindful of the high duties of his office and the dignity and proprieties thereof, and of the harmony and courtesies which ought to exist and be maintained between the executive and legislative branches of the Government of the United States, designing and intending to set aside the rightful authority and powers of Congress, did attempt to bring into disgrace, ridicule, hatred,

---

[1] Lorenzo Thomas (1804–1975) was Adjutant General in the U.S. Army from 1861–1869.

contempt, and reproach the Congress of the United States and the several branches thereof, to impair and destroy the regard and respect of all the good people of the United States for the Congress and legislative power thereof, (which all officers of the Government ought inviolably to preserve and maintain,) and to excite the odium and resentment of all the good people of the United States against Congress and the laws by it duly and constitutionally enacted: and in pursuance of said design and intent, openly and publicly, and before divers assemblages of the citizens of the United States convened in divers parts thereof to meet and receive said Andrew Johnson as the Chief Magistrate of the United States, did, on the 18th day of August, in the year of our Lord 1866, and on divers other days and times, as well before as afterward, make and deliver with a loud voice certain intemperate, inflammatory, and scandalous harangues, and did therein utter loud threats and bitter menaces as well against Congress amid the cries, jeers, and laughter of the multitudes then assembled and within hearing, which are set forth in the several specifications hereinafter written, in substance and effect, that is to say:

Specification First. In this, that at Washington, in the District of Columbia, in the Executive Mansion, to a committee of citizens who called upon the President of the United States, speaking of and concerning the Congress of the United States, said Andrew Johnson, President of the United States, heretofore, to wit, on the 18th day of August, in the year of our Lord 1866, did, in a loud voice, declare in substance and effect, among other things, that is to say:

"So far as the executive department of the Government is concerned, the effort has been made to restore the Union, to heal the breach, to pour oil into the wounds which were consequent upon the struggle, and (to speak in common phrase) to prepare as the learned and wise physician would, a plaster healing in character and coextensive with the wound. We thought, and we think, that we had partially succeeded; but as the work progresses, as reconstruction seemed to be taking place, and the country was becoming reunited, we found a disturbing and marring element opposing us. In alluding to that element, I shall go no further than your convention and the distinguished gentleman who has delivered to me the report of its proceedings. I shall make no reference to it that I do not believe the time and the occasion justify.

"We have witnessed in one department of the Government every endeavor to prevent the restoration of peace, harmony, and Union. We have seen hanging upon the verge of the government, as it were, a body called, or which assumes to be, the Congress of the Unites States, while in fact it is a Congress of only a part of the States. We have seen this Congress pretend to be for the Union, when its every step and act tended to perpetuate disunion and make a disruption of the States inevitable."

"We have seen Congress gradually encroach step by step upon constitutional rights, and violate, day after day and month after month, fundamental principles of the gGovernment. We have seen a Congress that seemed to forget that there was a limit to the sphere and scope of legislation. We have seen a Congress in a minority assume to exercise power which, allowed to be consummated, would result in despotism or monarchy itself."

Specification Second. In this, that at Cleveland, in the State of Ohio, heretofore, to wit, on the 3rd day of September, in the year of our Lord 1850, before a public assemblage of citizens and others, said Andrew Johnson, President of the United States, speaking of and concerning the Congress of the United States, did, in a loud voice, declare in substance and effect, among other things, that is to say:

"I will tell you what I did do. I called upon your Congress that is trying to break up the Government."

[Here, the text of the Articles of Impeachment indicates omitting a portion of the quoted speech.]

"In conclusion, besides that, Congress had taken much pains to poison their constituents against him. But what had Congress done? Have they done anything to restore the union of these States? No; on the contrary, they had done everything to prevent it; and because he stood now where he did when the rebellion commenced he had been denounced as a traitor. Who had run greater risks or made greater sacrifices than himself? But Congress, factions and domineering, had undertaken to poison the minds of the American people."

Specification Third. In this, that at St. Louis, in the State of Missouri, heretofore, to wit, on the 8th day of September, in the year of our Lord 1866, before a public assemblage of citizens and others, said Andrew Johnson, President of the United States, speaking of and concerning the Congress of the United States, did, in a loud voice, declare in substance and effect, among other things, that is to say:

"Go on. Perhaps if you had a word or two on the subject of New Orleans you might understand more about it than you do. And if you will go back—if you will go back and ascertain the cause of the riot at New Orleans, perhaps you will not be so prompt in calling out 'New Orleans.' If you will take up the riot at New Orleans and trace it back to its source or its immediate cause, you will find out who was responsible for the blood that was shed there. If you will take up the riot at New Orleans and trace it back to the Radical Congress you will find that the riot at New Orleans was substantially planned. If you will take up the proceedings in their caucuses you will understand that they there knew that a convention was to be called which was extinct by its power having expired; that it was said that the intention was that a new government was to be organized, and on the organization of that government the intention was to enfranchise one portion of the population, called the colored population, who had just been emancipated, and at the same time disfranchise white men. When you design to talk about New Orleans you ought to understand what you are talking about. When you read the speeches that were made, and take up the facts on the Friday and Saturday before that convention sat, you will there find that speeches were incendiary in their character, exciting that portion of the population, the black population, to arm themselves and prepare for the shedding of blood. You will also find that the convention did assemble in violation of law, and the intention of that convention was to supersede the reorganized authorities in the State government of Louisiana, which had been recognized by the Government of the United States; and every man engaged in that rebellion in that convention, with the intention of superseding and upturning the civil government which had been recognized by the Government of the United States, I say that he was a traitor to the Constitution of the United States and you find that another rebellion was commenced having its origin in the Radical Congress. [Here, the text of the Articles of Impeachment indicates omitting a portion of the quoted speech.]

"So much for the New Orleans riot. And there was the cause and the origin of the blood that was shed; and every drop of blood that was shed is upon their skirts, and they are responsible for it. I could test this thing a little closer but will not do it here tonight. But when you talk about the causes and consequences that resulted from proceedings of that kind, perhaps, as I have been introduced here, and you have provoked questions of this kind, though it does not provoke me, I will tell you a few wholesome things that have been done by this Radical Congress in connection with New Orleans and the extension of the elective franchise.

"I know that I have been traduced and abused. I know it has come in advance of me here, as elsewhere, that I have attempted to exercise an arbitrary power in resisting laws that were intended to be forced upon the Government; that I had exercised that power; that I had abandoned the party that elected me, and that I was a traitor, because I exercised the veto power in attempting and did arrest for a time a bill that was called a 'Freedman's Bureau' bill: yes, that I was a traitor. And I have been traduced. I have been slandered, I have been maligned, I have been called Judas Iscariot, and all that. Now, my countrymen here tonight, it is very easy to indulge in epithets; it is easy to call a man a Judas and cry out traitor; but when he is called upon to give arguments and facts he is very often found wanting. Judas Iscariot—Judas. There was a Judas and he was one of the twelve apostles. Oh yes, the twelve apostles had a Christ. The twelve apostles had a Christ, and he never could have had a Judas unless he had twelve apostles. If I have played the Judas, who has been my Christ that I have played the Judas with? Was it Thad. Stevens?[2] Was it Wendell Phillips?[3] Was it Charles Sumner?[4] These are the men that stop and compare themselves with the Savior: and everybody that differs with them in opinion, and to try and stay and arrest the diabolical and nefarious policy, is to be denounced as a Judas." [Here again, the text of the Articles of Impeachment indicates omitting a portion of the quoted speech.]

"Well, let me say to you, if you will stand by me in this action: if you will stand by me in trying to give the people a fair chance, soldiers and citizens, to participate in these offices, God being willing, I will kick them out. I will kick them out just as fast as I can.

"Let me say to you, in concluding, that what I have said I intended to say. I was not provoked into this, and I care not for their menaces, the taunts, and the jeers. I care not for threats. I do not intend to be bullied by my enemies nor overawed by my friends. But, God willing, with your help I will veto their measures whenever any of them come to me."

Which said utterances, declarations, threats, and harangues, highly censurable in any, are peculiarly indecent and unbecoming in the Chief Magistrate of the United States, by means whereof said Andrew Johnson has brought the high office of the President of the United States into contempt, ridicule, and disgrace, to the great scandal of all good citizens, whereby said Andrew Johnson, President of the United States, did commit, and was then and there guilty of, a high misdemeanor in office.

ARTICLE XI

That said Andrew Johnson, President of the United States, unmindful of the high duties of his office and of his oath of office, and in disregard of the

[2] Thaddeus Stevens (1792–1868) was a Radical Republican and Representative from Pennsylvania. from 1849–1868.
[3] Wendell Phillips (1811–1884) was a prominent abolitionist from Boston.
[4] Charles Sumner (1811–1874) was a Radical Republican and Senator from Massachusetts from 1851 to 1874.

Constitution and laws of the United States, did heretofore, to wit: on the 18th day of August, 1866, at the city of Washington, in the District of Columbia, by public speech, declare and affirm in substance that the Thirty-Ninth Congress of the United States was not a Congress of the United States authorized by the Constitution to exercise legislative power under the same: but, on the contrary, was a Congress of only part of the States, thereby denying and intending to deny that the legislation of said Congress was valid or obligatory upon him, the said Andrew Johnson, except in so far as he saw fit to approve the same, and also thereby denying and intending to deny the power of the said Thirty-Ninth Congress to propose amendments to the Constitution of the United States; and, in pursuance of said declaration, the said Andrew Johnson, President of the United States, afterward, to wit: on the 21st day of February, 1868, at the city of Washington, in the District of Columbia, did unlawfully and in disregard of the requirements of the Constitution, that he should take care that the laws be faithfully executed, attempt to prevent the execution of an act entitled "An act regulating the tenure of certain civil offices," passed March 2, 1867, by unlawfully devising and contriving, and attempting to devise and contrive, means by which he should prevent Edwin M. Stanton from forthwith resuming the functions of the office of Secretary for the Department of War, notwithstanding the refusal of the Senate to concur in suspension therefore made by said Andrew Johnson of said Edwin M. Stanton from said office of Secretary for the Department of War, and also by further unlawfully devising and contriving, and attempting to devise and contrive, means then and there to prevent the execution of an act entitled "An act making appropriations for the support of the Army for the fiscal year ending June 30, 1868 and for other purposes," approved March 2, 1867, and also to prevent the execution of an act entitled "An act to provide for the more efficient government of the rebel States," passed March 2, 1867: whereby the said president Andrew Johnson, President of the United States, did then, to wit: on the 21st day of February, 1865, at the city of Washington, commit and was guilty of a high misdemeanor in office.

And the House of Representatives, by protestation, saving to themselves the liberty of exhibiting at any time hereafter any further articles or other accusation or impeachment against the said Andrew Johnson, President of the United States, and also of replying to his answers which he shall make unto the articles herein preferred against him, and of offering proof to the same and every part thereof, and to all and every other article, accusation, or impeachment which shall be exhibited by them, as the case shall require, do demand that the said Andrew Johnson may be put to answer the high crimes and misdemeanors in office herein charged against him, and that such proceedings, examinations, trials, and judgements may be thereupon had and given as may be agreeable to law and justice.

Constitutional Government
in the United States

Woodrow Wilson

1908

W oodrow Wilson is the only political scientist to have served as president. His dissertation (1885) emphasized Congress as the most important part of the government. But in his Constitutional Government in the United States (1908), Wilson showed more interest in the presidency as an institution that could be shaped to meet what he saw as the demands of modern life. In this selection, Wilson links his critique of the Constitution of 1787 to his vision for a new and modern presidency. Although he was a Democrat, and Theodore Roosevelt was a Republican, both were Progressives who advocated reforms aimed at establishing direct democracy and increased regulation of commercial activity. In their view, the presidency would play an important role in these reforms, but for that to happen to the presidency would have to change.

SOURCE: Woodrow Wilson, *Constitutional Government in the United States* (New York: Columbia University Press, 1908), 54–62.

It is difficult to describe any single part of a great governmental system without describing the whole of it. Governments are living things and operate as organic wholes. Moreover, governments have their natural evolution and are one thing in one age, another in another. The makers of the Constitution constructed the federal government upon a theory of checks and balances which was meant to limit the operation of each part and allow to no single part or organ of it a dominating force; but no government can be successfully conducted upon so mechanical a theory. Leadership and control must be lodged somewhere; the whole art of statesmanship is the art of bringing the several parts of government into effective cooperation for the accomplishment of particular common objects—and party objects at that. Our study of each part of the federal system, if we are to discover our real government as it lives, must be made to disclose to us its operative coordination as a whole: its places of leadership, its method of action, how it operates, what checks it, what gives it energy and effect. Governments are what politicians make them, and it is easier to write of the President than of the presidency.

The government of the United States was constructed upon the Whig theory of political dynamics, which was a sort of unconscious copy of the Newtonian theory of the universe.[1] In our own day, whenever we discuss the structure or development of anything, whether in nature or in society, we consciously follow Mr. Darwin;[2] but before Mr. Darwin, they followed Newton. Some single law, like the law of gravitation, swung each system of thought and gave it its principle of unity. Every sun, every planet, every free body in the spaces of the heavens, the world itself, is kept in its place and reined to its course by the attraction of bodies that swing with equal order and precision about it, themselves governed by the nice poise and balance of forces which give the whole system of the universe its symmetry and perfect adjustment. The Whigs had tried to give England a similar constitution. They had had no wish to destroy the throne, no conscious desire to reduce the king to a mere figurehead but had intended only to surround and offset him with a system of constitutional checks and balances which should regulate his otherwise arbitrary course and make it at least always calculable.

They had made no clear analysis of the matter in their own thoughts; it has not been the habit of English politicians, or indeed of English-speaking politicians on either side of the water, to be clear theorists. It was left to a Frenchman[3] to point out to the Whigs what they had done. They had striven to make Parliament so influential in the making of laws and so authoritative in the criticism of the king's policy that the king could in no matter have his own way without their cooperation and assent, though they left him free, the

---

[1] The Whig party emerged in England during the seventeenth century; as Wilson points out, their primary aim was to curb the arbitrary element of the British monarchy by instituting a series of constitutional reforms. The adjective Newtonian refers to the group of scientific theories first developed by Sir Isaac Newton (1642–1727), the British polymath whose insights in the fields of mathematics, astronomy, and physics were critical to the opening of the Scientific Revolution.

[2] Charles Darwin (1809–1882), British naturalist best known as the author of *On the Origin of Species* (1859), the first widely publicized exposition of the theory of evolution

[3] Montesquieu (1689–1755) was a French philosopher whose *Spirit of the Laws* was quoted widely by early Americans for its recommendations of separation of powers and confederalism.

while, if he chose, to interpret an absolute veto upon the acts of Parliament. They had striven to secure for the courts of law as great an independence as possible, so that they might be neither overawed by Parliament nor coerced by the king. In brief, as Montesquieu pointed out to them in his lucid way, they had sought to balance executive, legislative, and judiciary off against one another by a series of checks and counterpoises, which Newton might readily have recognized as suggestive of the mechanism of the heavens.

The makers of our federal Constitution followed the scheme as they found it expounded in Montesquieu, followed it with genuine scientific enthusiasm. The admirable expositions of the *Federalist* read like thoughtful applications of Montesquieu to the political needs and circumstances of America. They are full of the theory of checks and balances. The President is balanced off against Congress, Congress against the President, and each against the courts. Our statesmen of the earlier generations quoted no one so often as Montesquieu, and they quoted him always as a scientific standard in the field of politics. Politics is turned into mechanics under his touch. The theory of gravitation is supreme.

The trouble with the theory is that government is not a machine, but a living thing. It falls, not under the theory of the universe, but under the theory of organic life. It is accountable to Darwin, not to Newton. It is modified by its environment, necessitated by its tasks, shaped to its functions by the sheer pressure of life. No living thing can have its organs offset against each other as checks, and live. On the contrary, its life is dependent upon their quick cooperation, their ready response to the commands of instinct or intelligence, their amicable community of purpose. Government is not a body of blind forces; it is a body of men, with highly differentiated functions, no doubt, in our modern day of specialization, but with a common task and purpose. Their cooperation is indispensable, their warfare fatal. There can be no successful government without leadership or without the intimate, almost instinctive, coordination of the organs of life and action. This is not theory, but fact, and displays its force as fact, whatever theories may be thrown across its track. Living political constitutions must be Darwinian in structure and in practice.

Fortunately, the definitions and prescriptions of our constitutional law, though conceived in the Newtonian spirit and upon the Newtonian principle, are sufficiently broad and elastic to allow for the play of life and circumstance. Though they were Whig theorists, the men who framed the federal Constitution were also practical statesmen with an experienced eye for affairs and a quick practical sagacity in respect of the actual structure of government, and they have given us a thoroughly workable model. If it had in fact been a machine governed by mechanically automatic balances, it would have had no history; but it was not, and its history has been rich with the influences and personalities of the men who have conducted it and made it a living reality. The government of the United States has had a vital and normal organic growth and has proved itself eminently adapted to express the changing temper and purposes of the American people from age to age.

That is the reason why it is easier to write of the President than the presidency. The presidency has been one thing at one time, another at another, varying with the man who occupied the office and with the circumstances that surrounded him. One account must be given of the office during the period 1789 to 1825, when the government was getting its footing both at home and abroad, struggling for its place among the nations as its full credit among its own people; when English precedents and traditions were strongest; and when the men chosen for the office were men bred to leadership in a way that attracted to them the attention and confidence of the whole country. Another account must be given of it during Jackson's time,[4] when an imperious man, bred not in deliberative assemblies or quiet councils, but in the field and upon a rough frontier, worked his own will upon affairs, with or without formal sanction of law, sustained by a clear undoubting conscience and the love of a people who had grown deeply impatient of the regime he had supplanted. Still another account must be given of it during the years 1836 to 1861, when domestic affairs of many debatable kinds absorbed the country, when Congress necessarily exercised the chief choices of policy, and when the Presidents who followed one another in office lacked the personal force and initiative to make for themselves a leading place in counsel. After that came the Civil War and Mr. Lincoln's unique task and achievement, when the executive seemed for a little while to become by sheer stress of circumstances the whole government, Congress merely voting supplies and assenting to necessary laws, as Parliament did in the time of the Tudors. From 1865 to 1898 domestic questions, legislative matters in respect of which Congress had naturally to make initial choice, legislative leaders the chief decisions of policy, came once more to the front, and no President except Mr. Cleveland[5] played

---

[4] Andrew Jackson (1767–1845) served as the seventh president of the United States from 1829 to 1837. See Documents 11–13 in this volume for examples of the evolution of the office of the president under his administration.

[5] Grover Cleveland (1837–1908) served as the twenty-second and twenty-fourth president of the United States, making him the only individual to have held that office for two non-consecutive terms (1885–89 and 1893–97).

a leading and decisive part in the quiet drama of our national life. Even Mr. Cleveland may be said to have owed his great role in affairs rather to his own native force and the confused politics of the time, than to any opportunity of leadership naturally afforded him by a system which had subordinated so many Presidents before him to Congress. The war with Spain again changed the balance of parts.[6] Foreign questions became leading questions again, as they had been in the first days of the government, and in them the President was of necessity leader. Our new place in the affairs of the world has since that year of transformation kept him at the front of our government, where our own thoughts and the attention of men everywhere is centered upon him.

Both men and circumstances have created these contrasts in the administration and influence of the office of President. We have all been disciples of Montesquieu, but we have also been practical politicians. Mr. Bagehot[7] once remarked that it was no proof of the excellence of the Constitution of the United States that the Americans had operated it with conspicuous success because the Americans could run any constitution successfully; and, while the compliment is altogether acceptable, it is certainly true that our practical sense is more noticeable than our theoretical consistency, and that, while we were once all constitutional lawyers, we are in these latter days apt to be very impatient of literal and dogmatic interpretations of constitutional principle.

The makers of the Constitution seem to have thought of the President as what the stricter Whig theorists wished the king to be: only the legal executive, the presiding and guiding authority in the application of law and the execution of policy. His veto upon legislation was only his 'check' on Congress—was a power of restraint, not of guidance. He was empowered to prevent bad laws, but he was not to be given an opportunity to make good ones. As a matter of fact, he has become very much more. He has become

---

[6] The Spanish-American War (April–August 1898) occurred during the presidency of William McKinley (1843–1901; in office, 1897–1901) and represented the first application of the Monroe Doctrine by which Americans proclaimed their interest in all actions taken by European powers in the Western Hemisphere. Under the guise of this interest, the United States intervened in the Cuban Independence movement against Spain, an act that eventually led to the United States gaining control of Cuba, Puerto Rico, Guam and the Philippines. Public debate on the propriety of the war and its outcomes was vociferous, and did not ignore the irony of McKinley's having used an anti-imperialist policy as the public justification for what became the nation's first foray into global expansion.

[7] Walter Bagehot (1826–1877), British journalist and political commentator best known for his long tenure as editor of *The Economist*.

the leader of his party and the guide of the nation in political purpose, and therefore in legal action. The constitutional structure of the government has hampered and limited his action in these significant roles, but it has not prevented it. The influence of the President has varied with the men who have been Presidents and with the circumstances of their times, but the tendency has been unmistakably disclosed, and springs out of the very nature of government itself. It is merely the proof that our government is a living, organic thing, and must, like every other government, work out the close synthesis of active parts which can exist only when leadership is lodged in some one man or group of men. You cannot compound a successful government out of antagonisms. Greatly as the practice and influence of Presidents has varied, there can be no mistaking the fact that we have grown more and more inclined from generation to generation to look to the President as the unifying force in our complex system, the leader both of his party and of the nation. To do so is not inconsistent with the actual provisions of the Constitution; it is only inconsistent with a very mechanical theory of its meaning and intention. The Constitution contains no theories. It is as practical a document as Magna Carta.

The role of the party leader is forced upon the President by the method of his selection. The theory of the makers of the Constitution may have been that the presidential electors would exercise a real choice, but it is hard to understand how, as experienced politicians, they can have expected anything of the kind. They did not provide that the electors should meet as one body for consultation and make deliberate choice of a President and Vice-President, but that they should meet "in their respective states" and cast their ballots in separate groups, without the possibility of consulting and without the least likelihood of agreeing, unless some such means as have actually been used were employed to suggest and determine their choice beforehand. It was the practice at first to make party nominations for the presidency by congressional caucus. Since the Democratic upheaval of General Jackson's time, nominating conventions have taken the place of congressional caucuses; and the choice of Presidents by party conventions has had some very interesting results.

We are apt to think of the choice of nominating conventions as somewhat haphazard. We know, or think that we know, how their action is sometimes determined, and the knowledge makes us very uneasy. We know that there is no debate in nominating conventions, no discussion of the merits of the respective candidates, at which the country can sit as audience and assess the wisdom of the final choice. If there is any talking to be done, aside from the formal addresses of the temporary and permanent chairmen and of those who present the platform and the names of the several aspirants for nomination, the assembly adjourns. The talking that is to decide the result must be done in private committee rooms and behind the closed doors of the headquarters of the several state delegations to the convention. . . .

On the Source of Executive Power

Theodore Roosevelt and William Howard Taft

An Autobiography, *1913, and* Our Chief Magistrate and His Powers, *1916*

A lthough they were once close political allies, Theodore Roosevelt and William Howard Taft came to embody different wings of the Republican Party. Roosevelt was a Progressive, who had come to embrace reforms such as the direct primary, the ballot initiative, the referendum, and the recall. Taft was more of a traditionalist, who believed that party government, with its emphasis on loyalty to party leadership, was an indispensable part of democratic life. The direct primary would allow individual members of the party, rather than party leaders at a convention, to choose the party nominee.

In the following selections from Roosevelt's An Autobiography of Theodore Roosevelt (1913) and Taft's Our Chief Magistrate and His Powers (1916), we can see the difference in their understandings of presidential power. Roosevelt's argument invites comparison with Jefferson (Document 10) and Lincoln (Documents 16 and 17).

SOURCE: Theodore Roosevelt, *An Autobiography of Theodore Roosevelt*, ed., Stephen Brennan (New York: Skyhorse Publishing, 2011), 304–10; William Howard Taft, *Our Chief Magistrate and His Powers* (New York: Columbia University Press, 1916), 138–40.

Theodore Roosevelt, *An Autobiography*, 1913

The most important factor in getting the right spirit in my Administration, next to the insistence upon courage, honesty, and a genuine democracy of desire to serve the plain people, was my insistence upon the theory that the executive power was limited only by specific restrictions and prohibitions appearing in the Constitution or imposed by the Congress under its Constitutional powers. My view was that every executive officer, and above all every executive officer in high position, was a steward of the people bound actively and affirmatively to do all he could for the people, and not to content himself with the negative merit of keeping his talents undamaged in a napkin. I declined to adopt the view that what was imperatively necessary for the Nation could not be done by the President unless he could find some specific authorization to do it. My belief was that it was not only his right but his duty to do anything that the needs of the Nation demanded unless such action was forbidden by the Constitution or by the laws. Under this interpretation of executive power I did and caused to be done many things not previously done by the President and the heads of the departments. I did not usurp power, but I did greatly broaden the use of executive power. In other words, I acted for the public welfare, I acted for the common well-being of all our people, whenever and in whatever manner was necessary, unless prevented by direct constitutional or legislative prohibition. I did not care a rap for the mere form and show of power; I cared immensely for the use that could be made of the substance. The Senate at one time objected to my communicating with them in printing, preferring the expensive, foolish, and laborious practice of writing out the messages by hand. It was not possible to return to the outworn archaism of hand writing; but we endeavored to have the printing made as pretty as possible. Whether I communicated with the Congress in writing or by word of mouth, and whether the writing was by a machine, or a pen, were equally, and absolutely, unimportant matters. The importance lay in what I said and in the heed paid to what I said. So as to my meeting and consulting Senators, Congressmen, politicians, financiers, and labor men. I consulted all who wished to see me; and if I wished to see any one, I sent for him; and where the consultation took place was a matter of supreme unimportance. I consulted every man with the sincere hope that I could profit by and follow his advice; I consulted every member of Congress who wished to be consulted, hoping to be able to come to an agreement of action with him; and I always finally acted as my conscience and common sense bade me act.

About appointments I was obligated by the Constitution to consult the Senate; and the long-established custom of the Senate meant that in practice this consultation was with individual Senators and even with big politicians who stood behind the Senators. I was only one-half the appointing power; I nominated; but the Senate confirmed. In practice, by what was called "the courtesy of the Senate," the Senate normally refused to confirm any appointment if the Senator from the State [of the nominee's residence] objected to it. In exceptional cases, where I could arouse public attention, I could force through the appointment in spite of the opposition of the Senators; in all ordinary cases this was impossible. On the other hand, the Senator could, of course, do nothing for any man unless I chose to nominate him. In consequence the Constitution itself forced the President and the Senators from each State to come to a working agreement on the appointments in and from that State.

My course was to insist on absolute fitness, including honesty, as a prerequisite to every appointment; and to remove only for a good cause, and, where there was such cause, to refuse even to discuss with the Senator in interest the unfit servant's retention. Subject to these considerations, I normally accepted each senator's recommendations for offices of a routine kind, such as most post-offices and the like, but insisted on myself choosing the men for the more important positions. I was willing to take any good man for postmaster; but in the case of a Judge or District Attorney or Canal Commissioner or Ambassador, I was apt to insist either on a given man or else on any man with a given class of qualifications. If the Senator deceived me, I took care that he had no opportunity to repeat the deception.

In a number of instances, the legality of executive acts of my Administration was brought before the courts. They were uniformly sustained. For example, prior to 1907 statutes relating to the dispositions of coal lands had been construed as fixing the flat price at $10 to $20 per acre. The result was that valuable coal lands were sold for wholly inadequate prices, chiefly to big corporations. By executive order the coal lands were withdrawn and not opened for entry until proper classification was placed thereon by Government agents. There was a great clamor that I was usurping legislative power; but the acts were not assailed in court until we brought suits to set aside entries made by persons and associations to obtain larger areas than the statutes authorized. This position was opposed on the ground that the restrictions imposed were illegal; that the executive orders were illegal. The Supreme Court sustained the Government. In the same way our attitude in the water power question was sustained, the Supreme Court holding that the Federal Government had the rights we claimed over streams that are or may be declared navigable by Congress. Again, when Oklahoma became a State we were obligated to use the executive power to protect Indian rights and property, for there had been an enormous amount of fraud in the obtaining of Indian lands by white men. Here we were denounced as usurping power over a State as well as usurping power that did not belong to the executive. The Supreme Court sustained our action.

In connection with the Indians, by the way, it was again and again necessary to assert the position of the President as steward of the whole people. I had a capital Indian Commissioner, Francis E. Leupp. I found that I could rely on his judgement not to get me into fights that were unnecessary, and therefore I always backed him to the limit when he told me that a fight was necessary. On one occasion, for example, Congress passed a bill to sell to settlers about a half a million acres of Indian land in Oklahoma at one and a half dollars an acre. I refused to sign it, and turned the matter over to Leupp. The bill was accordingly withdrawn, amended so as to safeguard the welfare of the Indians, and the minimum price raised to five dollars an acre. Then I signed the bill. We sold that land under sealed bids, and realized for the Kiowa, Comanche, and Apache Indians more than four million dollars— three millions and a quarter more than they would have obtained if I had signed the bill in its original form. In another case, where there had been a division among the Sac and Fox Indians, part of the tribe removing to Iowa, the Iowa delegation in Congress, backed by two Iowans who were members of my Cabinet, passed a bill awarding a sum of nearly a half million to the Iowa seceders. They had not consulted the Indian Bureau. Leupp protested against the bill, and I vetoed it. A subsequent bill was passed on the lines laid down by the Indian Bureau, referring the whole controversy to the courts, and the Supreme Court in the end justified our position by deciding against the Iowa seceders and awarding the money to the Oklahoma stay-at-homes.

As to all action of this kind there have long been two schools of political thought, upheld with equal sincerity. The division has not normally been along political, but temperamental, lines. The course I followed, of regarding the executive as subject only to the people, and under the Constitution, bound to serve the people affirmatively in cases where the Constitution does not explicitly forbid him to render the service, was substantially the course followed by both Andrew Jackson and Abraham Lincoln. Other honorable and well-meaning Presidents, such as James Buchanan, took the opposite and, as it seems to me, narrowly legalistic view that the President is the servant of Congress rather than of the people, and can do nothing, no matter how necessary it be to act, unless the Constitution explicitly commands the action. Most able lawyers who are past middle age take this view, and so do large numbers of well-meaning, respectable citizens. My successor in office[1] took this, the Buchanan, view of the President's powers and duties.

For example, under my Administration we found that one of the favorite methods adopted by the men desirous of stealing the public domain was to carry the decision of the Secretary of the Interior into court. By vigorously opposing such action, and only by so doing, we were able to carry out the policy of properly protecting the public domain.

---

[1] William Howard Taft (1857–1930).

I acted on the theory that the President could at any time in his discretion withdraw from entry any of the public lands of the United States and reserve the same for forestry, for water-power sites, for irrigation, and other public purposes. Without such action it would have been impossible to stop the activity of the land thieves. No one ventured to test its legality by lawsuit. My successor, however, himself questioned it, and referred the matter to Congress. Again Congress showed its wisdom by passing a law which gave the President the power which he had long exercised, and of which my successor had shorn himself....

William Howard Taft, *Our Chief Magistrate and His Powers*, 1916

While it is important to mark out the exclusive field of jurisdiction of each branch of the government, Legislative, Executive and Judicial, it should be said that in the proper working of the government there must be cooperation of all branches, and without a willingness of each branch to perform its function, there will follow a hopeless obstruction to the progress of the whole government. Neither [*sic*] branch can compel the other to affirmative action, and each branch can greatly hinder the other in the attainment of the object of its activities and the exercise of its discretion. The judicial branch has sometimes been said to be the most powerful branch of the government because in its decision of litigated cases it is frequently called upon to mark the limits of the jurisdiction of the other two branches. As already noted, by its continuity and the consistency of its decisions, the Court exercises much greater power in this regard than the other two branches. But it has no instruments to enforce its judgments, and if the Executive fails to remove the obstructions that may be offered to the execution of its decrees and orders, when its authority is defied, then the Court is helpless. It may not directly summon the army or the navy to maintain the supremacy of the law and order. So if the judges of the Court were to refuse to perform the judicial duties imposed by Congress, the object of Congress in much of its legislation might be defeated. And if Congress were to refuse to levy the taxes and make the appropriations which are necessary to pay the salaries of government officials, and to furnish the equipment essential in the performance of their duties, it could paralyze all branches of government. The life of the government, therefore, depends on the sense of responsibility of each branch in doing the parts assigned to it in the carrying on of the business of the people in the government, and ultimately as the last resource, we must look to public opinion as the moving force to induce affirmative action and proper team work. The power over the purse is, however, practically the greatest power, and that Congress exercises without control by either of the other branches. Therefore, when fear is expressed of the usurpation by other branches and the thieving of jurisdiction by either, we must keep in mind that the legislative power to withhold appropriations is that which in the history of constitutional government has always been the most powerful agency in the defense of the people's rights.

The true view of the Executive functions is, as I conceive it, that the President can exercise no power which cannot be fairly and reasonably traced to some specific grant of power or justly implied and included within such express grant as proper and necessary to its exercise. Such specific grant must be either in the Federal Constitution or in an act of Congress passed in pursuance thereof. There is no undefined residuum of power which he can exercise because it seems to him to be in the public interest, and there is nothing in the *Neagle* case and its definition of a law of the United States, or in other precedents, warranting such an inference.[2] The grants of Executive power are necessarily in general terms in order not to embarrass the Executive within the field of action plainly marked for him, but his jurisdiction must be justified and vindicated by affirmative constitutional or statutory provision, or it does not exist. . . .

---

[2] The *In re Neagle* case (1890) turned on the question whether the US attorney general could legally appoint a bodyguard for a Supreme Court justice. A federal marshal, appointed as bodyguard to a justice riding circuit in California, shot and killed a man he thought to be threatening the justice, and California officials arrested the marshal. When the US sued for the marshal's release, the state challenged the order, on the grounds that no national statute authorized the appointment of the bodyguard. The Supreme Court reasoned that the attorney general had the power to make the appointment since providing protection for the justice would further the execution of federal laws, and the president has the power to enforce the law even in the absence of specific laws passes by Congress

Myers v. US

Chief Justice William Howard Taft
(majority)

Associate Justice Oliver Wendell Holmes, Jr.
(dissenting)

1926

The Tenure of Office Act (Document 19) lingered beyond the presidency of Andrew Johnson. It was modified in 1869 and then repealed in 1887. The issue had become entangled with control of patronage. In 1876, however, Congress passed a law requiring the Senate's advice and consent for the removal of three classes of postmasters. President Woodrow Wilson violated this statute when he removed a Portland, Oregon postmaster, Fran Myers, before the end of his term. Myers sued in federal court to recover his lost salary, and the resulting Supreme Court opinion remains one of the fullest articulations of the position that the Constitution grants the removal power to the president.

In his full opinion of over seventy pages, Chief Justice William Howard Taft revisited the debates over the removal power in the first Congress to argue that the vote in fact endorsed Madison's position that the Constitution itself gave the power to the president. Taft's argument was joined by five other justices, and three justices dissented. Justice Oliver Wendell Holmes's dissenting opinion is also included here. Holmes's dissent focuses on the fact that the establishment and oversight of the post office (and thus, of the office of postmaster) is a responsibility of the legislative branch under Article I, Section 8. More broadly, because Congress can create and destroy the office, Holmes argues, Congress can determine who holds the power to remove.

Taft's opinion represents the high-water mark for executive power on this question, as the Court would narrow the president's power in less than ten years (Document 24).

SOURCE: *United States Reports*. Volume 272, *Cases Adjudged in the Supreme Court at October Term, 1926* (Washington, D.C.: Government Printing Office, 1927), 106, 109–110, 115–18, 177.

Mr. Chief Justice Taft delivered the opinion of the Court.

This case presents the question whether under the Constitution the President has the exclusive power of removing executive officers of the United States whom he has appointed by and with the advice and consent of the Senate....

The question where the power of removal of executive officers appointed by the President by and with the advice and consent of the Senate was vested, was presented early in the first session of the First Congress. There is no express provision respecting removals in the Constitution except as Section 4 of Article II, above quoted, provides for removal from office by impeachment. The subject was not discussed in the Constitutional Convention....

[Taft gives the history of a bill proposed by James Madison in the first Congress, establishing a Department of Foreign Affairs within the executive branch and allowing for its chief officer to be removable by the president.] The bill was discussed in the House at length and with great ability. The report of it in the Annals of Congress is extended. James Madison was then a leader in the House, as he had been in the Convention. His arguments in support of the President's constitutional power of removal independently of Congressional provisions, and without the consent of the Senate, were masterly, and he carried the House.

It is convenient in the course of our discussion of this case to review the reasons advanced by Mr. Madison and his associates for their conclusion, supplementing them, so far as may be, by additional considerations which lead the Court to concur therein.

First. Mr. Madison insisted that Article II by vesting the executive power in the President was intended to grant to him the power of appointment and removal of executive officers except as thereafter expressly provided for in that Article. He pointed out that one of the chief purposes of the Convention was to separate the legislative from the executive functions. He said:

If there is a principle in our Constitution, indeed in any free Constitution, more sacred than another, it is that which separates the Legislative, Executive, and Judicial powers. If there is any point in which the separation of the Legislative and Executive powers ought to be maintained with great caution, it is that which relates to officers and offices. (1 *Annals of Congress*, 581.)

Their union under the Confederation had not worked well, as the members of the convention knew. Montesquieu's view that the maintenance of independence as between the legislative, the executive, and the judicial branches was a security for the people had their full approval. (Madison in the Convention, 2 Farrand, *Records of the Federal Convention*, 56; *Kendall v.*

United States, 12 Peters 524, 610.) Accordingly, the Constitution was so framed as to vest in the Congress all legislative powers therein granted, to vest in the President the executive power, and to vest in one Supreme Court and such inferior courts as Congress may establish, the judicial power. From this division on principle, the reasonable construction of the Constitution should be expounded to blend them no more than it affirmatively requires. (Madison, 1 *Annals of Congress,* 497.) This rule of construction has been confirmed by this Court in *Meriwether v. Garrett,* 102 U.S. 472, 515; *Kilbourn v. Thompson,* 103 U.S. 168, 190; *Mugler v. Kansas,* 123 U.S. 623, 662.

The debates in the Constitutional Convention indicated an intention to create a strong executive, and after a controversial discussion the executive power of the government was vested in one person and many of his important functions were specified so as to avoid the humiliating weakness of the Congress during the Revolution and under the Articles of Confederation. (1 Farrand, 66–97.)

Mr. Madison and his associates in the discussion in the House dwelt at length upon the necessity there was for construing Article II to give the President the sole power of removal in his responsibility for the conduct of the executive branch, and enforced this by emphasizing his duty expressly declared in the third section of the Article to "take care that the laws be faithfully executed." (Madison, 1 *Annals of Congress,* 496, 497.)

The vesting of the executive power in the President was essentially a grant of the power to execute laws. But the President alone and unaided could not execute the laws. He must execute them by the assistance of subordinates. This view has since been repeatedly affirmed by this Court. (*Wilcox v. Jackson* 13 Peters 498, 513; *United States v. Eliason,* 16 Peters 291, 302; *Williams v. United States,* 1 How 290, 297; *Cunningham v. Neagle,* 135 U.S. 1, 63; *Russell Co. v. United States,* 261 U.S. 514, 523.) As he is charged specifically to take care that they be faithfully executed, the reasonable implication, even in the absence of express words, was that as part of his executive power he should select those who were to act for him under his direction in the execution of the laws. The further implication must be, in the absence of any express limitation respecting removals, that as his selection of administrative officers is essential to the execution of the laws by him, so must be his power of removing those for whom he cannot continue to be responsible. (Fisher Ames, 1 *Annals of Congress,* 474.) It was urged that the natural meaning of the term "executive power" granted the President included the appointment and removal of subordinate authorities. If such appointments and removals were not an exercise of the executive power, what were they? They certainly were not the exercise of legislative or judicial power in government as usually understood.

It is quite true that, in state and colonial governments at the time of the Constitutional Convention, power to make appointments and removals had sometimes been lodged in the legislatures of the courts, but such a disposition of it was really vesting part of the executive power in another branch of government. In the British system, the Crown, which was the executive, had the power of appointment and removal of executive officers, and it was natural, therefore, for those who framed our Constitution to regard the words "executive power" as including both. (*Ex Parte Grossman,* 267 U.S. 87, 110.) Unlike the power of conquest of the British Crown, considered and rejected as a precedent for us in *Fleming v. Page* (9 How. 603, 618), the association of removal with appointments of executive officers is not incompatible with our republican form of government.

The requirements of the second section of Article II that the Senate should advise and consent to the Presidential appointments, was to be strictly construed. The words of section 2, following the general grant of executive power under section 1, were either an enumeration and emphasis of specific functions of the executive, not all inclusive, or were limitations upon the general grant of the executive power, and as such, being limitations, should not be enlarged beyond the words used. (Madison, 1 *Annals,* 462, 463, 464.) The executive power was given in general terms, strengthened by specific terms where emphasis was regarded as appropriate, and was limited by direct expressions where limitation was needed, and the fact that no express limit was placed on the power of removal by the executive was convincing indication that none was intended. This is the same construction of Article II as that of Alexander Hamilton.[1]...

Mr. Justice Homes, dissenting.

My brothers McReynolds and Brandeis have discussed the question before us with exhaustive research and I say a few words merely to emphasize my agreement with their conclusion.

The arguments drawn from the executive power of the President, and

---

[1] See Hamilton's argument as Pacificus (Document 4) regarding the Vesting Clause of Article II.

from his duty to appoint officers of the United States (when Congress does not vest the appointment elsewhere), to take care that the laws be faithfully executed, and to commission all officers of the United States, seem to me spider's webs inadequate to control the dominant facts.

We have to deal with an office that owes its existence to Congress and that Congress may abolish tomorrow. Its duration and the pay attached to it while it lasts depend on Congress alone. Congress alone confers on the President the power to appoint to it and at any time may transfer the power to other hands. With such power over its own creation, I have no more trouble in believing that Congress has power to prescribe a term of life for it free from any interference than I have in accepting the undoubted power of Congress to decree its end. I have equally little trouble in accepting its power to prolong the term of an incumbent until Congress or the Senate shall have assented to his removal. The duty of the President to see that the laws be executed is a duty that does not go beyond the laws or require him to achieve more than Congress sees fit to leave within his power.

Humphrey's Executor v. United States

Associate Justice George Sutherland

1935

O nly nine years after Myers (Document 23), the Supreme Court revisited the removal power. This time, the question turned on a new law limiting the president's power to remove. In 1914, Woodrow Wilson signed the Federal Trade Commission Act. The law established a commission to prevent unfair trade practices. In order to ensure that the commission remained nonpartisan, the law stipulated that its commissioners could be removed by the president only for cause, that is, for "inefficiency, neglect of duty, or malfeasance in office." In the next several decades, Congress created more of these independent regulatory commissions (IRCs).

In 1934, Franklin D. Roosevelt removed William Humphrey, a Hoover appointee, who had been critical of the New Deal and with whom Roosevelt held deep differences over what constituted fair and unfair trade. After Humphrey's death in 1934, his executor sued to recover his salary. Writing for a unanimous court, Justice George Sutherland ruled against the president and upheld the constitutionality of the 1914 law. His argument has served as the foundation for IRCs and the modern regulatory state, but the case has left unsettled the extent to which Congress may limit the president's power to remove executive branch officials from office. Specifically, Justice Sutherland argued that Congress may create officials who may not be fired by the president because their duties are quasi-legislative or quasi-judicial rather than executive in nature.

SOURCE: *United States Reports*. Volume 295, *Cases Adjudged in the Supreme Court at October Term, 1934* (Washington, D.C.: Government Printing Office, 1935), 618, 627–30.

Mr. Justice Sutherland delivered the opinion of the Court....

The office of postmaster is so essentially unlike the office now involved that the decision in the *Myers* case cannot be accepted as controlling our decision here. A postmaster is an executive officer restricted to the performance of executive functions. He is charged with no duty at all related to either the legislative or the judicial power. The actual decision in the *Myers* case finds support in the theory that such an officer is merely one of the units in the executive department and, hence, inherently subject to the exclusive and illimitable power of removal by the Chief Executive, whose subordinate and aid he is. Putting aside *dicta*, which may be followed if sufficiently persuasive but which are not controlling, the necessary reach of the decision goes far enough to include all purely executive officers. It goes no farther;—much less does it include an officer who occupies no place in the executive department and who exercises no part of the executive power vested by the Constitution in the President.

The Federal Trade Commission is an administrative body created by Congress to carry into effect legislative policies embodied in the statute in accordance with the legislative standard therein prescribed, and to perform other specified duties as a legislative or as a judicial aid. Such a body cannot in any proper sense be characterized as an arm or an eye of the executive. Its duties are performed without executive leave and, in contemplation of the statute, must be free from executive control. In administering the provisions of the statute in respect of "unfair methods of competition"—that is to say, in filling in and administering the details embodied by that general standard— the commission acts in part quasi-legislatively and in part quasi-judicially. In making investigations and reports thereon for the information of Congress under §6, in aid of the legislative power, it acts as a legislative agency. Under §7, which authorizes the commission to act as a master in chancery under rules prescribed by the court, it acts as an agency of the judiciary. To the extent that it exercises any executive function—as distinguished from the executive power in the constitutional sense—it does so in the discharge and effectuation of its quasi-legislative or quasi-judicial powers, or as an agency of the legislative or judicial departments of government.

If Congress is without authority to prescribe causes for removal of members of the trade commission and limit executive power of removal accordingly, that power at once becomes practically all-inclusive in respect to civil officers with the exception of the judiciary provided for by the Constitution. The Solicitor General, at the bar, apparently recognizing this to be true, with commendable candor, agreed that this view in respect to the removability of members of the Federal Trade Commission necessitated a like view in respect of the Interstate Commerce Commission and the Courts of Claims. We are thus confronted with the serious question whether not only the members of these quasi-legislative and quasi-judicial bodies, but the judges of the legislative Court of Claims, exercising judicial power (*Williams v. United States*, 289 U.S. 553, 565–567), continue in the office only at the pleasure of the President.

We think it plain under the Constitution that illimitable power of removal is not possessed by the President in respect of officers of the character of those just named. The authority of Congress, in creating quasi-legislative or quasi-judicial agencies, to require them to act in discharge of their duties independently of executive control cannot well be doubted, and that authority includes, as an appropriate incident, power to fix the period during which they shall continue in office, and to forbid their removal except for cause in the meantime. For it is quite evident that one who holds his office only during the pleasure of another, cannot be depended to maintain an attitude of independence against the latter's will.

The fundamental necessity of maintaining each of the three general departments of government entirely free from the control or coercive influence, direct or indirect, of either of the others, has often been stressed and is hardly open to serious question. So much is implied in the very fact of the separation of powers of these departments by the Constitution; and in the rule which recognizes their essential co-equality. The sound application of a principle that makes one master in his own house precludes him from imposing his control in the house of another who is master there. James Wilson,[1] one of the framers of the Constitution and a former justice of this court, said that the independence of each department required that its proceedings "should be free from the remotest influence, direct or indirect, of either of the other two powers." (Andrews, *The Works of James Wilson* (1896), vol. 1, p. 367.) And Mr. Justice Story[2] in the first volume of his work on the Constitution, 4th ed., §530, citing No. 48 of the *Federalist*, said that neither of the departments in reference to each other "ought to possess, directly or indirectly, an overruling influence in the administration of their respective powers."...

The power of removal here claimed by the President falls within this principle, since its coercive influence threatens the independence of a commission, which is not only wholly disconnected from the executive department,

---

[1] James Wilson (1742–1798) is known mostly for being a signer of the Declaration of the Independence and the Constitution. His speeches on the presidency during the Constitutional Convention were especially influential. The reference here is to his *Lectures on Law*, delivered in 1790 and published in 1804.

[2] Joseph Story (1779–1845) was a Supreme Court Justice whose *Commentaries on the Constitution of the United States* (1833) endures as a classic study of the Constitution.

but which, as already fully appears, was created by Congress as a means of carrying into operation legislation and judicial powers, as an agency of the legislative and judicial departments.

In light of the question now under consideration, we have reexamined the precedents referred to in the *Myers* case, and find nothing in them to justify a conclusion contrary to that which we have reached. . . .

United States v. Curtiss-Wright Export Co.

Associate Justice George Sutherland

1936

I n 1934, Congress passed a joint resolution authorizing the president to prohibit the sale of arms by American companies to Bolivia and Paraguay because
the two nations were engaged in ongoing and brutal war. Franklin Roosevelt
quickly issued a proclamation to that effect. The American arms manufacturer
Curtiss-Wright violated Roosevelt's order, and, in its defense, the company's attorneys argued that the joint resolution was an unconstitutional delegation of legislative power to the president. In this, they were relying on a legal theory going back
to John Locke that the legislative and executive powers of a government had to be
not only placed but maintained in distinct hands. This theory had also provided
the undergirding for many of the Supreme Court's arguments in striking down
key New Deal provisions between 1935 and 1937. Instead of ruling against the president, however, a seven-to-one majority upheld the proclamation. In what follows,
Justice Sutherland makes an argument that has turned out to be the high-water
mark for executive power in foreign affairs. Along with Alexander Hamilton's
argument defending President George Washington's Neutrality Proclamation
(Document 4), Sutherland's opinion is frequently cited by those arguing for presidential control over war and peace (Document 37).

SOURCE: *United States Reports*. Volume 299, *Cases Adjudged in the Supreme Court at October
Term, 1936* (Washington, D.C.: Government Printing Office, 1937), 311–33.

Mr. Justice Sutherland delivered the opinion of the Court.

On January 27, 1936, an indictment was returned in the court below, the first
count of which charges that appellees, beginning with the 29th day of May,
1934, conspired to sell in the United States certain arms of war, namely fifteen machine guns, to Bolivia, a country then engaged in armed conflict in
the Chaco, in violation of the Joint Resolution of Congress approved May
28, 1934, and the provisions of a proclamation issued on the same day by the

President of the United States pursuant to authority conferred by §1 of the resolution....

The determination which we are called to make, therefore, is whether the Joint Resolution, as applied to the situation, is vulnerable to attack under the rule that forbids a delegation of the law-making power. In other words, assuming (but not deciding) that the challenged delegation, if it were confined to internal affairs, would be invalid, may it nevertheless be sustained on the ground that its exclusive aim is to afford a remedy for a hurtful condition within foreign territory?

It will contribute to the elucidation of the question if we first consider the differences between the powers of the federal government in respect of foreign or external affairs and those in respect of domestic or internal affairs. That there are differences between them, and that these differences are fundamental, may not be doubted.

The two classes of powers are different, both in respect of their origin and their nature. The broad statement that the federal government can exercise no powers except those specifically enumerated in the Constitution, and such implied powers as are necessary and proper to carry into effect the enumerated powers, is categorically true only in respect of our internal affairs. In that field, the primary purpose of the Constitution was to carve from the general mass of legislative powers *then possessed by the states* such portions as it was thought desirable to vest in the federal government, leaving those not included in the enumeration still in the states. *Carter v. Carter Coal Co.*, 298 U.S. 238, 294.[1] That this doctrine applies only to powers which the states had, is self-evident. And since the states severally never possessed international powers, such powers could not have been carved from the mass of state powers but obviously were transmitted to the United States from some other source. During the colonial period, those powers were possessed exclusively by and were entirely under the control of the Crown. By the Declaration of Independence, "the Representatives of the United States of America" declared the United [not the several] Colonies to be free and independent states, and as such to have "full Power to levy War, conclude Peace, contract Alliances, establish Commerce and to do all other Acts and Things which Independent States may of right do."

---

[1] In *Carter v. Carter Coal* (1936), the Supreme Court continued to hold a distinction between commerce and manufacturing in order to limit the reach of Congress's power to regulate interstate commerce. The presumptive logic at work is that the states retain the control over commerce if the Constitution does not give power to Congress to regulate it.

As a result of the separation from Great Britain by the colonies acting as a unit, the powers of external sovereignty passed from the Crown not to the colonies severally, but to the colonies in their collective and corporate capacity as the United States of America. Even before the Declaration, the colonies were a unit in foreign affairs, acting through a common agency—namely the Continental Congress, composed of delegates from the thirteen colonies. That agency exercised the power of war and peace, raised an army, created a navy, and finally adopted the Declaration of Independence. Rulers come and go; governments end and forms of government change; but sovereignty survives. A political society cannot endure without a supreme will somewhere. Sovereignty is never held in suspense. When, therefore, the external sovereignty of Great Britain in respect to the colonies ceased, it immediately passed to the Union. *See Penhallow v. Doane,* 3 Dall. 54, 80–81.[2] That fact was given practical application almost at once. The treaty of peace, made on September 23, 1783, was concluded between his Britannic Majesty and the "United States of America." 8 Stat.—European Treaties—80.

The Union existed before the Constitution, which was ordained and established among other things to form "a more perfect Union." Prior to that event, it is clear that the Union, declared by the Articles of Confederation to be "perpetual," was the sole possessor of external sovereignty and in the Union it remained without change save in so far as the Constitution in express terms qualified its exercise. The Framers' Convention was called and exerted its powers upon the irrefutable postulate that though the states were several their people in respect of foreign affairs were one. Compare *The Chinese Exclusion Case,* 130 U.S. 581, 604, 606. In that convention the entire absence of state power to deal with those affairs was thus forcefully stated by Rufus King:

> The states were not "sovereigns" in the sense contended for by some.
> They did not possess the peculiar features of sovereignty,—they could
> not make war, nor peace, nor alliances, nor treaties. Considering them
> as political beings, they were dumb, for they could not speak to any
> foreign sovereigns whatever. They were deaf, for they could not hear
> any propositions from such sovereign. They had not even the organs

---

[2] *Penhallow v. Doane's Administrators* (1795) is an obscure Supreme Court ruling that allowed federal courts in some instances to continue under the jurisdiction of laws passed under the Articles of Confederation.

or faculties of defence or offence, for they could not of themselves raise troops, or equip vessels, for war. 5 Elliott's Debates 212.

It results that the investment of the federal government with the powers of external sovereignty did not depend on the affirmative grants of the Constitution. The powers to declare and wage war, to conclude peace, to make treaties, to maintain diplomatic relations with other sovereignties, if they had never been mentioned in the Constitution, would have vested in the federal government as necessary concomitants of nationality. . . .

Not only, as we have shown, is the federal power over external affairs in origin and essential character different from that over internal affairs, but participation in the exercise of the power is significantly limited. In this vast external realm, with its important, complicated, delicate, and manifold problems, the President alone has the power to speak or listen as a representative of the nation. He *makes* treaties with advice and consent of the Senate; but he alone negotiates. Into the field of negotiation the Senate cannot intrude; and Congress itself is powerless to invade it. As Marshall said in his great argument of March 7, 1800, in the House of Representatives, "The President is the sole organ of the nation in its external relations, and its sole representative with foreign nations." *Annals*, 6th Cong., col. 613. The Senate Committee on Foreign Relations at a very early day in our history (February 15, 1816), reported to the Senate, among other things, as follows:

> The President is the constitutional representative of the United States with regard to foreign nations. He manages our concerns with foreign nations and must necessarily be most competent to determine when, how, and upon what subjects negotiations may be urged with the greatest prospect of success. For his conduct he is responsible to the Constitution. The committee consider this responsibility the surest pledge for the faithful discharge of his duty. They think the interference of the Senate in the direction of foreign negotiations calculated to diminish that responsibility and thereby to impair the best security for the national safety. The nature of transactions with foreign nations, moreover, requires causation and unity of design, and their success frequently depends on secrecy and dispatch. U.S. Senate, Reports, Committee on Foreign Relations, vol. 8, p. 24.

It is important to bear in mind that we are here dealing not alone with an authority vested in the President by an exertion of legislative power, but with such an authority plus the very delicate, plenary and exclusive power of the President as the sole organ of the federal government in the field of international relations—a power which does not require as a basis for its exercise an act of Congress but which, of course, like every governmental program, must be exercised in subordination to the applicable provisions of the Constitution. It is quite apparent that if, in the maintenance of our international relations, embarrassment—perhaps serious embarrassment—is to be avoided and success for our aims achieved, congressional legislation which is to be made effective through negotiation and inquiry within the international field must often accord to the President a degree of discretion and freedom from statutory restriction which would not be admissible were domestic affairs alone involved. Moreover, he, not Congress, has the better opportunity of knowing the conditions which prevail in foreign countries, and especially is this true in time of war. He has confidential sources of information. He has his agents in the form of diplomatic, consular, and other officials. Secrecy in respect of information gathered by them may be highly necessary, and the premature disclosure of it productive of harmful results. Indeed, so clearly is this true that the first President refused to accede to a request to lay before the House of Representatives the instructions, correspondence, and documents relating to the negotiation of the Jay Treaty—a refusal the wisdom of which was recognized by the House itself and has never since been doubted.[3]...

---

[3] Jay's Treaty (1795) prevented potential war with England but deepened partisan divisions between Federalists and Republicans. In the middle of this partisan maneuvering, President George Washington set an early precedent of something like executive privilege, refusing the House's request to turn over certain materials regarding the diplomatic negotiations between the two nations. However, Washington did give the documents to the Senate, and he eventually turned over some of the documents to the House.

First Inaugural Address

President Franklin D. Roosevelt

March 4, 1933

W*hen Franklin Roosevelt became president, the country was in its third year of the Great Depression. Nearly one fourth of workers were unemployed, and approximately one-half of banks had failed.*

As a candidate, Franklin Roosevelt argued that Americans needed to renegotiate their social contract to require that government secure economic rights for citizens in addition to political rights. In his 1932 address at the Commonwealth Club in San Francisco, Roosevelt had argued that this would require reorienting but not replacing the American constitutional tradition. As he put it, the country was still dedicated to the Jeffersonian end of equality, but instead of relying on the Jeffersonian means of a limited government, it should now employ more Hamiltonian means to achieve those ends. In other words, Roosevelt argued that the country needed a strong, activist government in order to be effective enough at securing rights.

In his First Inaugural, Roosevelt explained the expanded role that this would require of the national government and of the presidency.

SOURCE: Samuel I. Rosenman, ed., *Public Papers and Addresses of Franklin D. Roosevelt. Volume Two: The Year of Crisis, 1933* (New York: Random House, 1938), 11–16.

I am certain that my fellow Americans expect that on my induction into the Presidency I will address them with a candor and a decision which the present situation of our Nation impels.[1] This is preeminently the time to speak the truth, the whole truth, frankly and boldly. Nor need we shrink from honestly facing the conditions in our country today. This great Nation will endure as it has endured, will revive and will prosper. So, first of all, let me assert my firm belief that the only thing we have to fear is fear itself— nameless, unreasoning, unjustified terror which paralyzes needed efforts to

---

[1] the Great Depression

convert retreat into advance. In every dark hour of our national life a leadership of frankness and vigor has met with that understanding and support of the people themselves which is essential to victory. I am convinced that you will again give that support to leadership in these critical days.

In such a spirit on my part and on yours we face our common difficulties. They concern, thank God, only material things. [Monetary] values have shrunken to fantastic levels; taxes have risen; our ability to pay has fallen; government of all kinds is faced by serious curtailment of income; the means of exchange are frozen in the currents of trade; the withered leaves of industrial enterprise lie on every side; farmers find no markets for their produce; the savings of many years in thousands of families are gone.

Yet our distress comes from no failure of substance. We are stricken by no plague of locusts. Compared with the perils which our forefathers conquered because they believed and were not afraid, we have still much to be thankful for. Nature still offers her bounty and human efforts have multiplied it. Plenty is at our doorstep, but a generous use of it languishes in the very sight of the supply. Primarily this is because rulers of the exchange of mankind's goods have failed through their own stubbornness and their own incompetence, have admitted their failure, and have abdicated. Practices of the unscrupulous money changers stand indicted in the court of public opinion, rejected by the hearts and minds of men.[2]

True they have tried, but their efforts have been cast in the pattern of an outworn tradition. Faced by failure of credit they have proposed only the lending of more money. Stripped of the lure of profit by which to induce our people to follow their false leadership, they have resorted to exhortations, pleading tearfully for the restored confidence. They know only the rules of a generation of self-seekers. They have no vision, and when there is no vision the people perish.[3]

The money changers have fled from their high seats in the temple of our civilization. We many now restore that temple to the ancient truths. The measure of the restoration lies in the extent to which we apply social values more noble than mere monetary profit.

Happiness lies not in the mere possession of money; it lies in the joy of

---

[2] Roosevelt alludes to the story of Jesus throwing the moneychangers out of the temple in Jerusalem, found in Matthew 21:12–17, Mark 11:15–19, Luke 19:45–48, and John 2:13–16.

[3] A paraphrase of Proverbs 29:18.

achievement, in the thrill of creative effort. The joy and moral stimulation of work no longer must be forgotten in the mad chase of evanescent profits. These dark days will be worth all they cost us if they teach us that our true destiny is not to be ministered unto but minister to ourselves and to our fellow men.

Recognition of the falsity of material wealth as the standard of success goes hand in hand with the abandonment of the false belief that public office and high political position are to be valued only by the standards of pride of place and personal profit; and there must be an end to a conduct in banking and in business which too often has given to a sacred trust the likeness of callous and selfish wrongdoing. Small wonder that confidence languishes, for it thrives only on honesty, on honor, on the sacredness of obligations, on faithful protection, on unselfish performance; without them it cannot live.

Restoration calls, however, not for changes in ethics alone. This Nation asks for action, and action now.

Our greatest primary task is to put people to work. This is no unsolvable problem if we face it wisely and courageously. It can be accomplished in part by direct recruiting by the Government itself, treating the task as we would treat the emergency of a war, but at the same time, through this employment, accomplishing greatly needed projects to stimulate and reorganize the use of our national resources.

Hand in hand with this we must frankly recognize the overbalance of population in our industrial centers and, by engaging on a national scale in a redistribution, endeavor to provide a better use of the land for those best fitted for the land. The task can be helped by definite efforts to raise the values of agricultural products and with this the power to purchase the output of our cities. It can be helped by preventing realistically the tragedy of the growing loss through foreclosure of our small homes and our farms. It can be helped by insistence that the Federal, State, and local governments act forthwith on the demand that their costs be drastically reduced. It can be helped by the unifying of relief activities which today are often scattered, uneconomical, and unequal. It can be helped by national planning for and supervision of all forms of transportation and of communications and other utilities which have a definitely public character. There are many ways in in which it can be helped, but it can never be helped merely by talking about it. We must act and act quickly.

Finally, in our progress toward a resumption of work we require two safeguards against a return of the evils of the old order: there must be a strict supervision of all banking and credits and investments, so that there will be an end to speculation with other people's money; and there must be provision for an adequate but sound currency.

These are the lines of attack. I shall presently urge upon a new Congress, in special session, detailed measures for their fulfillment, and I shall seek the immediate assistance of the several States.

Through this program of action we address ourselves to putting our own national house in order and making income balance outgo. Our international trade relations, though vastly important, are in point of time and necessity secondary to the establishment of a sound national economy. I favor as a practical policy the putting of first things first. I shall spare no effort to restore world trade by international economic readjustment, but the emergency at home cannot wait on that accomplishment.

The basic thought that guides these specific means of national recovery is not narrowly nationalistic. It is the insistence, as a first consideration, upon the interdependence of the various elements in all parts of the United States—a recognition of the old and permanently important manifestation of the American spirit of the pioneer. It is the way of recovery. It is the immediate way. It is the strongest assurance that the recovery will endure.

In the field of world policy, I would dedicate this Nation to the policy of the good neighbor—the neighbor who resolutely respects himself and, because he does so, respects the rights of others—the neighbor who respects his obligations and respects the sanctity of his agreements in and with a world of neighbors.

If I read the temper of our people correctly, we now realize as we have never realized before our interdependence on each other; that we cannot merely take but we must give as well; that if we are to go forward, we must move as a trained and loyal army willing to sacrifice for the good of a common discipline, because without such discipline no progress is made, no leadership becomes effective. We are, I know, ready and willing to submit our lives and property to such discipline, because it makes possible a leadership which aims at a larger good. This I propose to offer, pledging that the larger purposes will bind upon us all as a sacred obligation with a unity of duty hitherto evoked only in time of armed strife.

With this pledge taken, I assume unhesitatingly the leadership of this great army of our people dedicated to a disciplined attack upon our common problems.

Action in this image and to this end is feasible under the form of government which we have inherited from our ancestors. Our Constitution is so simple and practical that it is possible always to meet extraordinary needs by changes in emphasis and arrangement without loss of essential form. That is why our constitutional system has proved itself the most superbly enduring political mechanism the modern has produced. It has met every stress of vast expansion of territory, of foreign wars, of bitter internal strife, of world relations.

It is to be hoped that the normal balance of Executive and legislative authority may be wholly adequate to meet the unprecedented task before us. But it may be that an unprecedented demand and need for undelayed action may call for temporary departure from that normal balance of public procedure.

I am prepared under my constitutional duty to recommend the measures that a stricken Nation in the midst of a stricken world may require. These measures, or such other measures as the Congress may build out of its experience and wisdom, I shall seek, within my constitutional authority, to bring to speedy adoption.

But in the event that the Congress shall fail to take one of these two courses, and in the event that the national emergency is still critical, I shall not evade the clear course of duty that will then confront me. I shall ask Congress for the one remaining instrument to meet the crisis - broad Executive power to wage a war against the emergency, as great as the power that would be given to me if we were in fact invaded by a foreign foe.

For the trust reposed in me I will return the courage and the devotion that befit the time. I can do no less.

We face the arduous days that lie before us in the warm courage of national unity; with the clear consciousness of seeking old and precious moral values; with the clean satisfaction that comes from the stern performance of duty by old and young alike. We aim at the assurance of a rounded and permanent national life.

We do not distrust the future of essential democracy. The people of the United States have not failed. In their need they have registered a mandate that they want direct, vigorous action. They have asked for discipline and direction under leadership. They have made me the present instrument of their wishes. In the spirit of the gift, I take it.

In this dedication of Nation we humbly ask the blessing of God. May He protect each and every one of us. May he guide me in the days to come.

The Brownlow Committee Report

The President's Committee on Administrative Management

1937

*I*n 1936, Franklin Roosevelt appointed a committee to recommend measures to reorganize the executive branch. The problem was that the New Deal created more offices and agencies in the executive branch than Roosevelt could oversee without help. The committee was chaired by Louis D. Brownlow, and it included two political scientists, Charles E. Merriam and Luther Gulick. The Brownlow Committee recommended a vast overhaul of the executive branch, the hiring of new assistants, and the creation of the Executive Office of the President (EOP). The report proved controversial, and Congress delayed approval until 1939. At that time, it approved a less ambitious plan for the reorganization of the Executive branch. Later presidents, however, would expand the EOP, fashioning it into the nerve center of the modern administrative state.

While it is true that the staff in the EOP serve at the pleasure of the president and are there to provide the president with expert advice, it is also true that the EOP is yet another layer of administration that the president has to manage. Moreover, although the authors of the Brownlow Committee argued that the staff in the EOP would be high in physical "vigor" and have a "passion for anonymity," the modern EOP is filled with men and women who sometimes have their own ambitions.

SOURCE: The President's Committee on Administrative Management, "Report of the Committee with Studies of Administrative Management in the Federal Government," (Washington, D. C.: United States Government Printing Office, 1937), 1–6.

The American Executive

The need for action in realizing democracy was as great in 1789 as it is today. It was thus not by accident but by deliberate design that the founding fathers set the American Executive in the Constitution on a solid foundation. Sad experience under the Articles of Confederation, with an almost headless Government and committee management, had brought the American Republic to the edge of ruin. Our forefathers had broken away from hereditary government and pinned their faith on democratic rule, but they had not found a way to equip the new democracy for action. Consequently, there was grim purpose in resolutely providing for a Presidency which was to be a national office. The President is indeed the one and only national officer representative of the entire Nation. There was hesitation on the part of some timid souls in providing the President with an election independent of the Congress; with a longer term than most governors of that day; with the duty of informing the Congress as to the state of the Union and of recommending to its consideration "such Measures as he shall judge necessary and expedient"; with a two-thirds veto; with a wide power of appointment; and with military and diplomatic authority. But this reluctance was overcome in the face of need and a democratic executive established.

Equipped with these broad constitutional powers, re-enforced by statute, by custom, by general consent, the American Executive must be regarded as one of the very greatest contributions made by our Nation to the development of modern democracy—a unique institution the value of which is as evident in times of stress and strain as in periods of quiet.

As an instrument for carrying out the judgment and will of the people of a nation, the American Executive occupies an enviable position among the executives of the states of the world, combining as it does the elements of popular control and the means for vigorous action and leadership—uniting stability and flexibility. The American Executive as an institution stands across the path of those who mistakenly assert that democracy must fail because it can neither decide promptly nor act vigorously.

Our Presidency unites at least three important functions. From one point of view the President is a political leader—leader of a party, leader of the Congress, leader of a people. From another point of view, he is head of the Nation in the ceremonial sense of the term, the symbol of our American national solidarity. From still another point of view the President is the Chief Executive and administrator within the Federal system and service. In many types of government these duties are divided or only in part combined, but in the United States they have always been united in one and the same person whose duty it is to perform all of these tasks.

Your Committee on Administrative Management has been asked to investigate and report particularly upon the last function; namely, that of administrative management—the organization for the performance of the duties imposed upon the President in exercising the executive power vested in him by the Constitution of the United States....

Modernizing our Governmental Management

In the light of these canons of efficiency, what must be said of the Government of the United States today? Speaking in the broadest terms at this point, and in detail later on, we find in the American Government at the present time that the effectiveness of the Chief Executive is limited and restricted, in spite of the clear intent of the Constitution to the contrary; that the work of the Executive Branch is badly organized; that the managerial agencies are weak and out of date; that the public service does not include its share of men and women of outstanding capacity and character; and that the fiscal and auditing systems are inadequate. These weaknesses are found at the center of our Government and involve the office of the Chief Executive itself.

While in general principle our organization of the Presidency challenges the admiration of the world, yet in equipment for administrative management our Executive Office is not fully abreast of the trend of our American times, either in business or in government. Where, for example, can there be found an executive in any way comparable upon whom so much petty work is thrown? Or who is forced to see so many persons on unrelated matters and to make so many decisions on the basis of what may be, because of the very press of work, incomplete information? How is it humanly possible to know fully the affairs and problems of over 100 separate major agencies, to say nothing of being responsible for their general direction and coordination?

These facts have been known for many years and are so well appreciated that it is not necessary for us to prove again that the President's administrative equipment is far less developed than his responsibilities, and that a major task before the American Government is to remedy this dangerous situation. What we need is not a new principle, but a modernizing of our managerial equipment.... On the basis of [prior experience reorganizing state governments] and our examination of the Executive Branch we conclude that the following steps should now be taken:

1. To deal with the greatly increased duties of executive management falling upon the President the White House staff should be expanded.

2. The managerial agencies of the Government, particularly those dealing with the budget, efficiency research, personnel, and planning, should be greatly strengthened and developed as arms of the Chief Executive.

3. The merit system should be extended upward, outward, and downward to cover all non-policy-determining posts, and the civil service system should be reorganized and opportunities established for a career system attractive to the best talent of the Nation.

4. The whole Executive Branch of the Government should be overhauled and the present 100 agencies reorganized under a few large departments in which every executive activity would find its place.

5. The fiscal system should be extensively revised in the light of the best governmental and private practice, particularly with reference to financial records, audit, and accountability of the Executive to the Congress.

These recommendations are explained and discussed in the following sections of this report.

The Purpose of Reorganization

In proceeding to the reorganization of the Government it is important to keep prominently before us the ends of reorganization. Too close a view of machinery must not cut off from sight the true purpose of efficient management. Economy is not the only objective, though reorganization is the first step to savings; the elimination of duplication and contradictory policies is not the only objective, though this will follow; a simple and symmetrical organization is not the only objective, though the new organization will be simple and symmetrical; higher salaries and better jobs are not the only objectives, though these too are demanded. There is but one grand purpose, namely, to make democracy work today in our National Government; that is, to make our Government an up-to-date, efficient, and effective instrument for carrying out the will of the Nation. It is for this purpose that the Government needs thoroughly modern tools of management....

The White House Staff

In this broad program of administrative reorganization the White House staff is involved. The President needs help. His immediate staff assistance is entirely inadequate. He should be given a small number of executive assistants who would be his direct aides in dealing with the managerial agencies and administrative departments of the Government. These assistants, probably not exceeding six in number, would be in addition to his present secretaries, who deal with the public, with the Congress, and with the press and the radio. These aides would have no power to make decisions or issue instructions in their own right. They would not be interposed between the President and the heads of his departments. They would not be assistant presidents in any sense. Their function would be, when any matter was presented to the President for action affecting any part of the administrative work of the Government, to assist him in obtaining quickly and without delay all pertinent information possessed by any of the executive departments so as to guide him in making his responsible decisions; and then when decisions have been made, to assist him in seeing to it that every administrative department and agency affected is promptly informed. Their effectiveness in assisting the President will, we think, be directly proportional to their ability to discharge their functions with restraint. They would remain in the background, issue no orders, make no decisions, emit no public statements. Men for these positions should be carefully chosen by the President from within and without the Government. They should be men in whom the President has personal confidence and whose character and attitude is such that they would not attempt to exercise power on their own account. They should be possessed of high competence, great physical vigor, and a passion for anonymity. They should be installed in the White House itself, directly accessible to the President. In the selection of these aides the President should be free to call on departments from time to time for the assignment of persons who, after a tour of duty as his aides, might be restored to their old positions.

Fireside Chat on the Reorganization of the Judiciary

President Franklin D. Roosevelt

March 9, 1937

F ranklin Roosevelt and the Democratic Party won a convincing victory in
1932 and an even more lopsided victory in 1936. Yet the Supreme Court had
ruled against key New Deal laws, often by a narrow five to four majority. Also,
Roosevelt had not yet had a chance to nominate a Justice to the Supreme Court.
In this radio message to the American people, Roosevelt explained his plan to
expand the number of Justices on the Supreme Court. In his view, the plan was
necessary in order to ensure that the Supreme Court was filled with Justices who
held a "modern" view of the Constitution. His plan was defeated, in part because
conservative Democrats agreed with Republicans who believed that the plan was
too direct an attack on the independent judiciary. Ironically, Roosevelt got his
way when one justice changed his view and began voting with the justices whose
more expansive reading of the Constitution was more favorable to Roosevelt's
policy agenda.

The conflict between Roosevelt and the Court is not the only one of its kind.
Other presidents whose parties have won realigning elections have discovered that
the Supreme Court is not necessarily guided by election returns.

SOURCE: Samuel I. Rosenman, ed., *Public Papers and Addresses of Franklin D. Roosevelt.* 1937
Volume: *The Constitution Prevails* (New York: MacMillan, 1941), 122–33.

Last Thursday I described in detail certain economic problems which everyone admits now face the Nation.[1] For the many messages which have come
to me after that speech, and which it is physically impossible to answer indi-
vidually, I take this means of saying "thank you." Tonight, sitting at my desk

---

[1] See Roosevelt's "Address at the Democratic Victory Dinner," March 4, 1937.

in the White House, I make my first radio report to the people in my second term of office.[2]

I am reminded of that evening in March, four years ago, when I made my first radio report to you. We were then in the midst of the great banking crisis.

Soon after, with the authority of the Congress, we asked the Nation to turn over all of its privately held gold, dollar for dollar, to the Government of the United States.

Today's recovery proves how right that policy was.

But when, almost two years later, it came before the Supreme Court its constitutionality was upheld only by a five-to-four vote. The change of one vote would have thrown all the affairs of this great Nation back into hopeless chaos. In effect, four Justices ruled that the right under a private contract to exact a pound of flesh was more sacred than the main objectives of the Constitution to establish an enduring Nation.

In 1933 you and I knew that we must never let our economic system get completely out of joint again—that we could not afford to take the risk of another great depression.

We also became convinced that the only way to avoid a repetition of those dark days was to have a government with power to prevent and to cure the abuses and the inequalities which had thrown that system out of joint.

We then began a program of remedying those abuses and inequalities—to give balance and stability to our economic system—to make it bomb-proof against the causes of 1929.

Today we are only part-way through that program—and recovery is speeding up to a point where the dangers of 1929 are again becoming possible, not this week or month perhaps, but within a year or two.

National laws are needed to complete that program. Individual or local or state effort alone cannot protect us in 1937 any better than ten years ago.

It will take time—and plenty of time—to work out our remedies administratively even after legislation is passed. To complete our program of protection in time, therefore, we cannot delay one moment in making certain that our National Government has power to carry through.

------

[2] On March 12, 1933, FDR began what became a tradition of direct addresses from the President to the American people when he took to the radio waves to explain his economic plan for helping the nation recover from the Great Depression. The informal nature of these reports led one journalist to dub them "fireside chats," and the term stuck.

Four years ago action did not come until the eleventh hour. It was almost too late.

If we learned anything from the depression we will not allow ourselves to run around in new circles of futile discussion and debate, always postponing the day of decision.

The American people have learned from the depression. For in the last three national elections an overwhelming majority of them voted a mandate that the Congress and the President begin the task of providing that protection—not after long years of debate, but now.

The Courts, however, have cast doubts on the ability of the elected Congress to protect us against catastrophe by meeting squarely our modern social and economic conditions.

We are at a crisis in our ability to proceed with that protection. It is a quiet crisis. There are no lines of depositors outside closed banks. But to the far-sighted it is far-reaching in its possibilities of injury to America.

I want to talk with you very simply about the need for the present action in this crisis—the need to meet the unanswered challenge of one-third of a Nation ill-nourished, ill-clad, ill-housed.

Last Thursday I described the American form of Government as a three-horse team provided by the Constitution of the American people so that their field might be plowed. The three horses are, of course, the three branches of government—the Congress, the Executive and the Courts. Two of the horses are pulling in unison today; the third is not. Those who have intimated that the President of the United States is trying to drive that team, overlook the simple fact that the President, as Chief Executive, is himself one of the three horses.

It is the American people themselves who are in the driver's seat.

It is the American people themselves who want the furrow plowed.

It is the American people themselves who expect the third horse to pull in unison with the other two.

I hope that you have re-read the Constitution of the United States in these past few weeks. Like the Bible, it ought to be read again and again.

It is an easy document to understand when you remember that it was called into being because the Articles of Confederation under which the original thirteen States tried to operate after the Revolution showed the need of a National Government with power enough to handle national problems. In its Preamble, the Constitution states that it was intended to form a more perfect Union and promote the general welfare; and the powers given to the

Congress to carry out those purposes can be best described by saying that they were all the powers needed to meet each and every problem which then had a national character and which could not be met by merely local action.

But the framers went further. Having in mind that in succeeding generations many other problems then undreamed of would become national problems, they gave to the Congress the ample broad powers "to levy taxes ... and provide for the common defense and general welfare of the United States."[3]

That, my friends, is what I honestly believe to have been the clear and underlying purpose of the patriots who wrote a Federal Constitution to create a National Government with national power, intended as they said, "to form a more perfect union ... for ourselves and our posterity."

For nearly twenty years there was no conflict between the Congress and the Court. Then Congress passed a statute which, in 1803, the Court said violated an express provision of the Constitution. The Court claimed the power to declare it unconstitutional and did so declare it. But a little later the Court itself admitted that it was an extraordinary power to exercise and through Mr. Justice Washington laid down this limitation upon it: "It is but a decent respect due to the wisdom, the integrity and the patriotism of the legislative body, by which any law is passed, to presume in favor of its validity until its violation of the Constitution is proved beyond all reasonable doubt."[4]

But since the rise of the modern movement for social and economic progress through legislation, the Court has more and more often and more and more boldly asserted a power to veto laws passed by the Congress and State Legislatures in complete disregard of this original limitation.

In the last four years the sound rule of giving statutes the benefit of all reasonable doubt has been cast aside. The Court has been acting not as a judicial body, but as a policy-making body.

When the Congress has sought to stabilize national agriculture, to improve the conditions of labor, to safeguard business against unfair competition, to protect our national resources, and in many other ways, to serve our clearly national needs, the majority of the Court has been assuming the power to pass on the wisdom of these Acts of the Congress—and to approve or disapprove the public policy written into these laws.

That is not only my accusation. It is the accusation of most distinguished Justices of the present Supreme Court. I have not the time to quote to you

[3] Article 1, Section 8
[4] Roosevelt has in mind *Marbury v. Madison* (1803) which overturned the Judiciary Act of 1789. The quotation comes from *Ogden v. Saunders* (1827).

all the language used by dissenting Justices in many of these cases. But in the case holding the Railroad Retirement Act unconstitutional, for instance, Chief Justice Hughes said in a dissenting opinion that the majority opinion was "a departure from sound principles" and placed "an unwarranted limitation upon the commerce clause." And three other Justices agreed with him.[5]

In the case holding the A.A.A. [Agricultural Adjustment Act] unconstitutional, Justice Stone said of the majority opinion that it was a "tortured construction of the Constitution." And two other Justices agreed with him.[6]

In the case holding the New York Minimum Wage Law unconstitutional, Justice Stone said that the majority were actually reading into the Constitution their own "personal economic predilections," and that if the legislative power is not left free to choose the methods of solving the problems of poverty, subsistence and health of large numbers in the community, then "government is to be rendered impotent." And two other Justices agreed with him.[7]

In the face of these dissenting opinions, there is no basis for the claim made by some members of the Court that something in the Constitution has compelled them regretfully to thwart the will of the people.

In the face of such dissenting opinions, it is perfectly clear, that as Chief Justice Hughes has said: "We are under a Constitution, but the Constitution is what the Judges say it is."[8]

The Court in addition to the proper use of its judicial functions has improperly set itself up as a third House of the Congress—a super-legislature, as one of the justices has called it—reading into the Constitution words and implications which are not there, and which were never intended to be there.

We have, therefore, reached a point as a Nation where we must take action to save the Constitution from the Court and the Court from itself. We must find a way to take an appeal from the Supreme Court to the Constitution itself. We want a Supreme Court which will do justice under the Constitution—not over it. In our Courts we want a government of laws and not of men.

---

[5] Charles Evans Hughes (1862–1948) served as Associate Justice on the Supreme Court (1910–1916), Secretary of State (1921–1925), and Chief Justice of the Supreme Court (1930–1941).

[6] See *United State v. Butler* (1936). Harlan Fiske Stone (1872–1946) was Associate Justice on the Supreme Court (1925–1941) and then Chief Justice (1941–1946).

[7] See *Morehead v. New York ex rel. Tipaldo* (1936)

[8] Charles Evans Hughes, "Speech at the Chamber of Commerce," Elmira, New York, May 3, 1907.

I want—as all Americans want—an independent judiciary as proposed by the framers of the Constitution. That means a Supreme Court that will enforce the Constitution as written—that will refuse to amend the Constitution by the arbitrary exercise of judicial power—amendment by judicial say-so. It does not mean a judiciary so independent that it can deny the existence of facts universally recognized.

How then could we proceed to perform the mandate given us? It was said in last year's Democratic platform, "If these problems cannot be effectively solved within the Constitution, we shall seek such clarifying amendment as will assure the power to enact those laws, adequately to regulate commerce, protect public health and safety, and safeguard economic security." In other words, we said we would seek an amendment only if every other possible means by legislation were to fail.

When I commenced to review the situation with the problem squarely before me, I came by a process of elimination to the conclusion that, short of amendments, the only method which was clearly constitutional, and would at the same time carry out other much needed reforms, was to infuse new blood into all our Courts. We must have men worthy and equipped to carry out impartial justice. But, at the same time, we must have judges who will bring to the Courts a present-day sense of the Constitution—Judges who will retain in the Courts the judicial functions of a court, and reject the legislative powers which the courts today have assumed.

In forty-five out of forty-eight States of the Union, Judges are chosen not for life but for a period of years. In many States Judges must retire at the age of seventy. Congress has provided financial security by offering life pensions at full pay for the Federal Judges on all Courts who are willing to retire at seventy. In the case of Supreme Court Justices, that pension is $20,000 a year. But all Federal Judges, once appointed, can, if they choose, hold office for life, no matter how old they may get to be.

What is my proposal? It is simply this: whenever a Judge or Justice of any Federal Court has reached the age of seventy and does not avail himself of the opportunity to retire on pension, a new member shall be appointed by the President then in office, with the approval, as required by the Constitution, of the Senate of the United States.

That plan has two chief purposes. By bringing into the judicial system a steady and continuing stream of new and younger blood, I hope, first, to make the administration of all Federal justice speedier and, therefore, less costly; secondly, to bring to the decision of social and economic problems younger men who have had personal experience and contact with modern facts and circumstances under which average men have to live and work. This plan will save our national Constitution from hardening of the judicial arteries.

The number of Judges to be appointed would depend wholly on the decision of present Judges now over seventy, or those who would subsequently reach the age of seventy.

If, for instance, any one of the six Justices of the Supreme Court now over the age of seventy should retire as provided under the plan, no additional place would be created. Consequently, although there never can be more than fifteen, there may be only fourteen, or thirteen, or twelve. And there may be only nine.

There is nothing novel or radical about this idea. It seeks to maintain the Federal bench in full vigor. It has been discussed and approved by many persons of high authority ever since a similar proposal passed the House of Representatives in 1869.

Why was the age fixed at seventy? Because the laws of many States, the practice of the Civil Service, the regulations of the Army and Navy, and the rules of many of our Universities and of almost every great private business enterprise, commonly fix their retirement age at seventy years or less.

The statute would apply to all the courts in the Federal system. There is general approval so far as the lower Federal courts are concerned. The plan has met opposition only so far as the Supreme Court of the United States itself is concerned. If such a plan is good for the lower courts it certainly ought to be equally good for the highest Court from which there is no appeal.

Those opposing this plan have sought to arouse prejudice and fear by crying that I am seeking to "pack" the Supreme Court and that a baneful precedent will be established.

What do they mean by the words "packing the Court?"

Let me answer this question with a bluntness that will end all *honest* misunderstandings of my purposes.

If by that phrase "packing the Court" it is charged that I wish to place on the bench spineless puppets who would disregard the law and would decide specific cases as I wished them to be decided, I make this answer: that no President fit for his office would appoint, and no Senate of honorable men would confirm, that kind of appointees to the Supreme Court.

But if by that phrase the charge is made that I would appoint and the Senate would confirm Justices worthy to sit beside present members of the Court who understand those modern conditions, that I will appoint Justices

who will not undertake to override the judgement of the Congress on legislative policy, that I will appoint Justices who will act as Justices and not as
legislators—if the appointment of such Justices can be called "packing the
Courts," then I say that I and with me the vast majority of the American
people favor doing just that thing—now.

Is it a dangerous precedent for the Congress to change the number of
Justices? The Congress has always had, and will have, that power. The number of Justices has been changed several times before, in the Administration
of John Adams and Thomas Jefferson—both signers of the Declaration of
Independence—Andrew Jackson, Abraham Lincoln and Ulysses S. Grant.

I suggest only the addition of Justices to the bench in accordance with
a clearly defined principle relating to a clearly defined age limit. Fundamentally, if in the future, America cannot trust the Congress it elects to
refrain from abuse of our Constitutional usages, democracy will have failed
far beyond the importance to it of any kind of precedent concerning the
Judiciary.

We think it is so much in the public interest to maintain a vigorous judiciary that we encourage the retirement of elderly Judges by offering them a
life pension at full salary. Why then should we leave the fulfillment of this
public policy to chance or make it dependent upon the desire or prejudice
of any individual Justice?

It is the clear intention of our public policy to provide for a constant
flow of new and younger blood into the Judiciary. Normally every President
appoints a large number of District and Circuit Judges and a few members
of the Supreme Court. Until my first term practically every President of the
United States had appointed at least one member of the Supreme Court.
President Taft appointed five members and named a Chief Justice; President
Wilson, three, President Harding, four, including a Chief Justice, President
Coolidge, one, President Hoover, three, including a Chief Justice.

Such a succession of appointments should have provided a Court
well-balanced as to age. But chance and the disinclination of individuals to
leave the Supreme bench have now given us a Court in which five Justices
will be over seventy-five years of age before next June and one over seventy.
Thus a sound public policy has been defeated.

I now propose that we establish by law an assurance against any such
ill-balanced Court in the future. I propose that hereafter, when a Judge
reaches the age of seventy, a new and younger Judge shall be added to the
Court automatically. In this way I propose to enforce a sound public policy by

law instead of leaving the composition of our Federal Courts, including the highest, to be determined by chance or the personal decision of individuals.

If such a law as I propose is regarded as establishing a new precedent, is it not a most desirable precedent?

Like all lawyers, like all Americans, I regret the necessity of this controversy. But the welfare of the United States, and indeed of the Constitution itself, is what we all must think about first. Our difficulty with the Court today rises not from the Court as an institution but from human beings within it. But we cannot yield our constitutional destiny to the personal judgement of a few men who, being fearful of the future, would deny us the necessary means of dealing with the present.

This plan of mine is no attack on the Court; it seeks to restore the Court to its rightful and historic place in our system of Constitutional Government and to have it resume its high task of building anew on the Constitution " a system of living law." The Court itself can best undo what the Court has done.

I have thus explained to you the reasons that lie behind our efforts to secure results by legislation within the Constitution. I hope that thereby the difficult process of constitutional amendment may be rendered unnecessary. But let us examine that process.

There are many types of amendment proposed. Each one is radically different from the other. There is no substantial group within the Congress or outside it who are agreed on any single amendment.

It would take months or years to get substantial agreement upon the type and language of an amendment. It would take months and years thereafter to get a two-thirds majority in favor of that amendment in *both* Houses of Congress.

Then would come the long course of ratification by three-fourths of all the States. No amendment which any powerful economic interests or the leaders of any powerful political party have had any reason to oppose has ever been ratified within anything like a reasonable time. And thirteen States which contain only five percent of the voting population can block ratification even though the thirty-five States with ninety-five percent of the population are in favor of it.

A very large percentage of newspaper publishers, Chambers of Commerce, bar Associations, Manufacturer's Associations, who are trying to give the impression that they really do want a constitutional amendment would be first to exclaim as soon as an amendment was proposed, "Oh! I was for an amendment all right, but this amendment that you have proposed is not the

174 FRANKLIN D. ROOSEVELT

kind of an amendment that I was thinking about. I am, therefore, going to spend my time, my efforts and my money to block that amendment, although I would be awfully glad to help get some other kind of amendment ratified."

Two groups oppose my plan on the ground that they favor a constitutional amendment. The first included those who fundamentally object to social and economic legislation along modern lines. This is the same group who during the campaign last Fall tried to block the mandate of the people.

Now they are making a last stand. And the strategy of that last stand is to suggest the time-consuming process of amendment in order to kill off by delay the legislation demanded by the mandate.

To them I say: I do not think you will be able long to fool the American people as to your purposes.

The other group is composed of those who honestly believe the amendment process is the best and who would be willing to support a reasonable amendment if they could agree on one.

To them I say: we cannot rely on an amendment as the immediate or only answer to our present difficulties. When the time comes for action, you will find that many of those who pretend to support you will sabotage any constructive amendment which is proposed. Look at these strange bed-fellows of yours. When before have you found them really at your side in your fights for progress?

And remember one thing more. Even if an amendment were passed, and even if in the years to come it were to be ratified, its meaning would depend upon the kind of Justices who would be sitting on the Supreme Court bench. An amendment, like the rest of the Constitution, is what the Justices say it is rather than what its framers or you might hope it is.

This proposal of mine will not infringe in the slightest upon the civil or religious liberties so dear to every American.

My record as Governor and as President proves my devotion to those liberties. You who know me can have no fear that I would tolerate the destruction by any branch of government of any part of our heritage of freedom.

The present attempt by those opposed to progress to play upon the fears of danger to personal liberty brings again to mind that crude and cruel strategy tried by the same opposition to frighten the workers of America in a pay-envelope propaganda against the Social Security Law. The workers were not fooled by that propaganda then. The people of America will not be fooled by such propaganda now.

I am in favor of action through legislation:

First, because I believe that it can be passed at this session of the Congress.

Second, because it will provide a reinvigorated, liberal-minded Judiciary necessary to furnish quicker and cheaper justice from bottom to top.

Third, because it will provide a series of Federal Courts willing to enforce the Constitution as written, and unwilling to assert legislative powers by writing into it their own political and economic policies.

During the past half century, the balance of power between the three great branches of the Federal Government, has been tipped out of balance by the Courts in direct contradiction of the high purposes of the framers of the Constitution. It is my purpose to restore that balance. You who know me will accept my solemn assurance that in a world in which democracy is under attack, I seek to make American democracy succeed. You and I will do our part.

House Debate on the 22nd Amendment

Representative John McCormack and Representative Chauncey Reed

1947

Franklin Roosevelt was elected president four times. In the elections of 1946, Republicans gained twelve seats in the Senate and fifty-five seats in the House to gain control of Congress, the first time this had occurred since FDR had taken office. They wasted little time in proposing an amendment to the Constitution limiting presidential tenure to two terms. No Republican voted against the amendment; the Democrats who voted for the amendment were largely conservative southerners.

In the debate in Congress, both supporters and opponents of the amendment argued that their respective positions were the better fit for constitutional tradition. Supporters argued that Roosevelt had violated the customary two-term limit that had existed going back to Washington and Jefferson, and opponents argued in response that the custom was actually to leave the option of multiple terms available. Most of the debate did not engage Hamilton's argument against a term limit in Federalist 72 (Document 1).

SOURCE: *Congressional Record*, 80th Congress, First Session, Volume 93, Part 1 (Washington D.C.: United States Government Printing Office, 1947), 842–43, 844, 853–54.

Mr. McCORMACK.[1] Mr. Speaker, this is one of the most important questions that any Member of this body will have to pass upon and I hope each Member will determine the question in accordance with his conscience. It is not my purpose to discuss politics in connection with the proposed amendment to the Constitution, an amendment which will not have any effect upon you and me of this generation but which might have a very important effect upon generations to come after you and I are dead and gone. If this amendment is incorporated in the Constitution, it will make the Constitution rigid.

---

[1] John William McCormack (1891–1980) was a Democratic Representative from Massachusetts from 1928 to 1971. He was also Speaker of the House from 1962–1971.

It ties the hands of future generations of Americans and deprives them of the opportunity to meet any problem that might confront them.

Of course, we have lived through the experience ourselves, but I can picture two generations from now, or one or three generations from now, when Americans may be enveloped in a war with their back to the wall. We will not be here. We will have passed on. But we will have imposed this prohibition upon them. They may be with their back to the wall with a President approaching the end of his second term. Let us assume the people of that future generation have complete confidence in their President. I do not know what his party may be. I do not care. That future President will be compelled to terminate his service as President of the United States when he may be the best man qualified to lead the people of our country at that time in meeting the crisis that confronts them. I beg of you as we sit here today to realize just what we are doing. I believe in custom. A custom is one thing, but a rigid prohibition is another thing. If this amendment becomes a part of the Constitution—and you cannot say, "We are sending it to the several State legislatures"; that is not the question; that is not the answer—if this amendment becomes a part of the Constitution, it imposes upon Americans for all time until and unless that Constitution is reamended the rigid hand of a rigid prohibition that no matter what crisis may confront America in the future when a President's second term is drawing to a close they cannot reelect him so that he may continue his service to the Nation which might be vitally necessary at that particular time.

I think it is too great a risk to take. For myself, I do not want to take it. Let us see what some of the eminent men of the past have said on this question. George Washington did not want a first term, even. He accepted it reluctantly as a patriotic duty. He expected to serve about two years. He reluctantly served a second term because of the conditions abroad. He withdrew voluntarily at the end of his second term. But what did Washington say? This is what he said in a letter to Marquis de Lafayette on April 28, 1788, in relation to the second term. This is probably the only quotation of George Washington in relation to this question which I think can be found. He said in discussing or writing about the limitation of the terms of a President: "Under an extended view of this part of the subject, I can see no propriety in precluding ourselves from the service of any man who on some great emergency shall be deemed universally most capable of serving the public."

What about Thomas Jefferson? Thomas Jefferson, historically, is the father of the two-term custom. There is no question about that. Thomas Jefferson, however, only wanted one term. He served a second term because of the calumnies hurled upon him by the Federalist Party and the effect they were having abroad at the time. He served patriotically. He could have had a third term. As we look back in history, I think we would all agree as to that. Jefferson retired at the end of his second term, but back in the days of the Constitutional Convention he believed in rotation in office. That was the big issue then. But what did Jefferson say about this? Jefferson himself said: "There is, however, but one circumstance that could engage my acquiescence in another election; to wit, such division about a successor as might bring in a monarchist. But this circumstance is impossible."

In other words, Jefferson himself recognized an emergency might exist where he would run for a third term, and in those days the emergency was the danger of a division existing that might establish a monarchy in our country. So Jefferson himself definitely saw that there was a distinction between custom and rigid prohibition. He recognized that in case of an emergency he might have been compelled, patriotically, to run for a third term, but he said this circumstance was impossible, because the danger of a monarchy did not exist at that time. But he said if there was such a danger he would have run for a third term.

John Quincy Adams said it should not be incorporated in the Constitution as a rigid prohibition....

In no part of the Constitution will you find any limitation, any prohibition except against Congress itself: Congress shall pass no law abridging the right of free speech, freedom of the press, freedom of assemblage. You will find limitations in the Constitution, but they are limitations upon Congress; and those limitations were imposed to protect the rights of individuals to assure that the legislative body would not take away the fundamental rights that our people believe in and for which the framers of the Constitution fought. This amendment is a limitation upon the people. This is not a limitation upon Congress. It is a limitation upon the action of the people of the future, no matter what the danger may be, no matter how urgent it may be that the second-term President continue, he cannot if this amendment becomes a part of the Constitution. O Mr. Speaker, it is too grave a danger to take this step, too grave a danger for us who will be dead at that time in all probability, to impose such a limitation upon future generations of Americans. Let their hands remain unshackled. Let us not put them into a strait-jacket, a strait-jacket that might be the factor resulting in the destruction of our country at some time in the future. Leadership is important. Leadership is the big thing and a President in his second term in the future might be the leader who will bring our people to victory. His going out at such a time might be the difference between victory and defeat. We are tying the hands of Americans in the future from exercising in a grave emergency the judgment which they may deem is for the best interests of our country.

Mr. REED of Illinois.[2] Mr. Chairman, the Presidential tenure of office is not a political question. It is a constitutional question of the highest order. In one form or another it occupied the attention of the Constitutional Convention from the introduction of Mr. Randolph's resolutions on May 29, 1787, until the adoption of the report of the Committee on Style submitted on September 12, five days before final adjournment.

In one form or another it has been before the people or the Congress, or both, ever since 1803—more than 140 years—when resolutions introduced after the election of 1800 came before the House of Representatives. Indeed, it has been calculated that between that date and 1889 more than 125 amendments were proposed to change the term of office of the President or to fix the period of eligibility; and it is estimated that almost as many have been introduced since.

It is hardly necessary to remind Members of Congress that when the matter of the Presidency was considered in the Convention the members of that body repeatedly expressed the importance of placing some limitation upon the tenure of the office. That was particularly so when it was contemplated that the Chief Executive was to be chosen by Congress and that long continuance in office would lead to autocracy, intrigue, or cabal. For a long time, the sentiment prevailed that the President should be limited to a single term of single years. When it became apparent that choice by the legislature would not be adopted, the plan of the Electoral College with a provision for a fixed term of four years was substituted.

Members of the Constitutional Convention feared autocracy. They feared perpetuation in the Executive Office. They had but emerged from war against a king with unlimited tenure of office. They had seen their State legislatures dissolved by royal governors appointed by a king. And they proposed that there should be no such usurpation of power in the Chief Executive they were about to create. And while they did not expressly prohibit reeligibility, they were not without the belief that the Electoral College, as they contemplated its operation, would provide an adequate check against perpetuation in office.

Regardless of the inadequacies of the Electoral College, however, the principle of a limitation upon the Presidential tenure came to develop by

---

[2] Chauncey William Reed (1890–1956) was a Republican Representative from Illinois, serving from 1935 to 1956.

tradition. Even though it be contended that Mr. Washington's refusal to accept a third term was based upon circumstances other than those intended to establish a precedent, the fact remains that his action was regarded as a precedent by his immediate successors, and the tradition of only two terms of 4 years each became attached to the Presidential office.

Jefferson expressed this sentiment in a letter dated January 1805, in which he wrote:

> My opinion originally was that the President of the United States should have been elected for 7 years, and forever ineligible afterward. I have since become sensible that 7 years is too long to be irremovable, and that there should be a peaceable way of withdrawing a man in midway who is doing wrong. The service for 8 years, with a power to remove at the end of the first four, comes nearly to my principle as corrected by experience; and it is in adherence to that that I determine to withdraw at the end of my second term. The danger is that the indulgence and attachments of the people will keep a man in the chair after he becomes a dotard, that reelection through life shall become habitual and election for life follow that. General Washington set the example of voluntary retirement after 8 years. I shall follow it. And a few more precedents will oppose the obstacle of habit to anyone after a while who shall endeavor to extend his term. Perhaps it may beget a disposition to establish it by an amendment of the Constitution.

In his first annual message, December 1829, President Jackson said:

> I would therefore recommend such an amendment of the Constitution as may remove all intermediate agency in the election of the President and Vice President.... In connection with such an amendment it would seem advisable to limit the service of the Chief Magistrate to a single term of either 4 or 6 years.

And he repeated that recommendation in several succeeding messages.

In his letter of August 18, 1884, accepting the nomination for the Presidency, President Cleveland wrote:

> When we consider the patronage of this great office, the allurements of power, the temptations to retain public place once gained, and, more than all, the availability a party finds in an incumbent whom a horde

of officeholders, with a zeal born of benefits received and fostered by the hope of favors yet to come, stand ready to aid with money and trained political service, we recognize in the eligibility of the President for reelection a most serious danger to that calm, deliberate, and intelligent political action which must characterize a government by the people.

And I would recall to my friends on the other side of the aisle that the Democratic National Convention, held in Baltimore, Md., in 1912, adopted the following resolution:

We favor a single Presidential term and to that end urge the adoption of an amendment to the Constitution making the President of the United States ineligible for reelection, and we pledge the candidate of this convention to this principle.

This historical feeling and tradition against unlimited tenure in the Presidential office, Mr. Chairman, is not based upon idle fear. The power and prestige of the President of the United States has grown constantly and increasingly since the first inauguration of Mr. Washington. Today, the President of the United States is perhaps the most powerful individual in the world. It is within the spirit of democracy that proper constitutional restraints be placed upon his tenure of office.

Special Message to Congress Reporting on the Situation in Korea

President Harry Truman

July 19, 1950

T he Constitution gives Congress the power to declare war, yet the president is made commander in chief. For early Americans this meant that Congress alone held the power to authorize war, that is, to bring the nation from a state of peace to a state of war. For example, during the debate over the Neutrality Proclamation (Document 4), Alexander Hamilton defended George Washington's power to declare that the nation was at peace, but he also went out of his way to say that only Congress could take the nation to war.

Since Harry Truman, however, presidents of both parties have assumed that it is the president who decides whether the nation will be at war. There are competing explanations for the emergence of this new understanding of the war power. One is that the United Nations provides a new and competing source of authority for military action. Another is that Cold War and the reality of atomic weapons rendered Congress's role less important. A third explanation is that wielding the war power is politically costly, so risk-adverse members of Congress are happy to let the president have it.

In the selection below, Truman announces his actions in Korea. Notice the role he assumes for the United Nations and the limited role he assumes for Congress.

SOURCE: *Public Papers of the Presidents of the United States. Harry S. Truman. Containing the Public Messages, Speeches, and Statements of the President, 1950* (Washington, D.C.: United States Government Printing Office, 1965), 527–37.

To the Congress of the United States:

I am reporting to the Congress on the situation which has been created in Korea, and on the actions which this Nation has taken, as a member of the United Nations, to meet this situation. I am also laying before the Congress my views concerning the significance of these events for this Nation and the world, and certain recommendations for legislative action which I believe should be taken at this time.

At four o'clock in the morning, Sunday, June 25th, Korean time, armed forces from north of the thirty-eighth parallel invaded the Republic of Korea....

This outright breach of the peace, in violation of the United Nations Charter, created a real and present danger to the security of every nation. This attack was, in addition, a demonstration of contempt for the United Nations, since it was an attempt to settle, by military aggression, a question which the United Nations had been working to settle by peaceful means.

The attack on the Republic of Korea, therefore, was a clear challenge to the basic principles of the United Nations Charter and to the specific actions taken by the United Nations in Korea. If this challenge had not been met squarely, the effectiveness of the United Nations would have been all but ended, and the hope of mankind that the United Nations would develop into an institution of world order would have been shattered.

Prompt action was imperative. The Security Council of the United Nations met, at the request of the United States, in New York at two o'clock in the afternoon, Sunday, June 25th, eastern daylight time. Since there is a 14-hour difference in time between Korea and New York, this meant that the Council convened just 24 hours after the attack began.

At this meeting, the Security Council passed a resolution which called for the immediate cessation of hostilities and for the withdrawal of the invading troops to the thirty-eighth parallel, and which requested the members of the United Nations to refrain from giving aid to the northern aggressors and to assist in the execution of this resolution. The representative of the Soviet Union to the Security Council stayed away from the meetings, and the Soviet Government has refused to support the Council's resolution.

The attack launched on June 25th moved ahead rapidly. The tactical surprise gained by the aggressors, and their superiority in planes, tanks and artillery, forced the lightly-armed defenders to retreat. The speed, the scale, and the coordination of the attack left no doubt that it had been plotted long in advance.

When the attack came, our Ambassador to Korea, John J. Muccio, began the immediate evacuation of American women and children from the danger zone. To protect this evacuation, air cover and sea cover were provided by the Commander in Chief of United States Forces in the Far East, General

of the Army Douglas MacArthur.[1] In response to urgent appeals from the
Government of Korea, General MacArthur was immediately authorized to
send supplies of ammunition to the Korean defenders. These supplies were
sent by air transport, with fighter protection. The United States Seventh
Fleet was ordered north from the Philippines, so that it might be available
in the area in case of need.

Throughout Monday, June 26th, the invaders continued their attack with
no heed to the resolution of the Security Council of the United Nations.
Accordingly, in order to support the resolution, and on the unanimous advice
of our civil and military authorities, I ordered United States air and sea forces
to give the Korean Government troops cover and support.

On Tuesday, June 27th, when the United Nations Commission in Korea
had reported that the northern troops had neither ceased hostilities nor withdrawn to the thirty-eighth parallel, the United Nations Security Council
met again and passed a second resolution recommending that members of
the United Nations furnish to the Republic of Korea such aid as might be
necessary to repel the attack and to restore international peace and security
in the area. The representative of the Soviet Union to the Security Council
stayed away from this meeting also, and the Soviet Government has refused
to support the Council's resolution.

The vigorous and unhesitating actions of the United Nations and the
United States in the face of this aggression met with an immediate and overwhelming response throughout the free world. The first blow of aggression
had brought dismay and anxiety to the hearts of men the world over. The
fateful events of the 1930's, when aggression unopposed bred more aggression
and eventually war, were fresh in our memory.

But the free nations had learned the lesson of history. Their determined
and united actions uplifted the spirit of free men everywhere. As a result,
where there had been dismay there is hope; where there had been anxiety
there is firm determination.

Fifty-two of the fifty-nine member nations have supported the United
Nations action to restore peace in Korea.

A number of member nations have offered military support or other types
of assistance for the United Nations action to repel the aggressors in Korea.

---

[1] Douglas MacArthur (1880–1964), was Supreme Commander of the Allied Powers in post war Japan. He was removed from his command by Truman in 1951, after
publicly disagreeing with the Truman Administration over the direction of the war
effort in Korea.

In a third resolution, passed on July 7th, the Security Council requested the United States to designate a commander for all the forces of the members of the United Nations in the Korean operation, and authorized these forces to fly the United Nations flag. In response to this resolution, General MacArthur has been designated as commander of these forces. These are important steps forward in the development of a United Nations system of collective security. Already, aircraft of two nations—Australia and Great Britain—and naval vessels of five nations—Australia, Canada, Great Britain, the Netherlands and New Zealand—have been made available for operations in the Korean area, along with forces of Korea and the United States, under General MacArthur's command. The other offers of assistance that have been and will continue to be made will be coordinated by the United Nations and by the unified command, in order to support the effort in Korea to maximum advantage.

All the members of the United Nations who have indorsed the action of the Security Council realize the significance of the step that has been taken. This united and resolute action to put down lawless aggression is a milestone toward the establishment of a rule of law among nations.

Only a few countries have failed to support the common action to restore the peace. The most important of these is the Soviet Union.

Since the Soviet representative had refused to participate in the meetings of the Security Council which took action regarding Korea, the United States brought the matter directly to the attention of the Soviet Government in Moscow. On June 27th, we requested the Soviet Government, in view of its known close relations with the north Korean regime, to use its influence to have the invaders withdraw at once.

The Soviet Government, in its reply on June 29th and in subsequent statements, has taken the position that the attack launched by the north Korean forces was provoked by the Republic of Korea, and that the actions of the United Nations Security Council were illegal.

These Soviet claims are flatly disproved by the facts.

The attitude of the Soviet Government toward the aggression against the Republic of Korea, is in direct contradiction to its often-expressed intention to work with other nations to achieve peace in the world.

For our part, we shall continue to support the United Nations action to restore peace in the Korean area.

As the situation has developed, I have authorized a number of measures to be taken. Within the first week of the fighting, General MacArthur reported, after a visit to the front, that the forces from north Korea were continuing to drive south, and further support to the Republic of Korea was needed. Accordingly, General MacArthur was authorized to use United States Army troops in Korea, and to use United States aircraft of the Air Force and the Navy to conduct missions against specific military targets in Korea north of the thirty-eighth parallel, where necessary to carry out the United Nations resolution. General MacArthur was also directed to blockade the Korean coast.

The attacking forces from the north have continued to move forward, although their advance has been slowed down. The troops of the Republic of Korea, though initially overwhelmed by the tanks and artillery of the surprise attack by the invaders, have been reorganized and are fighting bravely.

United States forces, as they have arrived in the area, have fought with great valor. The Army troops have been conducting a very difficult delaying operation with skill and determination, outnumbered many times over by attacking troops, spearheaded by tanks. Despite the bad weather of the rainy season, our troops have been valiantly supported by the air and naval forces of both the United States and other members of the United Nations.

In this connection, I think it is important that the nature of our military action in Korea be understood. It should be made perfectly clear that the action was undertaken as a matter of basic moral principle. The United States was going to the aid of a nation established and supported by the United Nations and unjustifiably attacked by an aggressor force. . . .

In these circumstances, we must take action to ensure that the increased national defense needs will be met, and that in the process we do not bring on an inflation, with its resulting hardship for every family.

At the same time, we must recognize that it will be necessary for a number of years to support continuing defense expenditures, including assistance to other nations, at a higher level than we had previously planned. Therefore, the economic measures we take now must be planned and used in such a manner as to develop and maintain our economic strength for the long run as well as the short run.

I am recommending certain legislative measures to help achieve these objectives. I believe that each of them should be promptly enacted. We must be sure to take the steps that are necessary now, or we shall surely be required to take much more drastic steps later on.

First, we should adopt such *direct measures as are now necessary to assure prompt and adequate supplies of goods for military and essential civilian use. I therefore recommend that the Congress now enact legislation authorizing the Government to establish priorities and allocate materials as necessary to promote the national security; to limit the use of materials for nonessential purposes; to prevent inventory hoarding; and to requisition supplies and materials needed for the national defense, particularly excessive and unnecessary inventories.

Second, we must promptly adopt some general measures to compensate for the growth of demand caused by the expansion of military programs in a period of high civilian incomes. I am directing all executive agencies to conduct a detailed review of Government programs, for the purpose of modifying them wherever practicable to lessen the demand upon services, commodities, raw materials, manpower, and facilities which are in competition with those needed for national defense. The Government, as well as the public, must exercise great restraint in the use of those goods and services which are needed for our increased defense efforts.

Nevertheless, the increased appropriations for the Department of Defense, plus the defense-related appropriations which I have recently submitted for power development and atomic energy, and others which will be necessary for such purposes as stockpiling, will mean sharply increased Federal expenditures....

The free world has made it clear, through the United Nations, that lawless aggression will be met with force. This is the significance of Korea—and it is a significance whose importance cannot be over-estimated.

I shall not attempt to predict the course of events. But I am sure that those who have it in their power to unleash or withhold acts of armed aggression must realize that new recourse to aggression in the world today might well strain to the breaking point the fabric of world peace.

The United States can be proud of the part it has played in the United Nations action in this crisis. We can be proud of the unhesitating support of the American people for the resolute actions taken to halt the aggression in Korea and to support the cause of world peace.

The Congress of the United States, by its strong, bi-partisan support of the steps we are taking and by repeated actions in support of international cooperation, has contributed most vitally to the cause of peace. The expressions of support which have been forthcoming from the leaders of both political parties for the actions of our Government and of the United Nations in dealing with the present crisis, have buttressed the firm morale of the entire free world in the face of this challenge.

The American people, together with other free peoples, seek a new era in world affairs. We seek a world where all men may live in peace and freedom, with steadily improving living conditions, under governments of their own free choice.

For ourselves, we seek no territory or domination over others. We are determined to maintain our democratic institutions so that Americans now and in the future can enjoy personal liberty, economic opportunity, and political equality. We are concerned with advancing our prosperity and our well-being as a Nation, but we know that our future is inseparably joined with the future of other free peoples.

We will follow the course we have chosen with courage and with faith, because we carry in our hearts the flame of freedom. We are fighting for liberty and for peace—and with God's blessing we shall succeed.

HARRY S. TRUMAN

Youngstown Sheet & Tube Co. v. Sawyer

Associate Justice Robert Jackson (concurring opinion)

1952

*I*n 1952, Harry Truman issued an executive order directing the Secretary of Commerce to take control of the nation's steel mills. Under this plan, the employees
of the steel mills would become employees of the US government. Truman issued
his order to prevent a slowdown in steel production, a slowdown caused by a
strike announced by United Steelworkers and a slowdown that Truman believed
would undermine the nation's war efforts in Korea. Under the Taft–Hartley Act
of 1947, Truman had the power to order the workers to return to work for eighty
days, but this law was passed over his veto by a Republican Congress and was
perceived as anti-Labor. Truman's seizure of the steel mills tested the outer limits
of the president's domestic powers during wartime. The steel companies took their
case to the federal courts.

The Supreme Court ruled against Truman in a six to three decision. Justice
Robert Jackson's concurring opinion has emerged as the most important of these
opinions. Jackson argues that the Constitution is unclear about the president's
authority, and instead offers a practical procedural framework for justices who
have to decide similar cases. Jackson's framework is still cited by presidents and
judges.

SOURCE: *United States Reports.* Volume 343, *Cases Adjudged in the Supreme Court at October
Term, 1951* (Washington, D.C.: United States Government Printing Office, 1952), 634–55.

Mr. Justice Jackson,[1] concurring ...

That comprehensive and undefined presidential powers hold both practical advantages and grave dangers for the country will impress anyone who
has served as legal adviser to a President in time of transition and public

---

[1] Robert Jackson (1892–1954), was an Associate Justice of the Supreme Court
from 1941 to 1954. He was appointed by Franklin Delano Roosevelt, in whose

anxiety. While an interval of detached reflection may temper teachings of that experience, they probably are a more realistic influence on my views than the conventional materials of judicial decision which may seem unduly to accentuate doctrine and legal fiction. But as we approach the question of presidential power, we half overcome mental hazards by recognizing them. The opinions of judges, no less than executives and publicists, often suffer the infirmity of confusing the issue of a power's validity with the cause it is invoked to promote, of confounding the permanent executive office with its temporary occupant. The tendency is strong to emphasize transient results upon policies—such as wages or stabilization—and lose sight of enduring consequences upon the balanced power structure of our Republic.

A judge, like an executive advisor, may be surprised at the poverty of really useful and unambiguous authority applicable to concrete problems of executive power as they actually present themselves. Just what our forefathers did envision, or would have envisioned had they foreseen modern conditions, must be divined from materials almost as enigmatic as the dreams Joseph was called upon to interpret for Pharaoh.[2] A century and a half of partisan debate and scholarly speculation yields no net results but only supplies more or less apt quotations from respected sources on each side of any question. They largely cancel each other. And court decisions are indecisive because of the judicial practice of dealing with the largest questions in the most narrow way.

The actual art of governing under this Constitution does not and cannot conform to judicial definitions of the power of any of its branches based on isolated clauses or even single Articles torn from context. While the Constitution diffuses power the better to secure liberty, it also contemplates that practice will integrate the dispersed powers into a workable government. It enjoins upon its branches separateness but interdependence, autonomy but reciprocity. Presidential powers are not fixed but fluctuate, depending on their disjunction or conjunction with those of Congress. We may well begin by a somewhat over-simplified grouping of practical situations in which a President may doubt, or others may challenge, his powers, and by distinguishing roughly the legal consequences of this factor of relativity.

1. When the President acts pursuant to an express or implied authorization

---

administration he served as Solicitor General and Attorney General. He is considered by many legal historians to be one of the leading Justices of the twentieth century.
[2] See Genesis 40–41.

of Congress, his authority is at its maximum, for it includes all that he possesses in his own right plus all that Congress can delegate. In these circumstances, and in these only, may he be said (for what it may be worth) to personify the federal sovereignty. If his act is held unconstitutional under these circumstances, it usually means that the Federal Government as an undivided whole lacks power. A seizure executed by the President pursuant to an act of Congress would be supported by the strongest of presumptions and the widest latitude of judicial interpretation, and the burden of persuasion would rest heavily upon any who might attack it.

2. When the President acts in absence of either a congressional grant or denial of authority, he can only rely upon his own independent powers, but there is a zone of twilight in which he and Congress may have concurrent authority, or in which its distribution is uncertain. Therefore, congressional inertia, indifference or quiescence may sometimes, at least as a practical matter, enable, if not invite, measures on independent presidential responsibility. In this area, any actual test of power is likely to depend on the imperatives of events and contemporary imponderables rather than on abstract theories of law.

3. When the President takes measures incompatible with the expressed or implied will of Congress, his power is at its lowest ebb, for then he can rely only upon his own constitutional powers minus any constitutional powers of Congress over the matter. Courts can sustain exclusive presidential control in such a case only by disabling the Congress from acting upon the subject. Presidential claim to a power at once so conclusive and preclusive must be scrutinized with caution, for what is at stake is the equilibrium established by our constitutional system.

Into which of these classifications does this executive seizure of the steel industry fit? It is eliminated from the first by admission, for it is conceded that no congressional authorization exists for this seizure. That takes away also the support or the many precedents and declarations which were made in relation, and must be confined, to this category.

Can it be defended under flexible tests available to the second category? It seems clearly eliminated from that class because Congress has not left seizure of private property an open field but has covered it by three statutory policies inconsistent with this seizure. In cases where the purpose is to supply the needs of the Government itself, two courses are provided: one, seizure of a plant which fails to comply with obligatory orders placed by the Government; another, condemnation of facilities, including temporary use under the eminent domain. The third is applicable where it is the general economy of the country that is to be protected rather than exclusive government interests. None of these were invoked. In choosing a different and inconsistent way of his own, the President cannot claim that it is necessitated or invited by failure of Congress to legislate upon the occasions, grounds and methods for seizure of industrial properties.

This leads the current seizure to be justified only by the severe tests under the third grouping, where it can be supported only by any remainder of executive power after subtraction of such powers as Congress may have over the subject. In short, we can sustain the President only by holding that seizure of such strike-bound industries is within his domain and beyond the control of Congress. Thus, this Court's first review of such seizures occurs under circumstances which leave presidential power most vulnerable to attack and in the least favorable of possible constitutional postures.

I did not suppose, and I am not persuaded, that history leaves it open to question, at least in the courts, that the executive branch, like the Federal Government as a whole, possesses only delegated powers. The purpose of the Constitution was not only to grant power, but to keep it from getting out of hand. However, because the President does not enjoy unmentioned powers does not mean that the mentioned ones should be narrowed by a niggardly construction. Some clauses could be made almost unworkable, as well as immutable, by refusal to indulge some latitude of interpretation for changing times. I have heretofore, and do now, give to the enumerated powers the scope and elasticity afforded by what seem to be reasonable, practical implications instead of the rigidity dictated by a doctrinaire textualism.

The Solicitor General seeks the power of seizure in three clauses of the Executive Article, the first reading, "The executive Power shall be vested in a President of the United States of America." Lest I be thought to exaggerate, I quote the interpretation which his brief puts upon it: "In our view, the clause constitutes a grant of all the executive powers of which the Government is capable." If that be true, it is difficult to see why the forefathers bothered to add several specific items, including some trifling ones. . . .

As to whether there is imperative necessity for such powers, it is relevant to note the gap that exists between the President's paper powers and his real powers. The Constitution does not disclose the measure of the actual controls wielded by the modern presidential office. That instrument must be understood as an Eighteenth-Century sketch of a government hoped for, not as a blueprint for the Government that is. Vast accretions of federal powers, eroded from that reserved by the states, have magnified the scope of presidential activity. Subtle shifts take place in the centers of real power that do not show on the face of the Constitution.

Executive power has the advantage of concentration in a single head in whose choice the whole nation has a part, making him the focus of public hopes and expectations. In drama, magnitude and finality his decisions so far overshadow any others that almost alone he fills the public eye and ear. No other personality in public life can begin to compete with him in access to the public mind through modern methods of communications. By his prestige as head of state and his influence upon the public opinion he exerts a leverage upon those who are supposed to check and balance his power which often cancels their effectiveness.

Moreover, the rise of the party system has made a significant extraconstitutional supplement to real executive power. No appraisal of his necessities is realistic which overlooks that he heads a political system as well as a legal system. Party loyalties and interests, sometimes more binding than law, extend his effective control into branches of government other than his own and he often may win, as a political leader, what he cannot command under the Constitution. Indeed, Woodrow Wilson, commenting on the President as leader both of his party and of his nation, observed, "If he rightly interpret the national thought and boldly insist upon it, he is irresistible. . . . His office is anything he has the sagacity and force to make it."[3] I cannot be brought to believe that this country will suffer if the Court refuses further to aggrandize the presidential office, already so potent and relatively immune from judicial review, at the expense of Congress.

But I have no illusion that any decision of this Court can keep power in the hands of Congress if it is not wise and timely in meeting its problems. A crisis that challenges the President equally, or perhaps primarily, challenges Congress. If not good law, there was worldly wisdom in the maxim attributed to Napoleon that "The tools belong to the man who can use them." We may say that power to legislate for emergencies belongs to the hands of Congress, but only Congress itself can prevent power from slipping through its fingers. . . .

---

[3] Woodrow Wilson makes this comment in a passage from his *Constitutional Government* (Document 21), although this passage is not included in this volume.

"The Presidency in 1960"

Senator John F. Kennedy

January 14, 1960

*I*n this speech at the National Press Club delivered in January 1960, Senator
*John F. Kennedy outlines his view of the proper role of the modern presidency.
But he characterizes this modern presidency by historical examples, citing several presidents as models and rejecting others. Moreover, Kennedy offers a view
of the constitutional order that ranks the presidency as the most important of the
three departments.*

*Kennedy's examples are wide-ranging, but readers should review Documents
17, 22, and 22 to appreciate Kennedy's remarks. Readers might also ask how Madison's (Document 4) or Taft's views (Document 22) might differ.*

SOURCE: Papers of John F. Kennedy, John F. Kennedy Presidential Library and Museum
(Pre-Presidential Papers, Senate Files, Speeches and the Press, Speech Files, 1953–1960:
National Press Club, Washington, D.C., 18 January 1960), JFKSEN-0905-022; https://goo.
gl/qNdLcP.

The modern Presidential campaign covers every issue in and out of the platform from cranberries to Creation. But the public is rarely alerted to a candidate's views about which all the rest turn. That central issue—and the point
of my comments this noon—is not the farm problem or defense of India. It
is the Presidency itself.

Of course, a candidate's views on specific policies are important—but Theodore Roosevelt and William Howard Taft shared policy views with entirely
different results in the White House. Of course, it is important to elect a good
man with good intentions—but Woodrow Wilson and Warren G. Harding were
both good men of good intentions—so were [both] Lincoln and Buchanan[1]—
but there is a Lincoln Room in the White House, and no Buchanan Room.

---

[1] James Buchanan (1791–1868) was fifteenth president of the United States. He is
normally ranked among the least effective presidents because of his failure to deal
with secession.

The history of this nation—its brightest and its bleakest pages—has been written largely in terms of the different views our Presidents have had of the Presidency itself. This history ought to tell us that the American people in 1960 have an imperative right to know what any man bidding for the Presidency thinks about the place he is bidding for—whether he is aware of and willing to use the powerful resources of that office—whether his model will be Taft—or Roosevelt—Wilson—or Harding.

Not since the days of Woodrow Wilson has any candidate spoken on the Presidency itself before the votes have been irrevocably cast. Let us hope that the 1960 campaign, in addition to discussing the familiar issues where our positions too often blur, will also talk about the Presidency itself—as an instrument for dealing with those issues—as an office with varying roles, powers and limitations.

During the past eight years, we have seen one concept of the Presidency at work. Our needs and hopes have been eloquently stated—but the initiative and follow-through have too often been left to others. And too often his own objectives have been lost by the President's failure to override objections from within his own party, in the Congress or even in his Cabinet.

The American people in 1952 and 1956 may well have preferred this detached, limited concept of the Presidency after twenty years of fast-moving, creative Presidential rule. Perhaps historians will regard this as necessarily one of these frequent periods of consolidation, a time to draw breath, to recoup our national energy. To quote the State of the Union Message: "No Congress . . . on surveying the State of the Nation, has met with a more pleasing prospect than that which appears at the present time." Unfortunately this is not Mr. Eisenhower's last message to the Congress, but Calvin Coolidge's. He followed to the White house Mr. Harding, whose "sponsor" declared very frankly that the times did not demand a first-rate President. If true, the times and the man met.

But the question is what do the times—and the people—demand for the next four years in the White House? They demand a vigorous proponent of the national interest—not a passive broker for conflicting private interests. They demand a man capable of acting as the Commander-in-Chief of the Grand Alliance, not merely a bookkeeper who feels that his work is done when the numbers on the balance sheet come out even. They demand that he be the head of a responsible party, not rise so far above politics as to be invisible—a man who will formulate and fight for legislative policies, not be a casual bystander to the legislative process.

Today a restricted concept of the Presidency is not enough. For beneath today's surface gloss of peace and prosperity are increasingly dangerous, unsolved, long-postponed [problems]—problems that will inevitably explode to the surface during the next four years of the next administration—the growing missile gap, the rise of Communist China, the despair of the under-developed nations, the explosive situations in Berlin and in the Formosa Straits, the deterioration of NATO, the lack of an arms control agreement, and all the domestic problems of our farms, cities and schools.

This Administration has not faced up to these and other problems. Much has been said—but I am reminded of the old Chinese proverb: "There is a great deal of noise on the stairs but nobody comes into the room."

The President's State of the Union Message reminded me of the exhortation from King Lear that goes: "I will do such things . . . what they are I know not . . . but they shall be the wonders of the earth."[2]

In the decade that lies ahead—in the challenging, revolutionary sixties—the American Presidency will demand more than ringing manifestoes issued from the rear of the battle. It will demand that the President place himself in the very thick of the fight, that he care passionately about the fates of the people he leads, that he be willing to serve them at the risk of incurring their momentary displeasure.

As Chief Executive

Whatever the political affiliation of our next President, whatever his views may be on all the issues and problems that rush in upon us, he must above all be the Chief Executive in every sense of the word. He must be prepared to exercise the fullest powers of his office—all that are specified and some that are not. He must master complex problems as well as receive one-page memoranda. He must originate action as well as study groups. He must reopen the channels of communication between the world of thought and the seat of power.

Ulysses Grant considered the President "a purely administrative officer." If he administered the government departments efficiently, delegated his functions smoothly, and performed his ceremonies of state with decorum and grace, no more was to be expected of him. But that is not the place the Presidency was meant to have in American life. The President is alone, at the top—the loneliest job there is, as Harry Truman has said.

If there is destructive dissension among the services, he alone can step

---

[2] See *King Lear*, Act II, scene iv, line 280.

in and straighten it out—instead of waiting for unanimity. If administrative agencies are not carrying out their mandate—if a brushfire threatens some part of the globe—he alone can act, without waiting for the Congress. If his farm program fails, he alone deserves the blame, not his Secretary of Agriculture.

"The President is at liberty, both in law and conscience, to be as big a man as he can."[3] So wrote *Professor* Woodrow Wilson. But *President* Woodrow Wilson discovered that to be a big man in the White house inevitably brings cries of dictatorship. So did Lincoln and Jackson and the two Roosevelts. And so may the next occupant of that office, if he is the man the times demand. But how much better it would be, in the turbulent sixties, to have a Roosevelt or a Wilson than to have another James Buchanan, cringing in the White House, afraid to move.

Nor can we afford a Chief Executive who is praised primarily for what he did not do, the disasters he prevented, the bills he vetoed—a President *wishing* his subordinates would produce more missiles or build more schools. We will need instead what the Constitution envisioned: a Chief Executive who is the vital center of action in our whole scheme of government.

As Legislative Leader

This includes the legislative process as well. The President cannot afford—for the sake of the office as well as the nation—to be another Warren G. Harding, described by one backer as a man who "would, when elected, sign whatever bill the Senate sent him—and not send bills for the Senate to pass." Rather he must know when to lead the Congress, when to consult it and when he should act alone.

Having served fourteen years in the Legislative Branch, I would not look with favor upon its domination by the Executive. Under our government of "power as the rival of power," to use Hamilton's phrase, Congress must not surrender its responsibilities. But neither should it dominate. However large its share in the formulation of domestic programs, it is the President alone who must make the major decisions of our foreign policy. That is what the Constitution wisely commands. And even domestically, the President must initiate policies and devise laws to meet the needs of the nation. And he must

---

[3] Woodrow Wilson makes this comment in *Constitutional Government* (Document 21), in a passage not included in this volume. Robert Jackson also quotes this passage in *Youngstown* (Document 31).

be prepared to use all the resources of his office to ensure the enactment of that legislation—even when conflict is the result.

By the end of his term, Theodore Roosevelt was not popular in the Congress—particularly when he criticized an amendment to the Treasury appropriation which forbade the use of Secret Servicemen to investigate Congressmen! And the feeling was mutual—Roosevelt saying: "I do not much admire the Senate, because it is such a helpless body when efficient work is to be done." And Woodrow Wilson was even more bitter after his frustrating quarrels—asked if he might run for the Senate in 1920, he replied: "Outside of the United States, the Senate does not amount to a damn. And inside the United States, the Senate is mostly despised. They haven't had a thought down there in 50 years."

But, however bitter their farewells, the facts of the matter are that Roosevelt and Wilson did get things done—not only through their executive powers, but through the Congress as well. Calvin Coolidge, on the other hand, departed Washington with the cheers of Congress still ringing in his ears. But when his World Court bill was under fire on Capitol hill, he sent no messages, gave no encouragement to the bill's leaders and paid little or no attention to the whole proceeding—and the cause of world justice was set back.

To be sure, Coolidge had held the usual White House breakfasts with Congressional leaders—but they were aimed, as he himself said, at "good fellowship," not a discussion of "public business." And at his press conferences, according to press historians, where he preferred to talk about the local flower show and its exhibits, reporters who finally extracted from him a single sentence—"I'm against that bill"—would rush to file tongue-in-cheek dispatches, proclaiming that: "President Coolidge, in a fighting mood, today served notice on Congress that he intended to combat, with all the resources at his command, the pending bill ...."

But in the coming years, we will need a *real* fighting mood in the White House—a man who will not retreat in the face of pressure from his Congressional leaders—who will not let down those supporting his views on the floor. Divided government over the past six years has only been further confused by this lack of legislative leadership. To restore it next year will help restore purpose to both the Presidency and the Congress.

As Party Leader

The facts of the matter are that legislative leadership is not possible without party leadership, in the most political sense—and Mr. Eisenhower prefers to stay above politics (although a weekly news magazine last fall reported the startling news, and I quote, that "President Eisenhower is emerging as a major political figure"). When asked, early in his first term, how he like the "game of politics", he replied with a frown that his questioner was using a derogatory phase: "Being President", he said, "is a very great experience.... But the word 'politics'... I have no great liking for that."

But no President, it seems to me, can escape politics. He has not only been chosen by the nation—he has been chosen by his party. And if he insists that he is "President of all the people" and should therefore offend none of them—if he blurs the issues and differences between the parties—if he neglects the party machinery and avoids his party's leadership—then he has not only weakened the political party as an instrument of the democratic process—he has dealt a blow to the Democratic process itself.

I prefer the example of Abe Lincoln, who loved politics with the passion of a born practitioner. For example, he waited up all night in 1863 to get the crucial returns on the Ohio Governorship. When the Unionist Candidate was elected, Lincoln wired: "Glory to God in the highest! Ohio has saved the nation!"

As a Moral Leader

But the White House is not only the center of political leadership. It must be the center of moral leadership—a "bully pulpit," as Theodore Roosevelt described it. For only the President represents the national interest. And upon him alone converge all the needs and aspirations of all parts of the country, all departments of the government, all nations of the world.

It is not enough merely to represent prevailing sentiment—to follow McKinley's practice, as described by Joe Cannon, of "keeping his ear so close to the ground he got it full of grasshoppers." We will need in the sixties a President who is willing and able to summon his national constituency to its finest hour—to alert the people to our dangers and our opportunities—demand of them the sacrifices that will be necessary. Despite the increasing evidence of a lost national purpose and a soft national will, F.D.R's words in his First Inaugural still ring true: "In every dark hour of our national life, a leadership of frankness and vigor has met with that understanding and support of the people themselves which is essential to victory."

Roosevelt fulfilled the role of moral leadership. So did Wilson and Lincoln, Truman and Jackson and Teddy Roosevelt. They led the people as well as the government—they fought for great ideals as well as bills. And the time has come to demand that kind of leadership again.

And so, as this vital campaign begins, let us discuss the issues the next President will face—but let us also discuss the powers and tools with which he must face them. For he must endow that office with extraordinary strength and vision. He must act in the image of Abraham Lincoln summoning his war-time Cabinet to a meeting on the Emancipation Proclamation. That Cabinet had been carefully chosen to please and reflect many elements in the country. But "I have gathered you together," Lincoln said, "to hear what I have written down. I do not wish your advice about the main matter—that I have determined for myself."

And later, when he went to sign it after several hours of exhausting handshaking that had left his arm weak, he said to those present: "If my name goes down in history, it will be for this act. My whole soul is in it. If my hand trembles when I sign this Proclamation, all who examine the document hereafter will say: 'He hesitated.'"

But Lincoln's hand did not tremble. He did not hesitate. He did not equivocate. For he was the President of the United States.

It is in this spirit that we must go forth in the coming months and years.

McGovern–Fraser Commission Report

1971

In 1968, the Democratic Party nominated Hubert Humphrey even though he did not win a single primary. Lyndon Johnson chose not to run for reelection after a narrower than expected victory over Minnesota Senator Eugene McCarthy. McCarthy was opposed to the Vietnam War and his surprising showing in New Hampshire, combined with Johnson's exit, brought in New York Senator Robert Kennedy, who also appealed to anti-war voters. After Kennedy's assassination, South Dakota Senator George McGovern entered the race, also campaigning against the war in Vietnam. At the Democratic Convention in Chicago, party leaders nominated Humphrey, sparking protests from the anti-war faction of the party.

Humphrey's victory was the last in the so-called mixed system of presidential nomination history, and its controversy ushered in reforms that would lead to the current system. From 1912 to 1968, many states held primaries, but these were largely non-binding contests to determine whom party members preferred. Candidates would enter select primaries to demonstrate their strength among voters to party leaders, but a victory in a primary was not a guarantee of the state's delegates. Discontent with this system led to the creation of the Democratic Party's Commission on Delegate Selection and Party Structure, also called the McGovern-Fraser Commission after its co-chairs. The Commission laid the foundation for the current nominating process, which requires that delegates be awarded based on results in primaries and caucuses. This move democratized the nomination process, taking it away from the control of party leaders.

SOURCE: *Congressional Record*, 92nd Congress, First Session, Volume 117, Part 25 (Washington D.C.: United States Government Printing Office, 1971), 32909–32910.

Mandate for Reform

The 1968 Democratic National Convention in Chicago exposed profound flaws in the presidential nominating process; but in so doing it gave our Party an excellent opportunity to reform its ways and to prepare for the problems of a new decade.

The delegates to the Convention, concerned by the chaos and divisiveness, shared a belief that the image of an organization impervious to the will of its rank and file threatened the future of the Party. Therefore, they took up the challenge of reform with a mandate requiring state Parties to give "all Democratic voters... a full, meaningful, and timely opportunity to participate" in the selection of delegates, and, thereby, in the decisions of the Convention itself.[1]

In order to ensure that this mandate would be implemented, the Convention directed the Democratic National Committee to establish a Commission to aid state Parties in meeting the Convention requirement.

In February 1969, Senator Fred Harris,[2] Chairman of the Democratic National Committee, appointed us to that body mandated by the Convention—*The Commission on Party Structure and Delegate Selection*. We are Democrats who represent every segment of our Party. We find common cause in our Party's history of fair play and equal opportunity. We believe that the continuing vitality of the Democratic Party depends upon its adherence to this heritage.

Since its inception, our Party has been an open party—open to new ideas and new people. From the days of Jefferson and Jackson, the Democratic Party has been committed to the broad participation of rank-and-file members in all of its major decision-making.

In the American two-party system, no decision is more important to the rank-and-file member than the choice of the party's presidential nominee. For this reason, popular control over the nominating process has been a principle of the Democratic Party since the birth of the National Convention 140 years ago.

This tradition for participation and popular control, however, has not always been adequately expressed. After a lengthy examination of the structures and processes used to select delegates to the National Convention in 1968, this is our basic conclusion: meaningful participation of Democratic voters in the choice of their presidential nominee was often difficult or costly, sometimes completely illusory, and, in not a few instances, impossible.

Among the findings the Commission has made about delegate selection in 1968 are the following:

---

[1] The 1968 Democratic National Convention adopted this resolution, required to be in place by 1972, as a concession to those who objected to the process by which Hubert Humphrey was nominated.

[2] Fred R. Harris (born in 1930), was Senator from Oklahoma from 1964–1973

In at least twenty states, there were no (or inadequate) rules for the selection of Convention delegates, leaving the entire process to the discretion of a handful of party leaders.

More than a third of the Convention delegates had, in effect, already been selected prior to 1968—before either the major issues or the possible presidential candidates were known. By the time President Johnson announced his withdrawal from the nomination contest, the delegate selection process had begun in all but twelve states.

Unrestrained use or application of majority rule was the cause of much strain among Democrats in 1968. The imposition of the unit rule from the first to final stage of the nominating process, the enforcement of binding instructions on delegates, and favorite-son candidacies were all devices used to force Democrats to vote against their stated presidential preferences. Additionally, in primary, convention and committee systems, majorities used their numerical superiority to deny delegate representation to the supporters of minority presidential candidates.

Secret caucuses, closed slate-making, widespread proxy voting—and a host of other procedural irregularities—were all too common at precinct, country, district, and state conventions.

In many states, the costs of participation in the process of delegate selection were clearly discriminatory; in others, they were prohibitive. Filing fees for entering primaries were often excessive, reaching $14,000 in one state, if a complete slate of candidates had been filed. "Hospitality" fees were often imposed on delegates to the convention, reaching $500 in one delegation. Not surprisingly, only 13% of the delegates to the National Convention had incomes of under $10,000 (whereas 70% of the population have annual incomes under that amount).

Representation of blacks, women and youth at the Convention was substantially below the proportion of each group in the population. Blacks comprised about five percent of the voting delegates, well above their numbers in 1964; since blacks make up 11% of the population and supplied at least 20% of the total vote for the Democratic presidential candidate, however, they were still underrepresented at the Convention. Women comprised only 13% of the delegates with only one of 55 delegations having a woman chairman. In a majority of delegations there was no more than a single delegate under 30 years of age, and in two delegations the average age was 54. The delegates to the 1968 Democratic National Convention, in short, were predominantly white, male, middle-aged, and at least middle-class.

As this information emerged, we recognized that two alternative courses of action were available to us. First, we could suggest that the institution of the National Convention had outlived its usefulness and should be discarded. To be sure, at our public hearings several Democrats gave testimony expressing the judgment that the convention system did not deserve to be saved. There was a substantial body of feeling, in fact, that a national primary within each Party would be the most democratic means of selecting presidential candidates.

Second, we could conclude that there was nothing inherently undemocratic about a National Convention: that 1968 was a culmination of years of indifference to the nominating process, rather than a startling aberration from previous years; that purged of its structural and procedural inadequacies, the National Convention was an institution well worth preserving. The Commission has taken this second course. The following are some of our reasons:

In view of the stringent demands made upon a President of the United States, the challenge imposed upon any contender for the nomination in seeking support in a wide variety of delegate selection systems should be maintained.

The face-to-face confrontation of Democrats of every persuasion in a periodic mass meeting is productive of healthy debate, important policy decisions (usually in the form of platform planks), reconciliation of differences, and realistic preparation for the fall presidential campaign.

The Convention provides a mechanism for party self-government through the election and instruction of a National Committee.

While endorsing the institution, the Commission believes that if delegates are not chosen in a democratic manner, the National Convention cannot perform its functions adequately. In order to ensure the democratic selection of delegates, the Commission has adopted Eighteen Guidelines binding on all state Parties.

These Guidelines represent the Commission's interpretation of its mandate to ensure that all Democrats are provided a full, meaningful, and timely opportunity to participate in the delegate selection process. To this end, the requirements and recommendations of the Guidelines are directed toward the elimination of regulation of:

(a) Rules or practices which inhibit access to the delegate selection process—items which compromise full and meaningful participation by inhibiting or preventing a Democrat from exercising his influence in the delegate selection process;

(b) Rules or practices which dilute the influence of a Democrat in the delegate selection process, after he has exercised all available resources to effect such influence.

(c) Rules and practices which have the combined effect of inhibiting access and diluting influence.

The Commission believes that there is no one selection system ideal for all states. Therefore, we did not find it desirable to lay down uniform rules for delegate selection in the Guidelines.

Instead, we have adopted certain minimum standards of fairness, that all states are expected to meet. Once these standards are met, state Parties are free to adopt any procedures they may prefer. The Commission believes that this preservation of local genius is an important element of a healthy National Convention.

These Guidelines are meant to serve no ideology and no geographic segment of our Party. They are designed to stimulate the participation of all Democrats in the nominating process and to re-establish public confidence in the National Convention.

The Commission has proceeded in its work against a backdrop of genuine unhappiness and mistrust of millions of Americans with our political system. We are aware that political parties are not the only way of organizing political life. Political parties will survive only if they respond to the needs and concerns of their members.

In adopting our Guidelines and in presenting this report, we have been guided by the firm belief that the Democratic Party is incapable of closing its eyes and ears to this unhappiness and mistrust. While the Republican response to popular demands for more participation and open processes has been indifference, the Democrats have chosen to face the matter head on.

Our Party's longevity is due in no small way to its capacity to respond to these demands in a positive fashion. We are confident that it will do so again.

War Powers Resolution and Veto

United States Congress and President Richard Nixon

1973

D iscontent with the war in Vietnam led to renewed attention to the question of war powers under the Constitution. In 1973, Congress attempted to clarify the matter and to reclaim a portion of the war power by passing the War Powers Resolution. The War Powers Resolution was meant to force presidents to seek approval for war by requiring them to report activities leading to hostile action and then setting a clock for either congressional approval or the removal of the troops.

Richard Nixon vetoed the Resolution on constitutional and policy grounds. Congress overrode Nixon's veto, and since then, Presidents of both parties have argued that the Resolution is an unconstitutional derogation of their powers as Commander in Chief. Judged by its own objectives, the War Powers Resolution has not succeeded in returning the war power to Congress. Presidents can do a lot in sixty days, and the Congress has proven to be reluctant to use its funding power to stop military action it has not authorized.

SOURCE: "H.J.Res. 542—93rd Congress: War Powers Resolution." www.GovTrack.us. 1973; https://goo.gl/b7NZwM.

War Powers Resolution, November 7, 1973

PURPOSE AND POLICY

SEC. 2. (a) It is the purpose of this joint resolution to fulfill the intent of the framers of the Constitution of the United States and insure that the collective judgment of both the Congress and the President will apply to the introduction of United States Armed Forces into hostilities, or into situations where imminent involvement in hostilities is clearly indicated by the circumstances, and to the continued use of such forces in hostilities or in such situations.

(b) Under Article I, section 8, of the Constitution, it is specifically pro-vided that the Congress shall have the power to make all laws necessary and proper for carrying into execution, not only its own powers, but also all other powers vested by the Constitution in the Government of the United States, or in any department or officer thereof.

(c) The constitutional powers of the President as Commander-in-Chief to introduce United States Armed Forces into hostilities, or into situations where imminent involvement in hostilities is clearly indicated by the circum-stances, are exercised only pursuant to (1) a declaration of war, (2) specific statutory authorization, or (3) a national emergency created by attack upon the United States, its territories or possessions, or its armed forces.

CONSULTATION

SEC. 3. The President in every possible instance shall consult with Congress before introducing United States Armed Forces into hostilities or into sit-uations where imminent involvement in hostilities is clearly indicated by the circumstances, and after every such introduction shall consult regularly with the Congress until United States Armed Forces are no longer engaged in hostilities or have been removed from such situations.

REPORTING

SEC. 4. (a) In the absence of a declaration of war, in any case in which United States Armed Forces are introduced—

(1) into hostilities or into situations where imminent involvement in hostilities is clearly indicated by the circumstances;

(2) into the territory, airspace or waters of a foreign nation, while equipped for combat, except for deployments which relate solely to sup-ply, replacement, repair, or training of such forces; or

(3) in numbers which substantially enlarge United States Armed Forces equipped for combat already located in a foreign nation;

the President shall submit within 48 hours to the Speaker of the House of Representatives and to the President pro tempore of the Senate a report, in writing, setting forth—

(A) the circumstances necessitating the introduction of United States Armed Forces;

(B) the constitutional and legislative authority under which such introduction took place; and

(C) the estimated scope and duration of the hostilities or involvement.

(b) The President shall provide such other information as the Congress may request in the fulfillment of its constitutional responsibilities with respect to committing the Nation to war and to the use of United States Armed Forces abroad.

(c) Whenever United States Armed Forces are introduced into hostilities or into any situation described in subsection (a) of this section, the President shall, so long as such armed forces continue to be engaged in such hostilities or situation, report to the Congress periodically on the status of such hostilities or situation as well as on the scope and duration of such hostilities or situation, but in no event shall he report to the Congress less often than once every six months.

CONGRESSIONAL ACTION

SEC. 5. (a) Each report submitted pursuant to section 4(a) (1) shall be transmitted to the Speaker of the House of Representatives and to the President pro tempore of the Senate on the same calendar day. Each report so transmitted shall be referred to the Committee on Foreign Affairs of the House of Representatives and to the Committee on Foreign Relations of the Senate for appropriate action. If, when the report is transmitted, the Congress has adjourned sine die[1] or has adjourned for any period in excess of three calendar days, the Speaker of the House of Representatives and the President pro tempore of the Senate, if they deem it advisable (or if petitioned by at least 30 percent of the membership of their respective Houses) shall jointly request the President to convene Congress in order that it may consider the report and take appropriate action pursuant to this section.

(b) Within sixty calendar days after a report is submitted or is required to be submitted pursuant to section 4 (a) (1), whichever is earlier, the President shall terminate any use of United States Armed Forces with respect to which such report was submitted (or required to be submitted), unless the Congress

(1) has declared war or has enacted a specific authorization for such use of United States Armed Forces,

(2) has extended by law such sixty-day period, or

(3) is physically unable to meet as a result of an armed attack upon the United States. Such sixty-day period shall be extended for not more

---

[1] indefinitely

than an additional thirty days if the President determines and certifies to the Congress in writing that unavoidable military necessity respecting the safety of United States Armed Forces requires the continued use of such armed forces in the course of bringing about a prompt removal of such forces.

(c) Notwithstanding subsection (b), at any time that United States Armed Forces are engaged in hostilities outside the territory of the United States, its possessions and territories without a declaration of war or specific statutory authorization, such forces shall be removed by the President if the Congress so directs by concurrent resolution.

CONGRESSIONAL PRIORITY PROCEDURES FOR JOINT RESOLUTION OR BILL

SEC. 6. (a) Any joint resolution or bill introduced pursuant to section 5(b) at least thirty calendar days before the expiration of the sixty-day period specified in such section shall be referred to the Committee on Foreign Affairs of the House of Representatives or the Committee on Foreign Relations of the Senate, as the case may be, and such committee shall report one such joint resolution or bill, together with its recommendations, not later than twenty-four calendar days before the expiration of the sixty-day period specified in such section, unless such House shall otherwise determine by the yeas and nays.

(b) Any joint resolution or bill so reported shall become the pending business of the House in question (in the case of the Senate the time for debate shall be equally divided between the proponents and the opponents), and shall be voted on within three calendar days there-after, unless such House shall otherwise determine by yeas and nays.

(c) Such a joint resolution or bill passed by one House shall be referred to the committee of the other House named in subsection (a) and shall be reported out not later than fourteen calendar days before the expiration of the sixty-day period specified in section 5(b). The joint resolution or bill so reported shall become the pending business of the House in question and shall be voted on within three calendar days after it has been reported, unless such House shall otherwise determine by yeas and nays.

(d) In the case of any disagreement between the two Houses of Congress with respect to a joint resolution or bill passed by both Houses, conferees shall be promptly appointed and the committee of conference shall make and file a report with respect to such resolution or bill not later than four calendar days before the expiration of the sixty-day period specified in section 5(b). In the event the conferees are unable to agree within 48 hours, they shall report back to their respective Houses in disagreement. Notwithstanding any rule in either House concerning the printing of conference reports in the Record or concerning any delay in the consideration of such reports, such report shall be acted on by both Houses not later than the expiration of such sixty-day period.

Richard Nixon's Veto, October 24, 1973

To the House of Representatives:

I hereby return without my approval House Joint Resolution 543—the War Powers Resolution. While I am in accord with the desire of the Congress to assert its proper role in the conduct of our foreign affairs, the restrictions which this resolution would impose upon the authority of the President are both unconstitutional and dangerous to the best interests of our Nation.

The proper roles of the Congress and the Executive in the conduct of foreign affairs have been debated since the founding of our country. Only recently, however, has there been a serious challenge to the wisdom of the Founding Fathers in choosing not to draw a precise and detailed line of demarcation between the foreign policy powers of the two branches.

The Founding Fathers understood the impossibility of foreseeing every contingency that might arise in this complex area. They acknowledged the need for flexibility in responding to changing circumstances. They recognized that foreign policy decisions must be made through close cooperation between the two branches and not through rigidly codified procedures.

These principles remain as valid today as they were when our Constitution was written. Yet House Joint Resolution 542 would violate those principles by defining the President's powers in ways which would strictly limit his constitutional authority.

CLEARLY UNCONSTITUTIONAL

House Joint Resolution 542 would attempt to take away, by a mere legislative act, authorities which the President has properly exercised under the Constitution for almost 200 years. One of its provisions would automatically cut off certain authorities after sixty days unless the Congress extended them. Another would allow the Congress to eliminate certain authorities merely by the passage of a concurrent resolution—an action which does not normally have the force of law, since it denies the President his constitutional role in approving legislation.

I believe that both these provisions are unconstitutional. The only way in which the constitutional powers of a branch of the Government can be altered is by amending the Constitution—and any attempt to make such alterations by legislation alone is clearly without force.

UNDERMINING OUR FOREIGN POLICY

While I firmly believe that a veto of House Joint Resolution 542 is warranted solely on constitutional grounds, I am also deeply disturbed by the practical consequences of this resolution. For it would seriously undermine this Nation's ability to act decisively and convincingly in times of international crisis. As a result, the confidence of our allies in our ability to assist them could be diminished and the respect of our adversaries for our deterrent posture could decline. A permanent and substantial element of unpredictability would be injected into the world's assessment of American behavior, further increasing the likelihood of miscalculation and war.

If this resolution had been in operation, America's effective response to a variety of challenges in recent years would have been vastly complicated or even made impossible. We may well have been unable to respond in the way we did during the Berlin crisis of 1961, the Cuban missile crisis of 1962, the Congo rescue operation in 1964, and the Jordanian crisis of 1970—to mention just a few examples. In addition, our recent actions to bring about a peaceful settlement of the hostilities in the Middle East would have been seriously impaired if this resolution had been in force.[2]

While all the specific consequences of House Joint Resolution 542 cannot yet be predicted, it is clear that it would undercut the ability of the United States to act as an effective influence for peace. For example, the provision automatically cutting off certain authorities after sixty days unless they are extended by the Congress could work to prolong or intensify a crisis. Until the Congress suspended the deadline, there would be at least a chance of United States withdrawal and an adversary would be tempted therefore to postpone serious negotiations until the sixty days were up. Only after the

---

[2] Here Nixon gives several types of examples meant to emphasize the structural advantages of the president in dealing with foreign affairs. The Berlin crisis and Cuban missile crisis are examples of a standoff with the Soviet Union. The Congo rescue involved American hostages, and the Jordanian crisis involved a civil war in the Middle East.

Congress acted would there be a strong incentive for an adversary to negotiate. In addition, the very existence of a deadline could lead to an escalation of hostilities in order to achieve certain objectives before the sixty days expired.

The measure would jeopardize our role as a force for peace in other ways as well. It would, for example, strike from the President's hand a wide range of important peace-keeping tools by eliminating his ability to exercise quiet diplomacy backed by subtle shifts in our military deployments. It would also cast into doubt authorities which Presidents have used to undertake certain humanitarian relief missions in conflict areas, to protect fishing boats from seizure, to deal with ship or aircraft hijackings, and to respond to threats of attack. Not the least of the adverse consequences of this resolution would be the prohibition contained in section 8 against fulfilling our obligations under the NATO treaty as ratified by the Senate.[3] Finally, since the bill is somewhat vague as to when the sixty-day rule would apply, it could lead to extreme confusion and dangerous disagreements concerning the prerogatives of the two branches, seriously damaging our ability to respond to international crises.

FAILURE TO REQUIRE POSITIVE CONGRESSIONAL ACTION

I am particularly disturbed by the fact that certain of the President's constitutional powers as Commander in Chief of the Armed Forces would terminate automatically under this resolution sixty days after they were invoked. No overt Congressional action would be required to cut off these powers—they would disappear automatically unless the Congress extended them. In effect, the Congress is here attempting to increase its policymaking role through a provision which requires it to take absolutely no action at all.

In my view, the proper way for the Congress to make known its will on such foreign policy questions is through a positive action, with full debate on the merits of the issue and with each member taking the responsibility of casting a yes or a no vote after considering those merits. The authorization and appropriations process represents one of the ways in which such influence can be exercised. I do not, however, believe that the Congress can responsibly contribute its considered, collective judgement on such grave questions without full debate and without a yes or no vote. Yet this is precisely what the joint resolution would allow. It would give every future Congress the ability to handcuff every future President merely by doing nothing and

---

[3] Section 8 included language stipulating that prior treaties could not be read as giving authority to the president for war.

sitting still. In my view, one cannot become a responsible partner unless one is prepared to take responsible action.

STRENGTHENING COOPERATION BETWEEN THE CONGRESS AND THE EXECUTIVE BRANCHES

The responsible and effective exercise of the war powers requires the fullest cooperation between the Congress and the Executive and the prudent fulfillment by each branch of its constitutional responsibilities. House Joint Resolution 542 includes certain constructive measures which would foster this process by enhancing the flow of information from the executive branch to the Congress. Section 3, for example, calls for consultations with the Congress before and during the involvement of the United States forces in hostilities abroad. This provision is consistent with the desire of this Administration for regularized consultations with the Congress in an even wider range of circumstances.

I believe that full and cooperative participation in foreign policy matters by both the executive and the legislative branches could be enhanced by a careful and dispassionate study of their constitutional roles. Helpful proposals for such a study have already been made in the Congress. I would welcome the establishment of a non-partisan commission on the constitutional roles of the Congress and the President in the conduct of foreign affairs. This commission could make a thorough review of the principal constitutional issues in Executive-Congressional relations, including the war powers, the international agreement powers, and the question of Executive privilege, and then submit its recommendations to the President and the Congress. The members of such a commission could be drawn from both parties—and could represent many perspectives including those of the Congress, the executive branch, the legal profession, and the academic community.

This Administration is dedicated to strengthening cooperation between the Congress and the President in the conduct of foreign affairs and to preserving the constitutional prerogatives of both branches of our Government. I know that the Congress shares that goal. A commission on the constitutional roles of the Congress and the President would provide a useful opportunity for both branches to work together toward that common objective.

Interview on the Huston Plan

Richard Nixon

1977

*I*n 1977, former president Richard Nixon agreed to be interviewed by British journalist David Frost for recordings broadcast on television. The interview tapes went over twenty-eight hours, and were produced as four television episodes, viewed by millions of people worldwide. In this selection, Nixon defends the Huston Plan, which included illegal efforts to monitor anti-war and countercultural activists.

In doing so, Nixon offers a theory of executive prerogative that goes beyond that offered by Jefferson and Lincoln (Documents 10 and 17). Unlike Jefferson, Nixon argues that the Constitution itself allows the president to break the law. Unlike Lincoln, Nixon assumes that this power can be used even when the Union is not at stake.

SOURCE: Sir David Frost, *Frost/Nixon: Behind the Scenes of the Nixon Interviews* (New York: Harper Perennial, 2007), 254–6, 266–71.

FROST: You called a meeting on June the fifth, 1970, about the Huston plan and eventually approved it in July. It got your okay on July the fourteenth, didn't it? And in the Huston plan it stated very clearly, with reference to the entry that was being proposed, it said very clearly, use of this technique is clearly illegal, it amounts to burglary ... however, it is also one of the most fruitful tools and it can produce the type of intelligence which cannot be obtained in any other fashion. Why did you approve a plan that included an element like that ... that was clearly illegal?

NIXON: Because as president of the United States ... ah ... I had to make a decision, as has faced most presidents, in fact, all of them, ah ... in which, ah ... the national security in terms of a threat from abroad, ah ... and the security of the individual ... individual violence at home had to be put first.[1] Ah ... I think Abraham Lincoln has stated it better than anybody else, as he does in so many cases. When he said, "Must a government be too strong for the liberties of its people? Or too weak to defend or maintain its own existence?"[2] That's the dilemma that presidents have had to face, ah ... Roosevelt had to face it in World War II. Truman and Eisenhower in the Cold War period. Kennedy and Johnson as Vietnam began to come in. And Kennedy, of course, even before Vietnam began to escalate, had the beginning of the violent racial disturbances ... ah ... which led to some activities in this category. Now let's first, let's second understand what the surreptitious entry is limited to. You will note that a surreptitious entry in cases involving national security and specifically mentions, ah ... two, ah ... groups of, ah ... internal organizations who had no foreign connections as far as we know. Ah ... the Weathermen and the Black Panthers.[3]

Now, why were we concerned? Let's look at the year, 1970. We had a situation where thirty-five thousand people, ah ... had been victims of assaults. A number of them had been killed. It was a year in which we had, ah ... sixteen airplane hijackings. There had been about eleven the year before. Ah ... but most significantly, it was a year in which there had been thirty thousand bombings and fifty thousand ... I mean, sorry, three thousands bombings, three thousand bombings and fifty thousand bomb threats ... which caused, ah ... the evacuation of buildings. Ah ... it was a year of turbulence in American society. Ah ... '68 ... '69 ... '70 ... the residue of the terrible period of '68. Washing over into '69 and continued through '70 and then, thank God, began to go down in '71 and '72, when calm was restored to the campuses. The cities did cease to be burned, and bombings did go down. And while we've argued about our crime statistics, where at least in '72 there was a decrease

---

[1] Frost indicates the pauses characteristic of Nixon's speaking style by means of ellipses. Hence, in this document excerpt, we indicate omitted text by means of footnotes.

[2] Nixon paraphrases a sentence from Lincoln's Special Message to Congress on July 4, 1861 (Document 16).

[3] The Black Panther Party was founded in Oakland, California in 1966, initially to monitor police treatment of black citizens; the group espoused a Marxist, black nationalist ideology and became involved in violent conflicts with police. The Weathermen, also known as the Weather Underground, formed in 1969 as a militant faction of the campus-based socialist organization Students for a Democratic Society. Seeing themselves as leaders of a revolutionary movement that would put an end to US "imperialism," they engaged in domestic terrorism.

rather than an increase. Alright, now, now in 1970, in the middle of 1970, ah ... we were faced with a situation here, first, where the intelligence agencies weren't working together. Ah ... there were CIA ... was not speaking to the FBI ... the NSA, the National Security Agency, which of course does all of our [cryptographic] work. That's the highly sensitive, technical work, you know, to break codes and that sort of thing ... had very little communication with the other two. Ah ... under the circumstances I felt that we had to coordinate these activities and get a more effective program for dealing with, first, foreign-directed, ah ... espionage, ah ... or foreign-supported, ah ... subversion. And in addition with domestic groups that used and advocated violence....

FROST: So, what in a sense you're saying is that there are certain situations and the Huston plan or that part of it was one of them where the president can decide that it's in the best interest of the nation or something and do something illegal.

NIXON: Well, when the president does it ... that means that it is not illegal.[4]

FROST: By definition—

NIXON: Exactly ... exactly ... if the president ... if, for example, the president approves something ... approves an action, ah ... because of the national security or in this case because of a threat to internal peace and order of, ah ... ah ... significant magnitude ... then ... the president's decision in that instance is one, ah ... that enables those who carry it out to carry it out without violating a law. Otherwise they're in an impossible position.

FROST: So that the black-bag jobs that were authorized in the Huston plan ... if they'd gone ahead, would have been made legal by your action?

NIXON: Well ... I think that we would ... I think that we're splitting hairs here. Burglaries per se are illegal. Let's begin with that proposition. Second, when a burglary, as you have described a black-bag job, ah ... when a burglary, ah ... is one that is undertaken because of an expressed policy decided by the president, ah ... in the interests of the national security ... or in the interests of domestic tranquility ... ah ... when those interests are very, very high ... and when the device will be used in a very limited and cautious manner and responsible manner ... when it is undertaken, then, then that means that what

---

[4] At this point in Frost's published transcript of the interview, he injects an editorial comment, which we omit.

would otherwise be technically illegal does not subject those who engage in such activity to criminal prosecution. That's the way I would put it. Now, that isn't trying to split hairs . . . but I do not mean to suggest the president is above the law . . . what I am suggesting, however, what we have to understand, is, in wartime particularly, war abroad, and virtually revolution in certain concentrated areas at home, that a president does have under the Constitution extraordinary powers and must exert them with . . . as little as possible. . . .

Articles of Impeachment Against President William Jefferson Clinton

House of Representatives

1998

I n December 1998, President Bill Clinton was impeached by the House for per-jury and obstruction of justice. The charges had to with his testimony denying a sexual relationship with White House intern Monica Lewinsky, testimony given during a deposition for a sexual harassment lawsuit filed by another woman, Paula Jones. In the Senate, the perjury charge received forty-five votes, and the obstruction of justice charge received fifty votes, both falling short of the two-thirds threshold for removal.

Note the understanding of impeachment offered by Clinton's defense. In this view, perjury about a private matter is not a sufficient condition for impeachment and removal from office.

SOURCE: 106 Congress, Impeachment of William Jefferson Clinton, 1st Session, Senate, Document 106-2 (Washington, D.C.: United States Government Printing Office, 1999), 15–19.

RESOLUTION

Impeaching William Jefferson Clinton, President of the
United States, for high crimes and misdemeanors.

Resolved, That William Jefferson Clinton, President of the United States, is impeached for high crimes and misdemeanors, and that the following articles of impeachment be exhibited to the United States Senate:

Articles of impeachment exhibited by the House of Representatives of the United States of America in the name of itself and of the people of the United States of America, against William Jefferson Clinton, President of the United States of America, in maintenance and support of its impeachment against him for high crimes and misdemeanors.

ARTICLE I

In his conduct while President of the United States, William Jefferson Clinton, in violation of his constitutional oath faithfully to execute the office of President of the United States and, to the best of his ability, preserve, protect, and defend the Constitution of the United States, and in violation of his constitutional duty to take care that the laws be faithfully executed, has willfully corrupted and manipulated the judicial process of the United States for his personal gain and exoneration, impeding the administration of justice, in that:

On August 17, 1998, William Jefferson Clinton swore to tell the truth, the whole truth, and nothing but the truth before a Federal grand jury of the United States. Contrary to that oath, William Jefferson Clinton willfully provided perjurious, false and misleading testimony to the grand jury concerning one or more of the following: (1) the nature and details of his relationship with a subordinate Government employee; (2) prior perjurious, false and misleading testimony he gave in a Federal civil rights action brought against him; (3) prior false and misleading statements he allowed his attorney to make to a Federal judge in that civil rights action; and (4) his corrupt efforts to influence the testimony of witnesses and to impede the discovery of evidence in that civil rights action.

In doing this, William Jefferson Clinton has undermined the integrity of his office, has brought disrepute on the Presidency, has betrayed his trust as President, and has acted in a manner subversive of the rule of law and justice, to manifest injury of the people of the United States.

Wherefore, William Jefferson Clinton, by such conduct, warrants impeachment and trial, and removal from office and disqualification to hold and enjoy any office of honor, trust, or profit under the United States.

ARTICLE II

In his conduct while President of the United States, William Jefferson Clinton, in violation of his constitutional oath faithfully to execute the office of President of the United States and, to the best of his ability, preserve, protect, and defend the Constitution of the United States, and in violation of his constitutional duty to take care that the laws be faithfully executed, has prevented, obstructed, and impeded the administration of justice, and has to that end engaged personally, and through his subordinates and agents, in a course of conduct or scheme designed to delay, impede, cover up, and conceal the existence of evidence and testimony related to a Federal civil rights action brought against him in a duly instituted judicial proceeding.

The means used to implement this course of conduct or scheme included one or more of the following acts:

(1) On or about December 17, 1997, William Jefferson Clinton corruptly encouraged a witness in a Federal civil rights action brought against him to execute a sworn affidavit in that proceeding that he knew to be perjurious, false and misleading.

(2) On or about December 17, 1997, William Jefferson Clinton corruptly encouraged a witness in a Federal civil rights action brought against him to give perjurious, false and misleading testimony if and when called to testify personally in that proceeding.

(3) On or about December 28, 1997, William Jefferson Clinton corruptly engaged in, encouraged, or supported a scheme to conceal evidence that had been subpoenaed in a Federal civil rights action brought against him.

(4) Beginning on or about December 7, 1997, and continuing through and including January 14, 1998, William Jefferson Clinton intensified and succeeded in an effort to secure job assistance to a witness in a Federal civil rights action brought against him in order to corruptly prevent the truthful testimony of that witness in that proceeding at a time when the truthful testimony of that witness would have been harmful to him.

(5) On January 17, 1998, at his deposition in a Federal civil rights action brought against him, William Jefferson Clinton corruptly allowed his attorney to make false and misleading statements to a Federal judge characterizing an affidavit, in order to prevent questioning deemed relevant by the judge. Such false and misleading statements were subsequently acknowledged by his attorney in a communication to that judge.

(6) On or about January 18 and January 20–21, 1998, William Jefferson Clinton related a false and misleading account of events relevant to a Federal civil rights action brought against him to a potential witness in that proceeding, in order to corruptly influence the testimony of that witness.

(7) On or about January 21, 23, and 26, 1998, William Jefferson Clinton made false and misleading statements to potential witnesses in a Federal grand jury proceeding in order to corruptly influence the testimony of those witnesses. The false and misleading statements made by William Jefferson Clinton were repeated by the witnesses to the grand jury, causing the grand jury to receive false and misleading information.

In all of this, William Jefferson Clinton has undermined the integrity of his office, has brought disrepute on the Presidency, has betrayed his trust as President, and has acted in a manner subversive of the rule of law and justice, to the manifest injury of the people of the United States.

Wherefore, William Jefferson Clinton, by such conduct, warrants impeachment and trial, and removal from office and disqualification to hold and enjoy any office of honor, trust, or profit under the United States.

Passed the House of Representatives December 19, 1998.

Newt Gingrich, *Speaker of the House of Representatives.*

Attest: Robin H. Carle, *Clerk.*

ANSWER OF PRESIDENT WILLIAM JEFFERSON CLINTON TO THE ARTICLES OF IMPEACHMENT

The Honorable William Jefferson Clinton, President of the United States, in response to the summons of the Senate of the United States, answers the accusations made by the House of Representatives of the United States in the two Articles of Impeachment it has exhibited to the Senate as follows:

PREAMBLE
THE CHARGES IN ARTICLES DO NOT CONSTITUTE
HIGH CRIMES OR MISDEMEANORS

The charges in the two Articles of Impeachment do not permit the conviction and removal from office of a duly elected President. The President has acknowledged conduct with Ms. Lewinsky that was improper. But Article II, Section 4 of the Constitution provides that the President shall be removed from office only upon "Impeachment for, and Conviction of, Treason, Bribery or other high Crimes and Misdemeanors." The charges in the articles do not rise to the level of "high Crimes and Misdemeanors" as contemplated by the Founding Fathers, and they do not satisfy the rigorous constitutional standard applied throughout our Nation's history. Accordingly, the Articles of Impeachment should be dismissed.

On the President's Constitutional Authority to Conduct Military Operations Against Terrorists

John C. Yoo

2001

After the terrorist attacks on September 11, 2001, George W. Bush asked the Office of Legal Counsel (OLC) to provide a legal opinion on the scope of his authority to respond to international terrorists who were not state actors. In this opinion, OLC attorney John Yoo puts forth a sweeping interpretation of the text and history of the Constitution that would lodge the war power firmly in the hands of the president. In particular, Yoo argues that Congress's power to declare war should not be read as the power to authorize war. In this, he goes beyond even Alexander Hamilton (Document 4). It also important to note that Congress in 2001 did pass an Authorization for the Use of Military Force for the president to respond to the attacks of September 11th. The scope of this AUMF would be a subject of controversy in the Supreme Court cases leading up to Boumediene v. Bush (Document 38).

Editors note: For the sake of readability, Yoo's in-text references have been relocated to footnotes, and Yoo's extensive footnotes have been deleted. For the sake of consistency, the substance of the references have not been changed. Readers who wish to learn more about the court cases Yoo cites should refer to www.oyez.org.

SOURCE: Nathan A. Forrester, ed., *Opinions of the Legal Counsel of the United States Department of Justice*. Volume 25 (Washington, D.C.: United States Government Printing Office, 2012), 188–96.

MEMORANDUM OPINION FOR THE DEPUTY COUNSEL TO THE PRESIDENT

You have asked for our opinion as to the scope of the President's authority to take military action in response to the terrorist attacks on the United States on September 11, 2001. We conclude that the President has broad constitutional power to use military force. Congress has acknowledged this inherent executive power in both the War Powers Resolution, Pub. L. No. 93-148, 87 Stat. 555 (1973), *codified at* 50 U.S.C. §§ 1541-5148 (the "WPR"), and in the Joint Resolution passed by Congress on September 14, 2001, Pub. L. No. 107-40, 115 Stat. 224 (2001). Further, the President has the constitutional power not only to retaliate against any person, organization, or state suspected of involvement in terrorist attacks on the United States, but also against foreign states suspected of harboring or supporting such organizations. Finally, the President may deploy military force preemptively against terrorist organizations or the states that harbor or support them, whether or not they can be linked to the specific terrorist incidents of September 11.

Our analysis falls into four parts. First, we examine the Constitution's text and structure. We conclude that the Constitution vests the President with the plenary authority, as Commander in Chief and the sole organ of the Nation in its foreign relations, to use military force abroad—especially in response to grave national emergencies created by sudden, unforeseen attacks on the people and territory of the United States. Second, we confirm that conclusion by reviewing the executive and judicial statements and decisions interpreting the Constitution and the President's powers under it. Third, we analyze the relevant practice of the United States, including recent history, that supports the view that the President has the authority to deploy military force in response to emergency conditions such as those created by the September 11, 2001 terrorist attacks. Finally, we discuss congressional enactments that, in our view, acknowledge the President's plenary authority to use force to respond to the terrorist attack on the United States.

I.

The President's constitutional power to defend the United States and the lives of its people must be understood in light of the Founders' express intention to create a federal government "clothed with all the powers requisite to [the] complete execution of its trust." Foremost among the objectives committed to that trust by the Constitution is the security of the Nation. As Hamilton explained in arguing for the Constitution's adoption, because "the circumstances which may affect the public safety are [not] reducible within certain determinate limits, . . . it must be admitted, as a necessary consequence that there can be no limitation of that authority which is to provide for the defense and protection of the community in any matter essential to its efficiency."[1]

"It is 'obvious and unarguable' that no government interest is more compelling than the security of the Nation."[2] Within the limits that the Constitution itself imposes, the scope and distribution of the powers to protect national security must be construed to authorize the most efficacious defense of the Nation and its interests in accordance "with the realistic purposes of the entire instrument."[3] Nor is the authority to protect national security limited to actions necessary for "victories in the field."[4] The authority over national security "carries with it the inherent power to guard against the immediate renewal of the conflict."[5]

We now turn to the more precise question of the President's inherent constitutional powers to use military force.

Constitutional Text. The text, structure and history of the Constitution establish that the Founders entrusted the President with the primary responsibility, and therefore the power, to use military force in situations of emergency. Article II, Section 2 states that the "President shall be Commander in Chief of the Army and Navy of the United States, and of the Militia of the several States, when called into the actual Service of the United States."[6] He is further vested with all of "the executive Power" and the duty to execute the laws.[7] These powers give the President broad constitutional authority to use military force in response to threats to the national security and foreign policy of the United States. During the period leading up to the Constitution's ratification, the power to initiate hostilities and to control the escalation of conflict had been long understood to rest in the hands of the Executive Branch.

By their terms, these provisions vest full control of the military forces of the United States in the President. The power of the President is at its zenith under the Constitution when the President is directing military operations of the armed forces because the power of Commander in Chief

---

[1] *The Federalist* No. 23, at [121–]122 (Alexander Hamilton) (Charles R. Kesler ed., 1999).
[2] *Haig v. Agee*, 453 U.S. 280, 307 (1981) (citation omitted).
[3] *Lichter v. United States*, 334 U.S. 742, 782 (1948).
[4] *Application of Yamashita*, 327 U.S. 1, 12 (1946).
[5] *Id.*
[6] U.S. Const. Art. II, § 2, cl. 1.
[7] U.S. Const. Art. II, § 1.

is assigned solely to the President. It has long been the view of this Office that the Commander-in-Chief Clause is a substantive grant of authority to the President and that the scope of the President's authority to commit the armed forces to combat is very broad.[8] The President's complete discretion in exercising the Commander-in-Chief power has also been recognized by the courts. In the *Prize Cases*, for example, the Court explained that, whether the President "in fulfilling his duties as Commander-in-Chief" had met with a situation justifying treating the southern States as belligerents and instituting a blockade, was a question "to be decided *by him*" and which the Court could not question, but must leave to "the political department of the Government to which this power was entrusted."[9]

Some commentators have read the constitutional text differently. They argue that the vesting of the power to declare war gives Congress the sole authority to decide whether to make war. This view misreads the constitutional text and misunderstands the nature of a declaration of war. Declaring war is not tantamount to making war—indeed, the Constitutional Convention specifically amended the working draft of the Constitution that had given Congress ... the power to "make" war. When it took up this clause on August 17, 1787, the Convention voted to change the clause from "make" to "declare."[10] A supporter of the change argued that it would "leav[e] to the Executive the power to repel sudden attacks."[11] Further, other elements of the Constitution describe "engaging" in war, which demonstrates that the Framers understood making and engaging in war to be broader than simply "declaring" war.[12] A state constitution at the time of the ratification included provisions that prohibited the governor from "making" war without legislative approval.[13] If the

---

[8] *See, e.g.,* Memorandum for Charles W. Colson, Special Counsel to the President, from William H. Rehnquist, Assistant Attorney General, Office of Legal Counsel, *Re: The President and the War Power: South Vietnam and the Cambodian Sanctuaries* (May 22, 1970) (the "Rehnquist Memo").

[9] 67 U.S. (2 Black) 635, 670 (1862) Ditto the above. [Editors Note: Yoo inserts a footnote to briefly explain the situations captured by those memo and the Prize cases.]

[10] 2 *The Records of the Federal Convention of 1787,* at 318–19 (Max Farrand ed., rev. ed. 1966).

[11] *Id.* at 318.

[12] *See* U.S. Const. Art. I, § 10, cl. 3 ("No State shall, without the Consent of Congress ... engage in War, unless actually invaded, or in such imminent Danger as will not admit of delay.")

[13] S.C. Const. Art. XXVI (1776), *reprinted in* 6 *The Federal and State Constitutions* 3247 (Francis Newton Thorpe ed., 1909).

Framers had wanted to require congressional consent before the initiation of military hostilities, they knew how to write such provisions.

Finally, the Framing generation well understood that declarations of war were obsolete. Not all forms of hostilities rose to the level of a declared war: during the seventeenth and eighteenth centuries, Great Britain and colonial America waged numerous conflicts against other states without an official declaration of war. As Alexander Hamilton observed during the ratification, "the ceremony of a formal denunciation of war has of late fallen into disuse."[14] Instead of serving as an authorization to begin hostilities, a declaration of war was only necessary to "perfect" a conflict under international law. A declaration served to fully transform the international legal relationship between two states from one of peace to one of war.[15] Given this context, it is clear that Congress's power to declare war does not constrain the President's independent and plenary constitutional authority over the use of military force.

Constitutional Structure. Our reading of the text is reinforced by analysis of the constitutional structure. First, it is clear that the Constitution secures all federal executive power in the President to ensure a unity in purpose and energy in action. "Decision, activity, secrecy, and dispatch will generally characterize the proceedings of one man in a much more eminent degree than the proceedings of any greater number."[16] The centralization of authority in the President alone is particularly crucial in matters of national defense, war, and foreign policy choices, where a unitary executive can evaluate threats, consider policy choices, and mobilize national resources with a speed and energy that is far superior to any other branch. As Hamilton noted, "Energy in the executive is a leading character in the definition of good government. It is essential to the protection of the community against foreign attacks."[17] This is no less true in war. "Of all the cares or concerns of government, the direction of war most peculiarly demands those qualities which distinguish the exercise of power by a single hand."[18]

Second, the Constitution makes clear that the process used for conducting military hostilities is different from other government decision-making. In the area of domestic legislation, the Constitution creates a detailed, finely wrought procedure in which Congress plays the central role. In foreign

---

[14] *The Federalist* No. 25, at 165 (Alexander Hamilton) (Clinton Rossiter ed., 1961).
[15] *See* William Blackstone, *Commentaries* 249–50.
[16] *The Federalist* No. 70, at 424 (Alexander Hamilton) (Clinton Rossiter ed., 1961).
[17] *Id.* at 423.
[18] *Id.* No. 74, at 447 (Alexander Hamilton).

affairs, however, the Constitution does not establish a mandatory, detailed, Congress-driven procedure for taking action. Rather, the Constitution vests the two branches with different powers—the President as Commander in Chief, Congress with control over funding and declaring war—without requiring that they follow a specific process in making war. By establishing this framework, the Framers expected that the process for warmaking would be far more flexible, and capable of quicker, more decisive action, than the legislative process. Thus, the President may use his Commander-in-Chief and executive power to use military force to protect the Nation, subject to congressional appropriations and control over domestic legislation.

Third, the constitutional structure requires that any ambiguities in the allocation of a power that is executive in nature—such as the power to conduct military hostilities—must be resolved in favor of the Executive Branch. Article II, Section I provides that "[t]he executive power shall be vested in a President of the United States."[19] By contrast, Article I's Vesting Clause gives Congress only the powers "herein granted."[20] This difference in language indicates that Congress's legislative powers are limited to the list enumerated in Article I, Section 8, while the President's powers include inherent executive powers that are unenumerated in the Constitution. To be sure, Article II lists specifically enumerated powers in addition to the Vesting Clause, and some have argued that this limits the "executive power" granted in the Vesting Clause to the powers on that list. But the purpose of the enumeration of executive powers in Article II was not to define and cabin the grant in the Vesting Clause. Rather, the Framers unbundled some plenary powers that had traditionally been regarded as "executive," assigning elements of those powers to Congress in Article I, while expressly reserving other elements as enumerated executive powers in Article II. So, for example, the King's traditional power to declare war was given to Congress under Article I, while the Commander-in-Chief authority was expressly reserved to the President in Article II. Further, the Framers altered other plenary powers of the King such as treaties and appointments, assigning the Senate a share in them in Article II itself. Thus, the enumeration in Article II marks the points at which several traditional executive powers were diluted or reallocated. Any other unenumerated executive powers, however, were conveyed to the President by the Vesting Clause.

There can be little doubt that the decision to deploy military force is

---

[19] U.S. Const. Art. II, § 1.
[20] Id. Art. I, § 1.

228

JOHN C. YOO

"executive" in nature, and was traditionally so regarded. It calls for action and energy in execution, rather than the deliberate formulation of rules to govern the conduct of private individuals. Moreover, the Framers understood it to be an attribute of the executive. "The direction of war implies the direction of the common strength," wrote Alexander Hamilton, "and the power of directing and employing the common strength forms a usual and essential part in the definition of the executive authority."[21] As a result, to the extent that the constitutional text does not explicitly allocate the power to initiate military hostilities to a particular branch, the Vesting Clause provides that it remain among the President's unenumerated powers.

Fourth, depriving the President of the power to decide when to use military force would disrupt the basic constitutional framework of foreign relations. From the very beginnings of the Republic, the vesting of the executive, Commander-in-Chief, and treaty powers in the Executive Branch has been understood to grant the President plenary control over the conduct of foreign relations. As Secretary of State Thomas Jefferson observed during the first Washington Administration, "[t]he constitution has divided the powers of government into three branches [and] has declared that the executive power shall be vested in the president, submitting only special articles of it to a negative by the senate."[22] Due to this structure, Jefferson continued, "[t]he transaction of business with foreign nations is executive altogether; it belongs, then, to the head of that department, except as to such portions of it as are specially submitted to the senate. Exceptions are to be construed strictly."[23] In defending President Washington's authority to issue the Neutrality Proclamation, Alexander Hamilton came to the same interpretation of the President's foreign affairs powers. According to Hamilton, Article II "ought ... to be considered as intended ... to specify and regulate the principal articles implied in the definition of Executive Power; leaving the rest to flow from the general grant of that power."[24] As future Chief Justice John Marshall famously declared a few years later, "The President is the sole organ of the nation in its external relations, and its sole representative with foreign nations.... The [executive] department ... is entrusted with the whole foreign

---

[21] *The Federalist* No. 74, at 447 (Alexander Hamilton) (Clinton Rossiter ed., 1961).
[22] Thomas Jefferson, Opinion on the Powers of the Senate (1790), reprinted in 5 *The Writings of Thomas Jefferson* at 161 (Paul L. Ford ed., 1895).
[23] *Id.*
[24] Alexander Hamilton, Pacificus No. I (1793), reprinted in 15 *The Papers of Alexander Hamilton* at 33, 39 (Harold C. Syrett et al. eds., 1969).

intercourse of the nation. . . ."[25] Given the agreement of Jefferson, Hamilton, and Marshall, it has not been difficult for the Executive Branch consistently to assert the President's plenary authority in foreign affairs ever since.

On the relatively few occasions where it has addressed foreign affairs, the Supreme Court has agreed with the Executive Branch's consistent interpretation. Conducting foreign affairs and protecting the national security are, as the Supreme Court has observed, "'central' Presidential domains."[26] The President's constitutional primacy flows from both his unique position in the constitutional structure, and from the specific grants of authority in Article II that make the President both the Chief Executive of the Nation and the Commander in Chief.[27] Due to the President's constitutionally superior position, the Supreme Court has consistently "recognized 'the generally accepted view that foreign policy [is] the province and responsibility of the Executive.'"[28] "The Founders in their wisdom made [the President] not only the Commander-in-Chief but also the guiding organ in the conduct of our foreign affairs," possessing "vast powers in relation to the outside world."[29] This foreign affairs power is exclusive: it is "the very delicate, plenary and exclusive power of the President as sole organ of the federal government in the field of international relations—a power which does not require as a basis for its exercise an act of Congress."[30]

Conducting military hostilities is a central tool for the exercise of the President's plenary control over the conduct of foreign policy. There can be no doubt that the use of force protects the Nation's security and helps it achieve its foreign policy goals. Construing the Constitution to grant such power to another branch could prevent the President from exercising his core constitutional responsibilities in foreign affairs. Even in the cases in which the Supreme Court has limited executive authority, it is also emphasized that we should not construe legislative prerogatives to prevent the Executive Branch "from accomplishing its constitutionally assigned functions."[31]

---

[25] 10 *Annals of Cong.* 613–14 (1800).

[26] *Harlow v. Fitzgerald*, 457 U.S. 800, 812 n.19 (1982).

[27] See *Nixon v. Fitzgerald*, 457 U.S. 731, 749–50 (1982).

[28] *Dept of Navy v. Egan*, 484 U.S. 518, 529 (1988) (quoting *Haig v. Agge*, 453 U.S. at 293–94).

[29] *Ludecke v. Watkins*, 335 U.S. 160, 173 (1948).

[30] *United States v. Curtis-Wright Export Corp.*, 299 U.S. 304, 320 (1936).

[31] *Nixon v. Adm'r of Gen. Servs.*, 433 U.S. 425, 443 (1977).

DOCUMENT 38

Boumediene v. Bush

Associate Justice Anthony Kennedy (majority) and
Associate Justice Antonin Scalia (minority)

2008

Lakhdar Boumediene, a Bosnian citizen born in Algeria, was arrested by Bosnian police for a plot to bomb the American embassy in Sarajevo and was being held by the United States at Guantanamo Bay. He was among a number of detainees who challenged their detention by filing for a writ of habeas corpus.

His Supreme Court case is best understood as part of larger negotiation between the Court and the political branches. In Rasul v. Bush (2004), a Supreme Court majority ruled that the detainees at Guantanamo could challenge their detentions in federal court and that they were entitled to some judicial process similar to the tribunals laid out by Congress in its Uniform Code of Military Justice. This was a defeat for George W. Bush who had argued that his detention of suspected terrorists was within Robert Jackson's first category (Document 31): Congress had authorized the action with its broad Authorization of the Use of Military Force against the terrorists of September 11th, and the president had authority under Article II of the Constitution. In response to Rasul, Congress passed the Detainee Treatment Act of 2005 (DTA), which seemed to limit judicial authority over the detainees in Guantanamo.

In Hamdan vs. Rumsfeld (2006), however, a divided Court read the DTA narrowly to mean that it did not apply to cases that were already pending. So Congress passed a new law, the Military Commissions Act of 2006, which explicitly stated that the detainees would not be eligible for habeas petitions.

In the opinion below, Justice Kennedy writes for a Court majority holding that the Congress in fact could not pass such a law. Justice Scalia's dissenting opinion is also included.

SOURCE: *United States Reports.* Volume 553, *Cases Adjudged in the Supreme Court at October Term, 2007* (Washington, D.C.: United States Government Printing Office, 1952), 732–33, 793–95, 796–98, 826–31.

Justice Kennedy[1] delivered the opinion of the Court.

Petitioners are aliens designated as enemy combatants and detained at the United States Naval Station at Guantanamo Bay, Cuba....

Petitioners present a question not resolved by our earlier cases relating to the detention of aliens at Guantanamo: whether they have the constitutional privilege of habeas corpus, a privilege not to be withdrawn except in conformance with the Suspension Clause, Art I, sec. 9, cl. 2. We hold these petitioners do have the habeas corpus privilege. Congress has enacted a statute, the Detainee Treatment Act of 2005 (DTA), 119 Stat. 2739, that provides certain procedures for review of the detainees' status. We hold that those procedures are not an adequate and effective substitute for habeas corpus. Therefore sec. 7 of the Military Commissions Act of 2006 (MCA), 28 U.S.C. sec. 2241(e), operates as an unconstitutional suspension of the writ. We do not address whether the President has the authority to detain these petitioners nor do we hold that the writ must issue. These and other questions regarding the legality of the detention are to be resolved in the first instance by the District Court....

In light of our conclusion that there is no jurisdictional bar to the District Court's entertaining petitioners' claims the question remains whether there are prudential barriers to habeas corpus review under these circumstances.

The Government argues petitioners must seek review of their CSRT [Combatant Status Review Tribunals] determinations in the Court of Appeals before they can proceed with their habeas corpus actions in the District Court. As noted earlier, in other contexts and for prudential reasons this Court has required exhaustion of alternative remedies before a prisoner can seek federal habeas relief. Most of these cases were brought by prisoners in state custody, e.g., Ex parte Royall, 117 U.S. 241, and thus involved federalism concerns that are not relevant here. But we have extended this rule to require defendants in courts-martial to exhaust their military appeals before proceeding with a federal habeas corpus action. See Schlesinger, 420 U.S. at 758.

The real risks, the real threats, of terrorist attacks are constant and not likely soon to abate. The ways to disrupt our life and laws are so many and unforeseen that the Court should not attempt even some general catalogue of crises that might occur. Certain principles are apparent, however. Practical

---

[1] Anthony Kennedy (1936–) was an Associate Justice of the Supreme Court from 1987 to 2018.

considerations and exigent circumstances inform the definition and reach of the law's writs, including habeas corpus. The cases and our tradition reflect this precept.

In cases involving foreign citizens detained abroad by the Executive, it likely would be both an impractical and unprecedented extension of judicial power to assume that habeas corpus would be available at the moment the prisoner is taken into custody. If and when habeas corpus jurisdiction applies, as it does in these cases, then proper deference can be accorded to reasonable procedures for screening and initial detention under lawful and proper conditions of confinement and treatment for a reasonable period of time. Domestic exigencies, furthermore, might also impose such onerous burdens on the Government that here, too, the Judicial Branch would be required to devise sensible rules for staying habeas corpus proceedings until the Government can comply with its requirements in a responsible way. Cf. *Ex parte Milligan*, 4 Wall., at 127 ("If, in foreign invasion or civil war, the courts are actually closed, and it is impossible to administer criminal justice according to law, *then*, on the theatre of active military operations, where war really prevails, there is a necessity to furnish a substitute for civil authority, thus overthrown, to preserve the safety of the army and society; and as no power is left but the military, it is allowed to govern by martial rule until the laws can have their free course").[2] Here, as is true with detainees apprehended abroad, a relevant consideration in determining the courts' role is whether there are suitable alternative processes in place to protect against the arbitrary exercise of governmental power.

The cases before us, however, do not involve detainees who have been held for a short period of time while awaiting their CSRT determinations. Were that the case, or were it probable that the Court of Appeals could complete a prompt review of their applications, the cause for requiring temporary abstention or exhaustion of alternative remedies would be much stronger. These qualifications no longer pertain here. In some of these cases six years have elapsed without the judicial oversight that habeas corpus or an adequate substitute demands. And there has been no showing that the Executive faces such onerous burdens that it cannot respond to habeas corpus actions. To require these detainees to complete DTA review before proceeding with their habeas corpus actions would be to require additional months, if not years, of delay. The first DTA review applications were filed over two years

---

[2] For an excerpt from this case, see Document 18.

ago, but no decision on the merits have been issued. While some delay in fashioning new procedures is unavoidable, the costs of delay can no longer be borne by those who are held in custody. The detainees in these cases are entitled to a prompt habeas corpus hearing.

Our decision today holds only that petitioners before us are entitled to seek the writ; that the DTA review procedures are an inadequate substitute for habeas corpus; and that petitioners in these cases need not exhaust the review procedures in the Court of Appeals before proceeding with their habeas actions in the District Court. The only law we identify as unconstitutional is MCA sec.7, 28 U.S.C. sec. 2241(e). Accordingly, both the DTA and the CSRT process remain intact. Our holding with regard to exhaustion should not be read to imply that habeas corpus should intervene the moment an enemy combatant steps foot in a territory where the writ runs. The Executive is entitled to a reasonable period of time to determine a detainee's status before a court entertains that detainees habeas corpus petition. The CRST process is the mechanism Congress and the President set up to deal with these issues. Except in cases of undue delay, federal courts should refrain from entertaining an enemy combatant's habeas corpus petition at least until after the Department, acting via the CSRT, has had a chance to review his status.... In considering both the procedural and substantive standards used to impose detention to prevent acts of terrorism, proper deference must be accorded to the political branches. See *United States v. Curtiss-Wright Export Corp.,* 229 U.S 304, 320 (1936).[3] Unlike the President and some designated members of Congress, neither the Members of this Court not most federal judges begin the day with briefings that may describe new and serious threats to our Nation and its people. The law must accord the Executive substantial authority to apprehend and detain those who pose a real danger to our security.

Officials charged with daily operational responsibility for our security may consider a judicial discourse on the history of the Habeas Corpus Act of 1679 and like matters to be far removed from the Nation's present, urgent concerns. Established legal doctrine, however, must be consulted for its teaching. Remote it time it may be; irrelevant to the present it is not. Security depends upon a sophisticated intelligence apparatus and the ability of our Armed Forces to act and to interdict. There are further considerations, however. Security subsists, too, in fidelity to freedom's first principles. Chief among

---

[3] See Document 25.

these are freedom from arbitrary and unlawful restraint and the personal liberty that is secured by adherence to the separation of powers. It is from these principles that the judicial authority to consider petitions for habeas corpus relief derives.

Our opinion does not undermine the Executive's powers as Commander in Chief. On the contrary, the exercise of those powers is vindicated, not eroded, when confirmed by the Judicial Branch. Within the Constitution's separation-of-powers structure, few exercises of judicial power are as legitimate or necessary as the responsibility to hear challenges to the authority of the Executive to imprison a person. Some of these petitioners have been in custody for six years with no definitive judicial determination as to the legality of their detention. Their access to the writ is a necessity to determine the lawfulness of their status, even if, in the end, they do not obtain the relief they seek.

Because our Nation's past military conflicts have been of limited duration, it has been possible to leave the outer boundaries of war powers undefined. If, as some fear, terrorism continues to pose dangerous threats to us for years to come, the Court might not have this luxury. This result is not inevitable, however. The political branches, consistent with their independent obligations to interpret and uphold the Constitution, can engage in a genuine debate about how best to preserve constitutional values while protecting the nation from terrorism. Cf. *Hamdan*, 548 U.S., at 636 (Breyer, J., concurring) ("[J]udicial insistence upon that consultation does not weaken our Nation's ability to deal with danger. To the contrary, that insistence strengthens the Nation's ability to determine—through democratic means—how best to do so").

It bears repeating that our opinion does not address the content of the law that governs petitioners' detention. That is a matter yet to be determined. We hold that petitioners may invoke the fundamental procedural protections of habeas corpus. The laws and Constitution are designed to survive, and remain in force, in extraordinary times. Liberty and security can be reconciled; and in our system they are reconciled within the framework of the law. The Framers decided that habeas corpus, a right of first importance, must be a part of the framework, a part of that law.

The determination by the Court of Appeals that the Suspension Clause and its protections are inapplicable to petitioners was in error. The judgement of the Court of Appeals is reversed. The cases are remanded to the Court of Appeals with instructions that it remand the cases to the District Court for proceedings consistent with this opinion.

It is so ordered.

Justice Scalia,[4] with whom the Chief Justice,[5] Justice Thomas,[6] and Justice Alito[7] join, dissenting.

Today, for the first time in our Nation's history, the Court confers the constitutional right to habeas corpus on alien enemies detained abroad by our military forces in the course of an ongoing war. The CHIEF JUSTICE's dissent, which I join, shows that the procedures prescribed by Congress in the Detainee Treatment Act provide the essential protections that habeas corpus guarantees; there has thus been no suspension of the writ, and no basis exists for judicial intervention beyond what the Act allows. My problem with today's opinion is more fundamental still: The writ of habeas corpus does not, and never has, run in favor of aliens abroad; the Suspension Clause thus has no application, and the Court's intervention in this military matter is entirely ultra vires.[8]

I shall devote most of what will be a lengthy opinion to the legal errors contained in the opinion of the Court. Contrary to my usual practice, however, I think it appropriate to begin with a description of the disastrous consequences of what the Court has done today.

I

America is at war with radical Islamists. The enemy began by killing Americans and American allies abroad: 241 at the Marine barracks in Lebanon, 19 at the Khobar Towers in Dhahran, 224 at our embassies in Dar es Salaam and Nairobi, and 17 on the USS Cole in Yemen. See National Commission on Terrorist Attacks Upon the United States, the 9/11 Commission Report, pp. 60–61,70,190 (2004). On September 11, 2001, the enemy brought the battle to American soil, killing 2,749 at the Twin Towers in New York City, 184 at the Pentagon in Washington, D.C., and 40 in Pennsylvania. See id., at 552, n. 188. It has threatened further attacks against our homeland; one need only walk about buttressed and barricaded Washington, or board a plane anywhere in the country, to know that the threat is a serious one. Our Armed Forces are

---

[4] Antonin Scalia (1936–2016) was an Associate Justice of the Supreme Court from 1986 to 2016.

[5] John G. Roberts (1955–) has been Chief Justice since 2005.

[6] Clarence Thomas (1948–) has been an Associate Justice since 1991.

[7] Samuel Alito (1950–) has been an Associate Justice since 2006.

[8] beyond the scope of its legal authority

now in the field against the enemy, in Afghanistan and Iraq. Last week, 13 of our countrymen in arms were killed.

The game of bait-and-switch that today's opinion plays upon the Nation's Commander in Chief will make the war harder on us. It will almost certainly cause more Americans to be killed. That consequence would be tolerable if necessary to preserve a time-honored legal principle vital to our constitutional Republic. But it is this Court's blatant *abandonment* of such a principle that produces the decision today. The President relied on our settled precedent in *Johnson v. Eisentrager,* 339 U.S. 763 (1950), when he established the prison at Guantanamo Bay for enemy aliens. Citing that case, the President's Office of Legal Counsel advised him "that the great weight of legal authority indicates that a federal district court could not properly exercise habeas jurisdiction over an alien detained at [Guantanamo Bay]." Memorandum from Patrick F. Philbin and John C. Yoo, Deputy Assistant Attorneys General, Office of Legal Counsel, to William J. Haynes II, General Counsel, Dept. of Defense, p. 1 (Dec 28, 2001). Had the law been otherwise, the military surely would not have transported prisoners there, but would have kept them in Afghanistan, transferred them to another of our foreign military bases, or turned them over to allies for detention. Those other facilities might well have been worse for the detainees themselves.

In the long term, then, the Court's decision today accomplishes little, except perhaps to reduce the well-being of enemy combatants that the Court ostensibly seeks to protect. In the short term, however, the decision is devastating. At least 30 of those prisoners hitherto released from Guantanamo Bay have returned to the battlefield. See S. Rep. No. 110-90, pt. 7, p. 13 (2007) (minority views of Sens. Kyl, Sessions, Graham, Cornyn, and Coburn) (hereinafter Minority Report). Some have been captured or killed. See *ibid,;* see also Mintz, Released Detainees Rejoining the Fight, Washington Post, Oct. 22, 2004, pp. A1, A12. But others have succeeded in carrying on their atrocities against innocent civilians. In one case, a detainee released from Guantanamo Bay masterminded the kidnaping of two Chinese dam workers, one of whom was later shot to death when used as a human shield against Pakistani commandos. See Khan & Lancaster, Pakistanis Rescue Hostage; 2nd Dies, Washington Post, Oct. 14, 2004, p. A18. Another former detainee promptly resumed his post as a senior Taliban commander and murdered a United Nations engineer and three Afghan soldiers. Mintz, *supra.* Still another murdered an Afghan judge. See Minority Report 13. It was reported only last month that a released detainee carried out a suicide bombing against Iraqi soldiers in Mosul, Iraq. See White, Ex-Guantanamo Detainee Joined Iraq Suicide Attack, Washington Post, May 8, 2008, p. A18.

These, mind you, were detainees whom *the military* had concluded were not enemy combatants. Their return to the kill illustrates the incredible difficulty in assessing who is and who is not an enemy combatant in a foreign theater of operations where the environment does not lend itself to rigorous evidence collection. Astoundingly, the Court today raises the bar, requiring military officials to appear before civilian courts and defend their decisions under procedural and evidentiary rules that go beyond what Congress has specified. As the CHIEF JUSTICE's dissent makes clear, we have no idea what those procedural and evidentiary rules are, but they will be determined by civil courts and (in the Court's contemplation at least) will be more detainee-friendly than those now applied, since otherwise there would be no reason to hold the congressionally prescribed procedures unconstitutional. If they impose a higher standard of proof (from foreign battlefields) than the current procedures require, the number of the enemy returned to combat will obviously increase.

But when the military has evidence that it can bring forward, it is often foolhardy to release that evidence to the attorneys representing our enemies. And one escalation of procedures that the Court is clear about is affording the detainees increased access to witnesses (perhaps troops serving in Afghanistan?) and to classified information. See *ante,* at 783–784. During the 1995 prosecution of Omar Abdel Rahman, federal prosecutors gave the names of 200 unindicted co-conspirators to the "Blind Sheik's" defense lawyers; that information was in the hands of Osama Bin Laden within two weeks. See Minority Report 14–15. In another case, trial testimony revealed to the enemy that the United States had been monitoring their cellular network, whereupon they promptly stopped using it, enabling more of them to evade capture and continue their atrocities. See *id.,* at 15.

And today it is not just the military that the Court elbows aside. A mere two Terms ago in *Hamdan v. Rumsfeld,* 548 U.S. 557 (2006), when the Court held (quite amazingly) that the Detainee Treatment Act of 2005 had not stripped habeas jurisdiction over Guantanamo petitioners' claims, four Members of today's five-Justice majority joined an opinion saying the following:

> Nothing prevents the President from returning to Congress to seek the authority [for trial by military commission] he believes necessary.

Where, as here, no emergency prevents consultation with Congress,
judicial insistence upon that consultation does not weaken our
Nation's ability to deal with danger. To the contrary, that insistence
strengthens the Nation's ability to determine—through democratic
means—how best to do so. The Constitution places its faith in those
democratic means. *Id.* at 636

(Breyer, J., concurring).

Turns out, they were just kidding. For in response, Congress, at the President's request, quickly enacted the Military Commissions Act, emphatically reasserting that it did not want these prisoners filing habeas petitions. It is therefore clear that Congress and the Executive—*both* political branches— have determined that limiting the role of civilian courts in adjudicating whether prisoners captured abroad are properly detained is important to success in the war that some 190,000 of our men and women are now fighting. As the Solicitor General argued, "the Military Commissions Act and the Detainee Treatment Act ... represent an effort by the political branches to strike an appropriate balance between the need to preserve liberty and the need to accommodate the weighty and sensitive governmental interests in ensuring that those who have in fact fought with the enemy during a war do not return to battle against the United States." Brief for Federal Respondents 10–11 (internal quotation marks omitted).

But it does not matter. The Court today decrees that no good reason to accept the judgement of the other two branches is "apparent." *Ante*, at 769. "The Government," it declares, "presents no credible arguments that the military mission at Guantanamo would be compromised if habeas corpus courts had jurisdiction to hear the detainees' claims." *Ibid.* What competence does the Court have to second guess the judgement of Congress and the President on such a point? None whatever. But the Court blunders in nonetheless. Henceforth, as today's opinion makes unnervingly clear, how to handle the enemy prisoners in this war will ultimately lie with the branch that knows least about the national security concerns that the subject entails....

Special Address to the Nation on Syria

President Barack Obama

September 10, 2013

A lthough no Congress has declared war since World War II, the United States
since then has been in several wars and multiple military conflicts. Some of
these wars were explicitly authorized by Congress, thus satisfying, perhaps, the
spirit if not the letter of the Constitution. For example, in 2002, Congress passed
an Authorization for the Use of Military Force in 2002, authorizing George W.
Bush to invade Iraq. The invasion of Afghanistan was similarly authorized by the
2001 AUMF passed by Congress after September 11th.

Barack Obama came to office criticizing George Bush's wars and his use of
executive power. Several legal analysts predicted that Obama would return the
war power to the control of Congress. But, as president, Obama defended military
action as beyond the scope of the War Powers Resolution and used a broad reading
of the 2002 AUMF to fight ISIS (the Islamic State of Iraq and Syria, a militant
terrorist Sunni organization claiming political and theological authority over the
world's Muslims). In the selection below, Obama reports to the nation on the civil
war in Syria. Notice his careful wording with respect to Congress and his authority
under the Constitution to use force against the Syrian regime.

SOURCE: Barack Obama, "Address to the Nation on Syria," September 10, 2013 , White House
Briefing Room, https://goo.gl/nWjT6t.

My fellow Americans, tonight I want to talk to you about Syria—why it matters, and where we go from here.

Over the past two years, what began as a series of peaceful protests against
the repressive regime of Bashar al-Assad[1] has turned into a brutal civil war.
Over 100,000 people have been killed. Millions have fled the country. In
that time, America has worked with allies to provide humanitarian support,
to help the moderate opposition, and to shape a political settlement. But I

---

[1] Bashar al-Assad (1965–) has been President of Syria since 2000.

have resisted calls for military action, because we cannot resolve someone else's civil war through force, particularly after a decade of war in Iraq and Afghanistan.

The situation profoundly changed, though, on August 21st, when Assad's government gassed to death over a thousand people, including hundreds of children. The images from this massacre are sickening: Men, women, children lying in rows, killed by poison gas. Others foaming at the mouth, gasping for breath. A father clutching his dead children, imploring them to get up and walk. On that terrible night, the world saw in gruesome detail the terrible nature of chemical weapons, and why the overwhelming majority of humanity has declared them off-limits—a crime against humanity, and a violation of the laws of war.

This was not always the case. In World War I, American GIs were among the many thousands killed by deadly gas in the trenches of Europe. In World War II, the Nazis used gas to inflict the horror of the Holocaust. Because these weapons can kill on a mass scale, with no distinction between soldier and infant, the civilized world has spent a century working to ban them. And in 1997, the United States Senate overwhelmingly approved an international agreement prohibiting the use of chemical weapons, now joined by 189 governments that represent 98 percent of humanity.[2]

On August 21st, these basic rules were violated, along with our sense of common humanity. No one disputes that chemical weapons were used in Syria. The world saw thousands of videos, cell phone pictures, and social media accounts from the attack, and humanitarian organizations told stories of hospitals packed with people who had symptoms of poison gas.

Moreover, we know the Assad regime was responsible. In the days leading up to August 21st, we know that Assad's chemical weapons personnel prepared for an attack near an area where they mix sarin gas. They distributed gasmasks to their troops. Then they fired rockets from a regime-controlled area into eleven neighborhoods that the regime has been trying to wipe clear of opposition forces. Shortly after those rockets landed, the gas spread, and hospitals filled with the dying and the wounded. We know senior figures in Assad's military machine reviewed the results of the attack, and the regime increased their shelling of the same neighborhoods in the days that followed. We've also studied samples of blood and hair from people at the site that tested positive for sarin.

---

[2] Obama is referring to the Chemical Weapons Convention (CWC), which went into effect in 1997.

When dictators commit atrocities, they depend upon the world to look the other way until those horrifying pictures fade from memory. But these things happened. The facts cannot be denied. The question now is what the United States of America, and the international community, is prepared to do about it. Because what happened to those people—to those children—is not only a violation of international law, it's also a danger to our security.

Let me explain why. If we fail to act, the Assad regime will see no reason to stop using chemical weapons. As the ban against these weapons erodes, other tyrants will have no reason to think twice about acquiring poison gases, and using them. Over time, our troops would again face the prospect of chemical warfare on the battlefield. And it could be easier for terrorist organizations to obtain these weapons, and to use them to attack civilians.

If fighting spills beyond Syria's borders, these weapons could threaten allies like Turkey, Jordan, and Israel. And a failure to stand against the use of chemical weapons would weaken prohibitions against other weapons of mass destruction, and embolden Assad's ally, Iran—which must decide whether to ignore international law by building a nuclear weapon, or to take a more peaceful path.

This is not a world we should accept. This is what's at stake. And that is why, after careful deliberation, I determined that it is in the national security interests of the United States to respond to the Assad regime's use of chemical weapons through a targeted military strike. The purpose of this strike would be to deter Assad from using chemical weapons, to degrade his regime's ability to use them, and to make clear to the world that we will not tolerate their use.

That's my judgment as Commander-in-Chief. But I'm also the President of the world's oldest constitutional democracy. So even though I possess the authority to order military strikes, I believed it was right, in the absence of a direct or imminent threat to our security, to take this debate to Congress. I believe our democracy is stronger when the President acts with the support of Congress. And I believe that America acts more effectively abroad when we stand together.

This is especially true after a decade that put more and more war-making power in the hands of the President, and more and more burdens on the shoulders of our troops, while sidelining the people's representatives from the critical decisions about when we use force.

Now, I know that after the terrible toll of Iraq and Afghanistan, the idea of any military action, no matter how limited, is not going to be popular. After all, I've spent four and a half years working to end wars, not to start them.

Our troops are out of Iraq. Our troops are coming home from Afghanistan. And I know Americans want all of us in Washington—especially me—to concentrate on the task of building our nation here at home: putting people back to work, educating our kids, growing our middle class.

It's no wonder, then, that you're asking hard questions. So, let me answer some of the most important questions that I've heard from members of Congress, and that I've read in letters that you've sent to me.

First, many of you have asked, won't this put us on a slippery slope to another war? One man wrote to me that we are "still recovering from our involvement in Iraq." A veteran put it more bluntly: "This nation is sick and tired of war."

My answer is simple: I will not put American boots on the ground in Syria. I will not pursue an open-ended action like Iraq or Afghanistan. I will not pursue a prolonged air campaign like Libya or Kosovo. This would be a targeted strike to achieve a clear objective: deterring the use of chemical weapons, and degrading Assad's capabilities.

Others have asked whether it's worth acting if we don't take out Assad. As some members of Congress have said, there's no point in simply doing a "pinprick" strike in Syria.

Let me make something clear: The United States military doesn't do pinpricks. Even a limited strike will send a message to Assad that no other nation can deliver. I don't think we should remove another dictator with force—we learned from Iraq that doing so makes us responsible for all that comes next. But a targeted strike can make Assad, or any other dictator, think twice before using chemical weapons.

Other questions involve the dangers of retaliation. We don't dismiss any threats, but the Assad regime does not have the ability to seriously threaten our military. Any other retaliation they might seek is in line with threats that we face every day. Neither Assad nor his allies have any interest in escalation that would lead to his demise. And our ally, Israel, can defend itself with overwhelming force, as well as the unshakeable support of the United States of America.

Many of you have asked a broader question: Why should we get involved at all in a place that's so complicated, and where—as one person wrote to me—"those who come after Assad may be enemies of human rights?"

It's true that some of Assad's opponents are extremists. But al Qaeda[3]

---

[3] An international terrorist network founded by Osama bin Laden in the late 1980s, Al-Qaeda seeks to rid Islamic countries of Western, particularly US, influence and

will only draw strength in a more chaotic Syria if people there see the world doing nothing to prevent innocent civilians from being gassed to death. The majority of the Syrian people—and the Syrian opposition we work with—just want to live in peace, with dignity and freedom. And the day after any military action, we would redouble our efforts to achieve a political solution that strengthens those who reject the forces of tyranny and extremism.

Finally, many of you have asked: Why not leave this to other countries, or seek solutions short of force? As several people wrote to me, "We should not be the world's policeman."

I agree, and I have a deeply held preference for peaceful solutions. Over the last two years, my administration has tried diplomacy and sanctions, warning and negotiations—but chemical weapons were still used by the Assad regime.

However, over the last few days, we've seen some encouraging signs. In part because of the credible threat of U.S. military action, as well as constructive talks that I had with President Putin, the Russian government has indicated a willingness to join with the international community in pushing Assad to give up his chemical weapons.[4] The Assad regime has now admitted that it has these weapons, and even said they'd join the Chemical Weapons Convention, which prohibits their use.

It's too early to tell whether this offer will succeed, and any agreement must verify that the Assad regime keeps its commitments. But this initiative has the potential to remove the threat of chemical weapons without the use of force, particularly because Russia is one of Assad's strongest allies.

I have, therefore, asked the leaders of Congress to postpone a vote to authorize the use of force while we pursue this diplomatic path. I'm sending Secretary of State John Kerry to meet his Russian counterpart on Thursday, and I will continue my own discussions with President Putin.[5] I've spoken to the leaders of two of our closest allies, France and the United Kingdom, and we will work together in consultation with Russia and China to put forward a resolution at the U.N. Security Council requiring Assad to give up his

---

establish Islamist fundamentalist regimes. The attack on the World Trade Center on September 11, 2001 was carried out by militants linked to Al-Qaeda, then based in Afghanistan.

[4] Vladimir Vladimirovich Putin (1952–) has been President of Russia since 2012. He was also President of Russia from 2000 to 2008.

[5] John Forbes Kerry (1943–) was Secretary of State from 2013 to 2017. He was also Senator from Massachusetts from 1985 to 2013, and ran for president as the Democratic nominee in 2004.

chemical weapons, and to ultimately destroy them under international control. We'll also give U.N. inspectors the opportunity to report their findings about what happened on August 21st. And we will continue to rally support from allies from Europe to the Americas—from Asia to the Middle East—who agree on the need for action.

Meanwhile, I've ordered our military to maintain their current posture to keep the pressure on Assad, and to be in a position to respond if diplomacy fails. And tonight, I give thanks again to our military and their families for their incredible strength and sacrifices.

My fellow Americans, for nearly seven decades, the United States has been the anchor of global security. This has meant doing more than forging international agreements—it has meant enforcing them. The burdens of leadership are often heavy, but the world is a better place because we have borne them.

And so, to my friends on the right, I ask you to reconcile your commitment to America's military might with a failure to act when a cause is so plainly just. To my friends on the left, I ask you to reconcile your belief in freedom and dignity for all people with those images of children writhing in pain, and going still on a cold hospital floor. For sometimes resolutions and statements of condemnation are simply not enough.

Indeed, I'd ask every member of Congress, and those of you watching at home tonight, to view those videos of the attack, and then ask: What kind of world will we live in if the United States of America sees a dictator brazenly violate international law with poison gas, and we choose to look the other way?

Franklin Roosevelt once said, "Our national determination to keep free of foreign wars and foreign entanglements cannot prevent us from feeling deep concern when ideals and principles that we have cherished are challenged."[6] Our ideals and principles, as well as our national security, are at stake in Syria, along with our leadership of a world where we seek to ensure that the worst weapons will never be used.

America is not the world's policeman. Terrible things happen across the globe, and it is beyond our means to right every wrong. But when, with modest effort and risk, we can stop children from being gassed to death, and thereby make our own children safer over the long run, I believe we should act. That's what makes America different. That's what makes us exceptional. With humility, but with resolve, let us never lose sight of that essential truth.

Thank you. God bless you. And God bless the United States of America.

---

[6] This quotation comes from a speech at San Diego, October 2, 1935.

Thematic Table of Contents

The Presidency and the Constitutional Order

Presidential Selection

Term Limit

Study Questions

For each of the Documents in this collection, we suggest below in section A questions relevant for that document alone and in Section B questions that require comparison between documents.

1. Alexander Hamilton, *The Federalist* Nos. 65, 68, 70–72, 1788

A. Why does Hamilton have to defend "energy" in the executive? What role does accountability play in Hamilton's discussion of executive energy? What does the discussion of duration in office reveal about the character of the people who will be president?

B. Does Hamilton's account of the impeachment process reflect the impeachment process as it has played out over time? Consider Documents 13, 20 and 26. What about the Electoral College? Is it "excellent," if "not perfect," as he claims? Given the developments discussed in Documents 8 and 33, to what extent does the Electoral College still function in the way that Hamilton and the other framers understood it would?

2. *Cato* No. 4, 1788

A. According to Cato, what will enhance the formal powers of the president? What is wrong with the procedures for electing the president and vice-president? What does he find fault with in the provision for a vice-president?

B. Do Cato and Publius (Document 1) have in mind the same kind of United States? Were Cato's concerns about the language of Article II misplaced? Did he, for example, anticipate Senator Henry Clay's critique of President Andrew Jackson (Document 12), or the difficulties Congress in the twentieth century would face in holding on to the war power (Documents 31 and 34)?

3. Representative James Madison, Remarks on the Removal Power: Speech in Congress, June 16, 1789 and Letter to Edmund Pendleton, June 21, 1789

A. The Constitution is silent on who holds the power to remove executive branch officials. What possible answers to the puzzle emerged in 1789? What is the logic of Madison's position, and how does the principle of responsibility fit into it?

B. Does Madison's argument here necessarily show an inconsistency with his argument as Helvidius? Can the two positions be made compatible?

4. Alexander Hamilton and James Madison, *Pacificus–Helvidius* Debate on the Neutrality Proclamation, June—August 1793

A. Who has the better understanding of the Constitution, Hamilton or Madison? If Hamilton is right, what are the limits to the president's powers of war and peace? If Madison is right, what are the implications for foreign policy?

B. Do Hamilton's arguments as Pacificus shed light on his arguments in *The Federalist*, Nos. 70–72 (Document 1)? Why didn't he mention the Vesting Clause in *The Federalist*?

5. President George Washington, Proclamation on the Whiskey Rebellion, August 7, 1794

A. What alternatives did Washington have in dealing with the Whiskey Rebellion? What might his opponents have found objectionable in the proclamation?

B. Is Washington's proclamation an example of unilateral activity, that is, of the president acting alone? Or is it an example of working with Congress? How is it like or unlike his Neutrality Proclamation (Document 4)?

6. President Thomas Jefferson, First Inaugural, March 4, 1801

A. Jefferson's address is famous today for being conciliatory toward Federalists, but in its day the Federalists found much to criticize in the address. What might they have found objectionable? What does Jefferson say should guide the country during moments of terror or alarm? What is the role of the president that is suggested near the end?

B. To what extent does Jefferson's address line up with the presentation of the president in *The Federalist*? How do Jefferson's arguments compare to those of Alexander Hamilton and James Madison in Document 4, or to the assumptions about executive power evident in Document 5?

7. President Thomas Jefferson, Letter to Elias Shipman and Others, July 12, 1801

A. Why did Jefferson have to defend his removal of Goodrich? What is the basis for this power according to Jefferson?

B. In what ways does Jefferson's explanation resemble James Madison's case for removal powers (Document 4)? In what ways is it different? How might this letter clarify Jefferson's First Inaugural (Document 6)?

8. Delaware General Assembly, Resolution Rejecting the 12th Amendment, 1804

A. According to Delaware's legislature, what is the problem with the Twelfth Amendment? Why does Delaware want to retain five as the number of candidates available to the House in the contingency election? How might this affect the separation of powers, or the relative influence of small and large states?

B. How does Delaware's understanding of presidential selection compare to Thomas Jefferson's vision for the presidency (Documents 6 and 7)? How does each line up with the logic of *Federalist* No. 68 (Document 1)?

9. President Thomas Jefferson, Letter to the New Jersey Legislature, December 10, 1807

A. How does Jefferson's public explanation of his decision to retire compare to or cast new light on President George Washington's precedent? What is implied about Washington in Jefferson's letter?

B. What would Alexander Hamilton, the author of *Federalist* No. 72 (Document 1), say in response to Jefferson? Does Jefferson's principle weaken the "will" necessary for presidents to carry out extensive and arduous enterprises?

10. Thomas Jefferson, Letter to John B. Colvin, September 20, 1810

A. How are Jefferson's first three examples of extra-legal actions similar to one another? In what way does his hypothetical about Florida differ from these examples? What are the requirements for the officer who acts beyond the law? For the people who judge the officer's action?

B. How does Jefferson's answer to Colvin compare to Alexander Hamilton's and James Madison's interpretations of the Vesting Clause in their respective arguments about the treaty power and the removal power (Documents 3 and 4) ?

11. President Andrew Jackson, First Annual Message, December 8, 1829

A. How does Jackson's proposal for direct election of the president correspond with the larger aims of Jackson's political coalition? The proposal did not become part of the Constitution. What might have been the concerns of those against the idea?

B. How would Jackson's proposal alter the logic of Alexander Hamilton in *Federalist* No. 68 (Document 1)? How might the Delaware legislature of 1804 respond to Jackson's proposal (Document 8)?

12. Senator Henry Clay, Speeches on the Removal Power, December 26, 1833 and March 7, 1834

A. Can Congress issue orders to a department head, orders that override the directives of the president? What is Clay's concern with President Andrew Jackson's argument about the purpose of presidential elections?

B. Why does Clay believe that James Madison was wrong in 1789 (Document 3) to argue that the Constitution gives the removal power to the president? Where might Madison place Clay's views among the competing stances on the removal power he outlines in his letter to Pendleton?

13. President Andrew Jackson, Message to the Senate Protesting the Censure Resolution, April 15, 1834

A. What is the problem with the censure from Jackson's perspective? Why did he have to remove Treasury Secretary William Duane and what does the election of 1832 have to do with it?

B. Do the essays in *The Federalist* leave a place for a motion of censure as an alternative to impeachment? Does Jackson's case for removing Duane most resemble the argument of James Madison (Document 3) or that of Thomas Jefferson (Document 7)? Or does Jackson offer his own theory?

14. President John Tyler, Speech on Assuming the Office of the President, April 9, 1841

A. Does Tyler leave open the possibility that he would not finish President William Henry Harrison's term? Is there another way he might have handled the situation? Can Tyler's political commitments be discerned from the speech? Do they easily align with either the Whig or Democratic parties?

B. In what ways does Tyler's speech resemble the inaugural addresses of Presidents Abraham Lincoln (Document 15) and Thomas Jefferson (Document 6)? What do these similarites suggest about parties and party platforms?

15. President Abraham Lincoln, First Inaugural Address, March 4, 1861

A. According to Lincoln, what does his party's platform reveal about his presidency? In his view, what does this platform suggest about the meaning of the election of 1860? What does this in turn reveal about the relationship between new presidents and the Supreme Court?

B. To what extent does Lincoln's treatment of his platform show continuity with the presidencies of Thomas Jefferson (Documents 6, 7, and 9) and Andrew Jackson (Documents 11 and 13)? To what extent does Lincoln's discussion of the Supreme Court accord with the views of Jefferson and Jackson?

16. President Abraham Lincoln, Message to Congress in Special Session, July 4, 1861

A. Why did critics say that Lincoln lacked the power to suspend habeas corpus? What is the significance of the oath of office in Lincoln's explanation why he has the power to suspend habeas corpus? Does it matter that the Constitution allows the president to call Congress into special session?

B. How does Lincoln's use of presidential power compare to that of Presidents Andrew Jackson and Thomas Jefferson? Does Lincoln rely on public opinion in this address, or does the source of his power reside elsewhere?

17. President Abraham Lincoln, Letter to Albert G. Hodges, April 4, 1864

A. What is the significance of the oath of office in Lincoln's understanding of his power? Why does Lincoln insist that he does not have the power to end slavery simply on the basis of his own antislavery stance?

B. How does Lincoln's justification of the Emancipation Proclamation fit with his defense of suspending habeas corpus in Document 16? How does it compare to Thomas Jefferson's approach to presidential prerogative in Document 10?

18. Associate Justice David Davis, *Ex parte Milligan*, December 1866

A. To what extent does this case rest on the fact that the war never came to Indiana and to what extent does it rest on the fact that the war was over?

B. Four Justices argued that the case turned on the fact that Congress had not specifically authorized the military commissions, while the majority argued that Congress could not make that authorization. How might the minority anticipate the logic of Associate Justice Robert Jackson's concurring opinion in *Youngstown* (Document 31)?

19. President Andrew Johnson, Third Annual Message, December 3, 1867

A. Why must the president have the power to remove, according to Johnson? Why is the Senate not the best institution for wielding the power?

B. Does Johnson's argument differ in any important respect from the arguments made by James Madison (Document 3), Thomas Jefferson (Document 7), and Andrew Jackson (Document 13)? Does the disagreement over Reconstruction complicate this constitutional controversy? Does it show that Senator Henry Clay was on to something in his speech in the Senate (Document 12)?

20. House of Representatives, The Trial of Andrew Johnson, President of the United States, 1868

A. In addition to violating the Tenure of Office Act, what were the charges against Johnson? Could those charges be made in the twentieth century, or do they suggest the expectations for presidents in the nineteenth century were different? What is the issue lurking underneath the stated charges?

B. Does Alexander Hamilton's discussion of impeachment in *Federalist* No. 65 (Document 1) anticipate the nature of the charges against Johnson? Does it matter that Johnson believed the Tenure of Office Act was unconstitutional?

21. Woodrow Wilson, *Constitutional Government in the United States*, 1908

A. What does Wilson mean by a Newtonian theory of the Constitution? What does he mean by a Darwinian theory? How will the latter change the presidency?

B. How does Wilson's call for a new presidency fit within a call for a new theory of the Constitution? Does this argument fit within any of the others in this volume or is it one of a kind?

22. On the Source of Executive Power: Theodore Roosevelt, *An Autobiography*, 1913; and William Howard Taft, *Our Chief Magistrate and His Powers*, 1916

A. Are there any limits on executive power under Roosevelt's understanding? Is there any room for a strong president under Taft's understanding?

B. To what extent does Roosevelt's understanding fit within Alexander Hamilton's presentation of executive power in *Federalist* No. 70 (Document 1) and Pacificus (Document 4)?

23. Chief Justice William Howard Taft (majority) and Associate Justice Oliver Wendell Holmes, Jr. (dissenting), *Myers v. US*, 1926

A. What is the role of accountability (or responsibility) in Taft's reasoning? What is the role of the Take Care Clause?

B. Does Taft's opinion contradict his argument in Document 21? Which is closest to Taft's logic, the arguments of James Madison (Document 3), Thomas Jefferson (Document 7), or Andrew Jackson (Document 13)? How does Justice Holmes's dissenting opinion line up with Henry Clay's critique (Document 12) of presidential removal powers?

24. Associate Justice George Sutherland, *Humphrey's Executor v. United States*, 1935

A. According to the Court, what is the difference between a member of the Federal Trade Commission and a postmaster? Who gets to determine the difference? What if Congress believes one thing and the president another?

B. To what extent does the decision in *Humphrey's Executor* continue the logic of Senator Henry Clay's critique of President Andrew Jackson (Document 22) and to what extent does it continue the logic of Associate Justice Oliver Holmes's dissent in *Myers* (Document 23)? To what extent does it argue something new?

25. Associate Justice George Sutherland, *United States v. Curtiss-Wright Export Co.*, 1936

A. Why does the non-delegation doctrine not apply in this case, according to the Court? What is the significance of the argument about the historical location of sovereignty during the Revolution and during the framing and ratification of the Constitution? What are the limits to the president's foreign policy powers under this argument?

B. Does Sutherland go beyond even Alexander Hamilton as Pacificus (Document 4)? What might James Madison say in response to the Court in 1936?

26. President Franklin D. Roosevelt, First Inaugural Address, March 4, 1933

A. President Roosevelt argued in one of his campaign addresses that the social contract had to be renegotiated. Specifically, the country needed to use Hamiltonian means (a strong central government) to achieve Jeffersonian ends (equality). What measures will the government undertake to bring about this renegotiation? What is the role of the president in this process? Will this change our system of separated powers?

B. Presidents Thomas Jefferson, Abraham Lincoln, and Franklin Roosevelt resemble each other in certain ways. For example, each was a victor in a transformative election. Consider their inaugural addresses. How are they similar, and how are they different?

27. The President's Committee on Administrative Management, "The Brownlow Committee Report," 1937

A. According to the members of the Brownlow Commission, what is new about the federal government in the 1930's? What does this entail for the presidency? How likely is it that the president's advisors would have a "passion for anonymity"?

B. How do the Brownlow Commission's recommendations square with the arguments on the removal power in Documents 3, 7, 13, 23 and 24? To what extent do its recommendations fall in line with Wilson's call for a new presidency in Document 22?

28. Franklin D. Roosevelt, Fireside Chat On the Reorganization of the Judiciary, March 9, 1937

A. What is the significance of President Roosevelt's three-horse team analogy? Where is the Constitution in that image? Roosevelt's proposal promoted a backlash from conservative members of his own party. Why?

B. To what extent is Roosevelt's criticism of the Supreme Court similar to Abraham Lincoln's in his First Inaugural Address (Document 15)? To what extent does Roosevelt go beyond Lincoln?

29. Representative John McCormack and Representative Chauncey Reed, House Debate on the 22nd Amendment, 1947

A. What is argument for the amendment? What is the argument against it? Does either argument presuppose the existence of a modern presidency?

B. Based on *Federalist* No. 72 (Document 1) and on the letter to the New Jersey Legislature (Document 9), how might Alexander Hamilton and Thomas Jefferson have argued had they been present in 1947?

30. President Harry Truman, Special Message to the Congress Reporting on the Situation in Korea, July 19, 1950

A. Why does Truman place importance on the United Nations in his speech? By comparison, what is the role of Congress? What is the importance of the larger strategic imperatives of the Cold War? Of the fact that the conflict involved an aggressor nation?

B. Does Truman's presumption of authority over the war power go beyond that outlined by Hamilton in Pacificus (Document 4)? Does it go beyond that outlined by Justice Sutherland in *Curtiss-Wright* (Document 25)?

31. Associate Justice Robert Jackson (concurring), *Youngstown Sheet & Tube Co. v. Sawyer*, 1952

A. Is Jackson's opinion a ruling against Truman or a ruling against presidential power? What does he recommend that a judge do in each of the three practical situations he outlines?

B. Can Jackson's opinion be squared with the result in *Curtiss-Wright* (Document 25)? Is the difference that the question involves domestic action rather than foreign action? Or is the difference more fundamental?

32. Senator John F. Kennedy, "The Presidency in 1960," January 14, 1960

A. Where is the Constitution in Senator Kennedy's conception of the presidency? Where is Congress? Does Kennedy believe that the modern presidency is somehow different from the constitutional presidency? Is Kennedy primarily concerned with presidential temperament or with a theory of power?

B. Are there any differences between what Theodore Roosevelt described as having guided his presidency (Document 21) and what Kennedy promises will guide his?

33. The McGovern–Fraser Commission Report, 1971

A. The McGovern-Fraser Commission created the process by which we nominate presidential candidates today. What were the Commission's goals?

B. The Constitution did not anticipate national political parties, and so it could not have anticipated our nomination process today. That being said, to what extent does our nominating process line up with the expectations and goals outlined by Alexander Hamilton in *Federalist* No. 68 (Document 1)?

34. The War Powers Resolution and President Richard Nixon's Veto, 1973

A. Congress overrode Nixon's veto, but did he have the better argument? Or did Congress? Where does the Constitution place the war power? Why hasn't the War Powers Resolution lived up to its purpose?

B. How would Justices George Sutherland (Document 25) and Robert Jackson (Document 31) respond to the War Powers Resolution?

35. Richard Nixon, Interview on the Huston Plan, 1977

A. Does it matter whether the Huston Plan was designed to counteract foreign espionage or domestic opposition? Could Nixon have sought approval from Congress for this operation?

B. Nixon's assertion of executive prerogative clearly goes beyond that of Thomas Jefferson (Document 10) and Abraham Lincoln (Documents 16 and 17). But the more interesting question is whether Lincoln and Jefferson's arguments necessarily lead to something like Nixon's claim. Is there a way to make their arguments without leading to what Nixon says? Or, does either Jefferson or Lincoln offer the safer path for constitutional government?

36. House of Representatives, Articles of Impeachment Against President William Jefferson Clinton, 1998

A. Why was President Bill Clinton impeached? Why didn't a supermajority of the Senate support removal from office?

B. Clinton's defense argues that his crime was not "high" enough to be an impeachable offense. Does *Federalist* No 65 (Document 1) support that argument? In what ways are the charges against Clinton like those against President Andrew Johnson (Document 20)? In what ways are they different?

37. John C. Yoo, On the President's Constitutional Authority to Conduct Military Operations Against Terrorists, 2001

A. According to Yoo, what is the meaning of "declare" in Congress's power to declare war? What evidence does he employ to make this argument? What evidence does he ignore? Accoridng to Yoo, which provision of the Constitution better describes Congress's power over war?

B. Would Alexander Hamilton (Documents 1 and 4) agree with Yoo's reading of the Constitution with respect to the war power? Would Justice George Sutherland (Document 25)?

38. Associate Justice Anthony Kennedy (majority) and Associate Justice Antonin Scalia (minority), *Boumediene v. Bush*, 2008

A. What, precisely, is at stake in the differences between Justices Kennedy and Scalia? Does it matter that the war on terror is different from conventional wars with specific nations?

B. Does Justice Kennedy seem to have used the framework recommended by Justice Jackson in Youngstown (Document 31) in reaching his decision? If so, how?

39. President Barack Obama, Special Address to the Nation on Syria, September 10, 2013

A. Does Obama believe he needs Congressional approval for military action against Syria? If not, what is the purpose of the message?

B. How does Obama's message compare to President Harry Truman's speech on Korea (Document 30)? Which is more deferential to Congress? Which leaves the most room for executive authority?

Errata

page   for   read
vii, author Abrahama   Abraham

Suggestions for Further Reading

Alvis, J. David, Jeremy D. Bailey, and F. Flagg Taylor. *The Contested Removal Power, 1789–2010*. Lawrence: University Press of Kansas, 2013.

Bailey, Jeremy D. *Thomas Jefferson and Executive Power*. New York: Cambridge University Press, 2007.

Ceaser, James W. *Presidential Selection: Theory and Development*. Princeton: Princeton University Press, 1979.

Ellis, Richard. *The Development of the American Presidency*. New York: Routledge, 2012.

Fisher, Louis. *Presidential War Power*. Lawrence: University Press of Kansas, 2013.

Goldsmith, Jack. *The Terror Presidency: Law and Judgment Inside the Bush Administration*. New York: Norton, 2007.

Howell, William D. *Power Without Persuasion: The Politics of Direct Presidential Action*. Princeton: Princeton University Press, 2003.

Kleinerman, Benjamin A. *The Discretionary President: The Promise and Peril of Executive Power*. Lawrence: University Press of Kansas, 2009.

Knott, Stephen F. *Secret and Sanctioned: Covert Operations and the American Presidency*. New York: Oxford University Press, 1996.

Landy, Marc and Sidney M. Milkis, *Presidential Greatness*. Lawrence: University Press of Kansas, 2000.

Milkis, Sidney M. *The President and the Parties: The Transformation of the American Party System Since the New Deal*. New York: Oxford University Press, 1993.

Nichols, David K. *The Myth of the Modern Presidency*. University Park, PA: Pennsylvania State Press, 1994.

Schlesinger, Arthur M., Jr., *The Imperial Presidency*. Boston: Houghton Mifflin, 1973.

Skowronek, Stephen. *The Politics Presidents Make: Leadership from John Adams to George Bush*. Cambridge, MA: Harvard University Press, Belknap Press, 1993.

Slonim, Shlomo. "The Electoral College at Philadelphia: The Evolution of an Ad Hoc Congress for Selection of President," *Journal of American History* 73: 1 (1986): 35–58.

Tulis, Jeffrey K. *The Rhetorical Presidency.* Princeton, NJ: Princeton University Press, 1998.